落笔生花

新托福综合写作
高分范文精讲

TOEFL
Integrated
Writing

万炜 编著

本书针对的是冲击托福写作高分的同学，旨在全方位为 TPO1~75 综合写作试题给出翔实的答案解析。第一部分总结考生在实际备考和考试中遇到的关于综合写作的若干问题，并以此为出发点剖析托福综合写作题型，给出高效的复习和解题思路、答题技巧。第二部分精讲每套 TPO 综合写作。首先对阅读文章进行核心信息提炼，对听力可能的反驳策略进行粗略预期。接着，对听力进行解析，分析哪些信息符合预期，哪些信息重要、需要记录，哪些信息不重要，并整理听力的反驳策略。最后给出满分范文，将先前阅读与听力部分的关键信息重现出来。

本书在语言上地道但不华丽，有效而不炫技。作者希望通过这本书，对处在 TOEFL 综合写作优秀边缘的同学们给予最后的助力，使写作成为大家的拿分点、冲分点。

图书在版编目（CIP）数据

落笔生花：新托福综合写作高分范文精讲 / 万炜编著. -- 北京：机械工业出版社，2023.12

（娓娓道来出国考试系列丛书）

ISBN 978-7-111-74702-4

Ⅰ. ①落… Ⅱ. ①万… Ⅲ. ①TOEFL-写作-自学参考资料 Ⅳ. ①H315

中国国家版本馆 CIP 数据核字（2024）第 006525 号

机械工业出版社（北京市百万庄大街 22 号　邮政编码 100037）

策划编辑：苏筛琴　　责任编辑：苏筛琴

责任校对：张晓娟　　责任印制：单爱军

保定市中画美凯印刷有限公司印刷

2024 年 9 月第 1 版·第 1 次印刷

184mm×260mm·16.5 印张·1 插页·369 千字

标准书号：ISBN 978-7-111-74702-4

定价：68.00 元

电话服务　　　　　　　　网络服务

客服电话：010-88361066　　机　工　官　网：www.cmpbook.com
　　　　　010-88379833　　机　工　官　博：weibo.com/cmp1952
　　　　　010-68326294　　金　书　网：www.golden-book.com

封底无防伪标均为盗版　　机工教育服务网：www.cmpedu.com

Preface 前言

　　托福写作目前由综合写作与学术写作两部分构成，本书的定位是从综合写作方面帮助同学们冲击 TOEFL 写作高分。

　　本书作为一本系统性的综合写作方法论，本身就填补了市场上巨大的空白。首先，我们必须承认，对于综合写作听力部分都无法听懂大概的同学来说，TOEFL 综合写作的提分要务是提高听力能力。否则，一切技巧、策略等对他们来说都是纸上谈兵。这部分同学也不是本书所针对的主要群体，他们首先应该突破的不是 TOEFL 写作部分，而是 TOEFL 听力部分。当然，也有一些同学，TOEFL 听力已经能够获得 25 分以上，甚至更高，但是在综合写作中却举步维艰，这就不可能是纯粹听力不足造成的结果了。

　　事实上，综合写作的听力部分远比 TOEFL 听力部分的听力要简单得多，原因有二：第一，篇幅更短；第二，更重要的是，TOEFL 听力是没有提示信息的，而 TOEFL 综合写作一上来先看一篇短文，其实已经对听力部分可能反驳些什么有极其强的暗示了。然而，很多同学仍然把 TOEFL 综合写作的听力部分当作纯听力来听，记下一切可能听到的信息，这其实非常干扰主线思路，甚至导致在写作中无法突出重点。

　　本书的核心理念是，**TOEFL 综合写作其实是整个 TOEFL 考试中最讲求逻辑性的一部分测试**。相比而言，TOEFL 学术写作主要要求考生有自己的想法，逻辑不离谱，语言地道，这三点是得高分的关键。而 TOEFL 综合写作可不仅仅要表现自己的语言能力，我们必须尊重阅读与听力原文。有的同学说了，把阅读和听力复制出来不就完了，这还有什么逻辑思维要求呢？问题来了，由于词数限制，我们只能选择最精练的语言去概述文章，因此，对于高端考生来说，什么要复述、什么不要复述就成了重中之重。这里最大的误区就是：只复述内容，不复述逻辑。而这个问题其实可能覆盖了 90% 以上的考生。

　　我们在听听力部分时记下来的笔记基本上都是一些实词，比如，名词、形容词、动词；而在写作中，我们所做的就是把这些信息罗列出来。但其实，这些词在听力当中是如何组织的，某个信息和上个信息之间是什么关系，比如，让步、递进、质疑、证明等，这些都是要反映出来的。

　　事实上，在我自己的考试经历当中，由于我从来不做笔记，因此几乎完全没法复制原文所使用的名词、形容词和动词，我使用的全部是同义替换，但最终仍然能够轻易拿到满分。这是因为我真正尊重原文的复述，并不是东施效颦地去拷贝原词，而是把原文核心的论证逻辑和论证形式表现出来。很多人以为听力和阅读之间就是个取反关系，这实在是对听力部分的过分简化。比如，阅读说 TOEFL 很难，理由是得高分的考生很少。那么，听力要去反驳，一定要说 TOEFL 不难，因为得高分的考生不少吗？显然，听力可以说，就算得高分的考生少，也不代表 TOEFL 很难。事实上，综合写作的听力部分的反驳会有不同的逻辑线路可走，而我们对听力的复述，就不仅仅是复述出某些信息本身，而更重要的是这些信息的组织能够反映出原文的反驳策略。

本书想要传递给大家的三个重要理念是：

第一，如何根据逻辑选择阅读中的重要信息和信息关系去复述，从而完美地体现听力和阅读之间的逻辑对应性，完美地体现听力的反驳策略。

第二，如何选择正确的句型，以体现出我们刚才所设计好的完美思路。

第三，从逻辑上把握阅读部分，以对听力将会说的信息进行逻辑预期，从而降低听力的难度，以便更容易把握到听力的关键信息。这是一个隐性的帮助。

本书的每一套 TPO 综合写作讲解将由以下部分组成。首先，对每篇阅读进行核心信息提炼，这种提炼要求准确判断阅读文章的目标，并对三个分论点高度概括，找到和文章目标相符的结合点，同时，对听力可能的反驳策略进行粗略预期。接着，对听力进行解析，这种解析不是听完之后的解析，而是呈现听的过程中的思考，分析哪些信息符合预期，哪些信息重要需要留下印象，哪些信息不重要，并整理听力的反驳策略。接着，给出范文，将先前阅读与听力部分的关键信息重现出来。

我们希望通过这本书能为处在 TOEFL 综合写作优秀边缘的同学们给予最后的助力，使得综合写作成为大家的拿分点、冲分点。

万　炜

2023 年 10 月

Instructions 使用说明

对于每套 TPO 的综合写作，本书都会首先概括阅读内容，预测听力可能的反驳策略，然后分析听力过程，并给出高分范文。

请同学们不要急于先看解析。自己读一读阅读的开头部分，看看是否有某些关键词可以体现该阅读文章的类型。并思考在几个展开段中你希望寻找到什么样的关键信息，以及听力的目标会是什么。最后再和解析比对。这么做是为了培养大家快速寻找综合写作阅读部分主旨的能力。

看阅读文章时可做一些笔记，但紧记只记录关键信息中的关键词，主要是要预测听力可能采取的反驳策略。此部分带 📝 图标的内容是作者做的阅读笔记，带 🎧 图标的内容是作者预测的听力反驳策略。

请先尝试用最快的速度找到三个段落中与文章目的最相关的三个论点。然后，预判对于每个论点听力可能实施的宏观反驳策略。最后再和解析比对。这么做是为了培养大家在阅读部分快速找到关键信息的能力，以及对听力的预判能力。

听听力时请记笔记，结合自己先前的预期，谨慎选择笔记内容，一切可以被预见的信息都不要记录。听完听力，再去和解析比对，看看自己对关键信息的选择是否准确。这个部分是在逐渐培养大家听听力时的目的性。

在看范文时，请大家着重学习作者对句型的选择，一定要思考这种句型适合什么样的文章类型或反驳类型。

阅读解析与听力预测

▶ **总　论：**
公司应该提供员工每周工作4天的选择。[1] 阅读接下来肯定会给三个理由支持这个建议，所以这是典型的"观点+三个理由"的文章。听听力时应该注意到底是在否定前提还是在否定逻辑。

▶ **理由1：**
这会让公司利润增加，因为员工工作状态会更好；并且，公司支出不会增多，因为虽然员工多了，但每个人的工资减少了。[2]

▶ **理由2：**
这会降低失业率。[3]

▶ **理由3：**
提高员工生活水平，因为有更多的自由支配的时间。[4]

📝 5 → 4-day week
🎧 听力肯定不支持这个选择

📝 $ ↑ ← rested, alert, error ↓; more staff, less pay
🎧 这个理由很有意思，分为两个部分，所以理论上可以讨论。

📝 unemployment ↓
🎧 可能会直接否定前提，说并不能减少失业；或者否定逻辑，说就算减少失业，这个变化也不大。当然，这个说法听起来有点不符合常理。

📝 life quality ↑ ← family, leisure
🎧 最可能说的是，就算有更多空闲时间，也不见得会提高生活质量；理论上可以否定前提，但是乎这个前提看起来是事实，估计很难否定。

听力解析

Offering ... a 4-day workweek won't affect company profits, economic conditions, or the lives of employees in the ways the reading suggests, 直接与阅读对抗，我们已经预见到了，不需记录。[5]

First, 准备听公司利润. spend more, 导致支出增加。... more money... training, and medical benefits... costs... the same whether

满分范文

The article presents three arguments why companies should offer employees the option of a four-day work week, all of which are contested in the lecture. [9]

[8] 很鲜明的"观点+三个理由"的文章。这个开头明显体现的是理由型文章的开头形式。到了别的文章中，同学们就会学到

Contents 目 录

前言
使用说明

Part 1　综合写作的本质　/ 001
　　01　综合写作是什么？　/ 003
　　02　优秀的综合写作回答应该做到
　　　　什么？　/ 004
　　03　综合写作有什么应对方案？　/ 007

Part 2　综合写作高分范文精讲　/ 025
TPO 1　/ 027
TPO 2　/ 030
TPO 3　/ 033
TPO 4　/ 036
TPO 5　/ 039
TPO 6　/ 042
TPO 7　/ 045
TPO 8　/ 048
TPO 9　/ 051
TPO 10　/ 054
TPO 11　/ 057
TPO 12　/ 060
TPO 13　/ 063
TPO 14　/ 066
TPO 15　/ 069
TPO 16　/ 072
TPO 17　/ 075
TPO 18　/ 078

TPO 19　/ 081
TPO 20　/ 084
TPO 21　/ 087
TPO 22　/ 091
TPO 23　/ 094
TPO 24　/ 098
TPO 25　/ 102
TPO 26　/ 105
TPO 27　/ 108
TPO 28　/ 111
TPO 29　/ 115
TPO 30　/ 118
TPO 31　/ 121
TPO 32　/ 124
TPO 33　/ 127
TPO 34　/ 130
TPO 35　/ 133
TPO 36　/ 136
TPO 37　/ 139
TPO 38　/ 142
TPO 39　/ 145
TPO 40　/ 148
TPO 41　/ 151
TPO 42　/ 154
TPO 43　/ 157

TPO 44	/ 160	TPO 61	/ 210
TPO 45	/ 163	TPO 62	/ 213
TPO 46	/ 166	TPO 63	/ 216
TPO 47	/ 169	TPO 64	/ 219
TPO 48	/ 172	TPO 65	/ 222
TPO 49	/ 175	TPO 66	/ 225
TPO 50	/ 178	TPO 67	/ 228
TPO 51	/ 181	TPO 68	/ 231
TPO 52	/ 184	TPO 69	/ 234
TPO 53	/ 187	TPO 70	/ 237
TPO 54	/ 190	TPO 71	/ 240
TPO 55	/ 192	TPO 72	/ 243
TPO 56	/ 195	TPO 73	/ 246
TPO 57	/ 198	TPO 74	/ 249
TPO 58	/ 201	TPO 75	/ 252
TPO 59	/ 204		
TPO 60	/ 207		

Part 1

落笔生花——
新托福综合写作高分范文精讲

综合写作的本质

- 综合写作是什么?
- 优秀的综合写作回答应该做到什么?
- 综合写作有什么应对方案?

Part 1

01 综合写作是什么？

在进入 TOEFL 考试的写作部分后，考生们首先面对的就是综合写作（Integrated Writing）的任务，其分数占整个 TOEFL 写作部分的一半。在这项任务中，考生们首先有 3 分钟时间阅读一篇学术文章（约 200 词）。在文章第一段，作者通常会清楚地表达一个目标，接下来用三个分论点对这个目标进行展开论述。接着，这篇阅读文章会从屏幕上消失，进入一段听力文章（约 2 分钟），其中的说话者首先会针对阅读文章的总目标发表（支持或反对的）看法，然后对阅读部分的各分论点（通常为三个展开段）依次进行讨论，当然，这一定与听力总目标（支持或反对）保持一致。在听力结束后，屏幕上会出现以下写作要求：

> *You have 20 minutes to plan and write your response. Your response will be judged on the basis of the quality of your writing and on how well your response presents the points in the lecture and their relationship to the reading passage. Typically, an effective response will be 150 to 225 words.*
>
> *Summarize the points made in the lecture you just heard, explaining how they cast doubt on points made in the reading passage.*
>
> （上面这段话可能有其他写法。）

考生将会有 20 分钟时间写一篇作文（推荐词数为 150~225），该作文**考生不表达自己的立场**，而是对听力文段进行概述，并体现出听力与阅读的关系。接下来，计时开始，**屏幕左方会重新出现阅读文段，右方为答题位置**。

理论上，如果听力是在对阅读进行反驳，则写作要求会显示以下三种之一：

> *Summarize the points made in the lecture, being sure to explain how they cast doubt on specific points made in the reading passage.*
>
> *Summarize the points made in the lecture, being sure to explain how they challenge specific claims/arguments made in the reading passage.*
>
> *Summarize the points made in the lecture, being sure to specifically explain how they answer the problems raised in the reading passage.*

如果听力是在对阅读进行支持，则写作要求会显示以下两种之一：

Summarize the points made in the lecture, being sure to specifically explain how they support the explanations in the reading passage.

Summarize the points made in the lecture, being sure to specifically explain how they strengthen specific points made in the reading passage.

但现实是，在所有官方 TPO 题目以及考生们经历的考试当中，几乎所有的听力文段都是在对阅读进行反驳，所以在复习准备阶段，考生们大可只考虑反驳的情况。

02 优秀的综合写作回答应该做到什么？

本书针对的是冲击写作高分（28 分以上）的考生，所以不涉及 20 分以下考生所面对的极其基础的问题，比如阅读完全看不懂，听力什么都听不出来，或者写作常规句子都写不了。有很多学生长久停留在 fair 这个档次，却觉得自己好像什么都看懂了，听力也听得差不多，感觉自己也把这些都写出来了，却始终到不了 good，这是本章要探讨的问题。

我们首先需要明确一篇完美的综合写作文章会产生什么效果。它是对听力的完美复述，而不是对阅读的复述。我们可以选择性地挑选阅读的最关键信息进行复述，或者干脆完全不复述阅读，这都是没有问题的。重要的是，我们不可能把听力的内容全部写下来。首先，时间不允许；其次，篇幅也不允许。这意味着我们的复述是选择性的。选什么？考试要求写得很清楚，我们的复述要体现听力与阅读的关系，我们主要考虑反驳关系。完美的复述恰好会选择听力当中最能够对阅读进行反驳的点，并且把听力对这些反驳的论据准确表现出来。这么说也许听起来有些空洞，那就让我们按照考试的发展过程来逐步讨论一下同学们会遇到的问题。

▶ 阅读部分的常见问题

阅读第一段通常会清楚表达自己的目标，比如：提出一个观点，用三个段落去支持；提出一个现象，给出三个解释；遇到一个问题，给出三种解决方案。很多同学一直习惯性以为阅读都是"一个观点+三个理由"，这是一种严重的误解，可能会造成连带性的恶果。首先，可能在写作中就把阅读目的复述错了；其次，由于阅读一开始目标定位错误，导致阅读三个展开段落中无法迅速找到最关键的信息，继而无法预见听力可能会攻击的点，自然在漫长的听力当中无法确定什么信息是最重要的。

阅读的三个正文段落理论上每个段落在 30 秒钟之内可以看完，这个时间有时甚至更短，且在这个时间内我们还理应已经挑出了最关键信息。阅读的 3 分钟时间非常充裕，我们应该有一定的时间去大概预判听力的反驳策略。然而，大部分人做不到，就算阅读速度本身没有问题的同学也做不到，为什么？这种挑关键信息是有目的性的，这是由开篇的全文目标决定的。

我们拿 TPO 48 举例。开篇就说明了，本文要去寻找拯救 frogs 的方法。那么，三个正文段落最重要的事情就是拯救方案。需要我们记下来的、听力会去反驳的，就一定只能是这三个方案。第一段中，Frogs are being harmed by pesticides 是解决方案吗？显然不是。which are 引导的定语从句就更不会是解决方案了，直接扫过去。Pesticides often spread 这个主句一看就不是解决方案。Once…they attack nervous system，明显也不是。"If laws prohibit farmers from using pesticides, it would reduce harm to frogs…" 这一句中明显出现了解决方案，就是建议立法禁止使用 pesticides。这一下就非常明确，等会儿听力中相应的第一段讨论的一定会是为什么禁止使用 pesticides 不是一个好的举措。同样，在下面两段中，我们应该快速找到的关键信息分别是：第二段建议使用 antifungal medication and treatment，第三段建议 protect water habitats from excessive water use and development。

举这个例子想传达给同学们什么道理呢？那就是，阅读的时候我们是带着开头的目的去找信息读的，这会让我们的阅读速度加快，且它会让我们读得更准确。同学们必须认识到一个关键的事情，一个阅读段落也许写了三四句话，但一定只有一句才是最关键的信息，其他都是辅助，我们要做的关键的事就是把一个段落压缩成那一句话。其实，这种目的性阅读最重要的价值是辅助听力。做过综合写作的同学们能普遍感受到，真正压力大的是其中的听力环节，如果不记笔记，听完就忘；但如果记了笔记，又干扰听下文。所以，我们阅读精确性的价值在于对于听力的预测，它可以让我们做听力时更有目的性，不需要每个词都听出来。

可是很多同学是没有能力进行预测的，可能还是因为对阅读核心信息把握不准，当然还有可能是对常见的反驳模式缺乏总结。有的同学可能说，时间太紧，怎么可能预测呢？请注意，我们并不需要精细预测，这是时间上不允许的，并且风险太大。但是，每一种话题都有共同的反驳策略，这是大家必须熟悉的，因为它可以帮助我们在五秒钟之内就可以对大体的反驳方向有所定位。比如，TPO 48 这篇文章我们将会听到对三个建议的反驳。

> 在综合写作当中，对一个建议进行否定，一共有且仅有三种可能策略：
> 1. 方案不可行，因为某些原因（时间、金钱）导致根本做不到；
> 2. 该方案无效，即并不能够解决相应的问题；
> 3. 该方案虽然可行且有效，但危害严重，副作用大过其正作用。

这种反驳策略不仅适用于这道题，也适用于所有综合写作的问题解决型文章。针对 TPO 48 这篇文章让我们赶紧开动脑筋，一起来预判。如果可能，可以排除明显不合理的信息。首先，针对第一个建议，禁止使用 pesticide，反驳它，要么没有条件所以无法禁止，要么禁止了也许无法帮助 frogs，要么禁止了会造成更大危害；这同样适用剩下的两条建议。这个预测的价值在于，听力必然会落入其中一种策略，其额外价值在于，我们写作时要写出来的正是听力到底采用哪种策略否定了阅读的建议。

▶ 听力部分的常见问题

上面已经说过了，听力最大的问题就是听和记的协调。记笔记的简单原则就是：

> 阅读会帮助预期，听力已经听到的东西也会帮助预期，只要能完美验证预期的内容，都不用记，因为逻辑上可以推断出来。根据上下文逻辑能够推断出来的内容，也一定不用记。对于例子，不是不记笔记，而是不应该罗列不展开的名词例子。比如，听力说人类喜欢吃水果，像苹果、梨子、香蕉等。那么只需记录人类喜欢吃水果，而苹果等例子是无所谓的，因为听力不会展开。

回到 TPO 48 综合写作的听力当中。文章一开头就听到关键词：none, offer, solution，这显然不用记，我们不听都知道听力要说刚才的建议都不行，所以这是一定不要记的。

听到 first，肯定要准备听禁止使用 pesticide。...not economically practical or fair，这基本上已经把反驳策略说出来了，这是刚才三种策略当中的第一种——成本过高，代价大，不可行。这个信息必须记录，因为这排除了其他反驳的可能。接下去，说话者最多只能对代价进行展开了，这个段落已经不太可能发生大的变化了，一定要对刚才的这个信息有印象，其统领本段接下来的内容。接着听，Farmers rely on pesticide to decrease crop loss and to stay competitive in market，这基本是常识，而且肯定是说禁止了 pesticide，农民收成不保，经济利益不保，是对该点的展开，可以选择性不记录。下一句，听到 "If...strict regulations...then...at a severe disadvantage compared to farmers in other areas. They...lose more crops and have lower yield..."，这基本上是无用信息，这不就是刚才的信息逻辑上反过来说吗？肯定不需要记录。所以，这一段下来，我们记下来的应该只是"该建议成本过高，伤害农民"。

同理，在第二点当中，我们听到的应该是，给 frogs 涂 antifungal medication 不可行，因为需要给每个都涂，而且每一代还得重新涂。在第三点中，我们听到的应该是，该建议根本无效，因为危害 frogs 栖息地的根本原因是全球变暖，不是人为破坏。（具体分析请参见 TOP 48 的综合写作解析。）

总的来说，听力听不好，对于本来能听出个大概的同学来说，最大的原因很可能是把太多任务交给了耳朵。实际上，我们的阅读，我们的逻辑，都应该帮助我们缓解听力的压力，让我们有目的地听到个别关键的逻辑词和信息词，这样我们就可以确定已经听到最重要的东西。

▶ 写作部分的常见问题

写作部分是综合写作当中最简单的部分了。这个部分出问题，可能是因为语法、拼写等。另外，这个部分最可能出问题的原因还是阅读和听力做不好所导致的，上面已分析过，在这里最值得提出的问题，就是选择适合听力逻辑的句型。

大家一定要注意，我们需要复述的不仅仅是听力所说的信息，还有听力的逻辑。听力的反驳中有可能有让步、对比、类比、举例、理由等各种逻辑关系存在，我们必须用恰当的逻辑词把这些信息都结合在一起。而不是写成"The lecturer says... then he says... and then he says..."这种写法只有信息,没有信息关系,是残缺的。同时,不同的文章类型,不同的反驳策略,采取的句型肯定也不同。比如,TPO 48 综合写作范文是否定建议的,那和否定解释的文章肯定不一样。第二段否定建议可行性和最后一段否定建议有效性,所采用的句型也不应该一样。这些语言细节都是冲击高分的同学不应该忽视的。下面分析一下 TPO 48 综合写作的范文:

> 开头段:The article offers / proposes three possible solutions to the decline of frog populations, all of which are questioned in the lecture. 一目了然,这显然是反驳问题解决方案的文章开头。
>
> 第二段的开头"The lecturer believes that the anti-fungal medication is extremely costly and impractical."和第三段的开头"The lecturer does not believe that strict regulation on water use and development is going to affect frogs significantly."分别清晰地体现了不同的反驳策略。
>
> 第二段指出建议不可行性,第三段指出建议无效。

总的来说,在综合写作中,同学们需要训练出来的能力就是,给你任何一种文章逻辑与反驳逻辑,你都能够瞬间用相应的句型把这些逻辑表现出来。

03 综合写作有什么应对方案?

说完了同学们在综合写作中需要做到的事情,那到底如何实现这些目标呢?现在我们就来详细谈一谈综合写作的方法体系。

首先,我们需要认识综合写作中的文章类型,然后我们将按不同类型的文章分别探讨整个阅读、听力,以及写作的具体过程。

不同阅读文章的备考策略

文章类型的区分,如前文所说,通常在阅读部分的第一段就能体现。粗略划分,最常见的有三类文章:观点理由型、现象解释型、问题(困难)解决型。精细划分,观点理由型还可以继续划分子类,但这并不是必需的,所有这些子类可以共用同样的方法体系,所以对我们影响不大。

观点理由型文章（TPO 绝大多数文章是这种类型），就是第一段首先抛出一个观点，接下来将有几个理由支持这个观点。正文三个段落各自提出一个理由对该观点进行支持；听力部分将否定该观点，并且分别削弱三个理由对该观点的支持。

现象解释型文章（如：TPO 5、23、27、32、33、34、56），就是第一段首先抛出一个现象，一定是一个已知事实，本身是不能反驳的，接下来将有针对这个现象的几个解释。正文三个段落各自给出对该现象的解释，即造成该现象的原因，这三个解释一定是互相独立、互不相干的；听力部分不会说该现象是假的，而会说这三个解释都无法解释该现象的发生。

问题（困难）解决型文章（TPO 15、18、42、48），就是第一段首先抛出一个困难，接下来将有几个方案可以解决这个困难，正文就会分别给出这几个解决方案；听力部分一定会指出这些方案各自的缺陷。

（1）观点理由型文章的备考策略

Q1：怎样辨识观点理由型文章？>>

首先，第一段一定会有观点。观点是与事实区分开来的，当作者表达观点的时候，他会用一些鲜明的标志词来表示这件事情是他或其他某些人的看法，比如：表示观点的词 view, claim, position 等；表示推断的词 must, should 等。**但是，最明显的标志是段尾会说，有以下几个 reasons/arguments/evidences 可以支持/反对这个立场。**比如，TPO 47 中的 "Several arguments have been made against powered flight"，TPO 45 中的 "The skeptics support their view with several arguments"，TPO 44 中的 "There are three main reasons why some archaeologists believe that the coin is not genuine historic evidence"，TPO 41 中的 "They use the following arguments to support their position"，等等。看到这么明显的信号，我们自然可以大胆地确定，下文将会是三个理由或证据，都将支持前文的观点。

Q2：怎样有效地阅读观点理由型文章？>>

我们可以将看到的核心观点简称为 C（conclusion 的缩写），接下来看每个段落的目的就是以最快的速度找出那个核心理由 P（premise 的缩写）。从逻辑上讲，理由 P 要能支持观点 C，需要一个背后的前提，即 P 和 C 之间的关系。某个理由段当中，通常只有一句最关键的语句是点出这个 P 的，而剩下的信息要么是展开 P（比如，论述 P 背后的子理由 P'），要么是展开 P 与 C 的关系。

以 TPO 47 综合写作的阅读文章为例：

第一段开始就说明阅读的目的是证明 pterosaurs 不会 powered flight。那三个理由段落一定分别有一个核心理由，我们称为 P1、P2、P3。

第一段紧接着说出了这个 P1，pterosaurs 是 cold-blooded。那下文还能说什么？要么是 pterosaurs 为什么是 cold-blooded，要么就是说 cold-blooded 和不能 powered flight 之间的关系。往下一看，下面说的是 powered flight 需要 energy，而 cold-blooded 不能提供 energy，这就建立了 cold-blooded 和不能 powered flight 之间的关系。所以，这个阅读段落对我们最有用的信息就是 cold-blooded。

再看第二段，因为很短，很容易看出核心理由是 too heavy。

第三段，会飞的生物能 take off，而这些 take off 的方法不适合 pterosaurs，那简而言之，就是 pterosaurs 不能 take off。接下来展开讲 pterosaurs 为什么不能 take off。

三段的核心关键词分别是：P1 — cold-blooded；P2 — heavy；P3 — 不能 take off。

好，这些关键词有什么用？第一，在写作中，如果你选择复述阅读（可以不复述），则复述得最多的就是这些关键词。第二，更重要的是，我们已经可以提前预估听力的反驳方案了。

> 在观点理由型（即 C + 3P）文章中，针对每一个 P，听力有且仅有两种反驳策略：❶ P 是错的；❷ P 不支持 C，换句话说，就算 P 是对的，C 也是错的；再换句话说，否定 P 和 C 之间的逻辑关系。否定某理由对某观点的支持，要么否定该理由，要么否定该理由的充分性。

再深入每个理由，如果 P 背后还有子理由 P' 去支持 P，即 P 支持 C，而 P' 支持 P，那听力可以否定 P 和 C 间的关系，可以否定 P，而否定 P 的方式可以是否定 P 与 P' 的关系，或者否定 P'。这个步骤可以循环进行，当然，在我们这个长度的阅读中，最多不过两层。

回到 TPO 47。对于理由 1，我们知道，听力只有两种选择：否定 cold-blooded，或者承认 cold-blooded，坚持 powered flight；对于理由 2，听力仍然只有两种选择：否定 heavy，或者承认 heavy，坚持 powered flight；对于理由 3，听力还是只有两种选择：坚持能 take off，或者承认无法 take off，坚持 powered flight。

预测到这个程度，其实已经很厉害了。在一些情况下，这两种策略并不都是开放的，我们甚至可以确定只有一种方案是有可能的。简单来说，这个原则是：听力永远不会否定事实。如果 P 是事实，听力是不能否定的，只能否定 P 和 C 之间的关系；如果 P 和 C 之间的关系是事实，听力只能否定 P 本身。

Q3：怎样 get 到观点理由型文章的听力重点？>>

《托福官方指南》对综合写作的介绍强调了要注意听力与阅读之间的关系，而鉴于我们刚才说过了，观点理由型文章的听力反驳策略只有两个——否定 P 或否定 P 和 C 之间的关系，那么，听听力时，关键就在于听出到底采取的是哪种策略。

我们以 TPO 47 综合写作的听力部分为例。

> 第一个正文段，听到 dense hair covering like fur, typical of warm-blooded animals 时，我们应该明确知道，这是在否定理由本身，即认为 pterosaurs 本身是 warm-blooded，意味着有足够的能量，意味着可以 powered flight，剩下这个段落的听力内容基本就是走过场。
>
> 第二段，听到 anatomic features that made them unusually light for their size 时，我们可以明确，这是在否定 pterosaurs heavy，即否定了阅读的理由本身，剩下这个段落的听力内容是对这个信息的展开而已。
>
> 最后一段，takeoff would be a problem, if they took off the way birds do, there are differences between birds and pterosaurs，这些明显是在说 takeoff is not a problem for pterosaurs，也是在否定阅读中的前提本身。

这篇文章三个段落采取的都是否定前提的策略，为什么呢？因为这三个理由本身都不是事实，本身就是阅读文章做的猜测。怎么判断的呢？回到阅读部分，请寻找一下三个理由中标志观点的词。第一个理由段的 probably，第二个理由段的 probably，第三段的 would not have，这些词都表示作者做判断时自己的推断，而不是客观事实。

再看下一篇观点理由型文章，即 TPO 45。

> 阅读为了证明发现的古树化石不是蜂巢，用了三个核心理由：1. 没有发现蜜蜂化石；2. 那时没有开花植物；3. 古树化石中没有发现某个 cap 结构。
>
> 听力的第一个理由段，一开始就听到让步词 it's true，接着听到 no fossil bees，已经表明了反驳策略，即承认前提，那接下来只能否定逻辑关系，即没有 fossil bees，但不代表该结构不是蜂巢。剩下的信息一定是对破坏这个逻辑关系的展开。
>
> 第二段，也是一开始听到了让步词 while it's true，接着听到 close relationship with flowering plants today（如今的蜜蜂和开花植物相关），紧接着是 early bees existed on non-flowering plants，这等于是在否定逻辑关系。承认当年可能没有开花植物，但仍然可以有 bees，因为当年的 bees 不需要 flowering plants。
>
> 最后一段，even though lack caps，同样承认阅读前提，接下来则只能说为什么没有 caps 仍然可以是蜂巢。

这篇文章我们发现，听力的三个反驳都采取了否定阅读逻辑的策略，为什么？因为阅读给出的三个证据都是事实，没有办法否定。与 TPO 47 的三个理由段的语气相比，TPO 45 三个阅读理由段的证据提出都没有使用任何推断性的字眼，因为当人们在陈述事实时，是不需要任何语气词的。请大家对比中文的两句话："TOEFL 考语言"和"TOEFL 考的肯定是语言"，前者明显是陈述事实的口气，而后者是发表自己看法的口气。当然，这种精细的判断，在能力不到位时不需要强迫自己做到。

TPO 45 中否定逻辑的三个理由段一开始都使用了让步。我们应该知道各种让步词，如 while, although, even though, it's true, indeed 等。否定逻辑为什么会可能使用到让步呢？我们想象一下，阅读观点是 C，理由是 P。如果听力要否定 P，是不是可以直接说 P 错就好了？但如果否定逻辑呢？那是不是要先承认 P 是对的，接着展开说为什么 P 对不代表 C 对啊？这时，很可能开始就说"诚然，P 有道理，但是……"。

就算有让步词，也不代表质疑的一定是前文的逻辑！我们需要做的是，听到让步之后，注意接下来的信息是否完美对应阅读理由，如果是，则可以确定是否定逻辑。比如：TPO 45 综合写作听力文章的第二个理由段，while 让步之后其实紧跟着的不是阅读理由本身，即当年没有开花植物。所以，第二段的论述方式和第一、三两段是不同的。

我们举一个非常日常的例子。

> 阅读说：万炜这个人很优秀，理由分别是高、帅、富。如果我要否定他优秀，并且要否定三个理由，我们该怎么反驳？假想听力这么说：诚然他帅，但是……那这个省略号肯定只能是否定帅与优秀之间的关系了。假设听力这么说：诚然他小时候长得很帅……这个省略号要否定帅与优秀的关系吗？肯定不是！因为这个帅伴随了一个定语或状语，即小时候，接下来很可能说他现在不帅，这还是否定前提本身。

所以，请注意，在听到让步词后，要留意让步的内容是否完全等同于阅读理由，如果是，我们可以确定听力的反驳策略是反驳逻辑。但如果听到的信息虽然部分等同于阅读理由，但伴随了定语或状语，可能是在进行对比，采取的策略仍然是反驳理由本身。这种策略其实非常常见，我们会在稍后听力部分的对比展开法当中详细讨论。

记笔记的时候，基本原则是，已经预见的东西一定不要记，这是浪费时间，因为我们都知道记笔记会影响听下文，所以只需记必要的东西。那么，在这种类型文章的听力当中，我们记什么呢？

第一，记大的策略方向，尽快听出来是否定 P 还是否定 P 与 C 的关系，做相应标记就好；接着，重点记否定 P 或者 P 与 C 的关系的理由。

Q4：怎样展开观点理由型文章的写作？>>

所有对话题的区分，对反驳策略的区分，目的是能够在写作中形成形式上的区别。很多人以为综合写作有所谓的"模板",以为套用几句"The reading claims that ... but the lecturer does not agree..."就万事俱备了。这简直是对这项考试的侮辱。真正得高分的学生在写作中不仅精确地复述了听力信息本身,更重要的是精确地使用了某些句型,准确地捕捉了听力的反驳逻辑,完美复现了听力与阅读之间的关系。

观点理由型文章是 TPO 的重点,同学们可以在之后的范文库中进一步学习更丰富的句型,现在我们只介绍一些形式,足够大家使用。

首先,开头段。假设阅读观点为 C(C 为句子,不是名词;如果是名词,句型需要变),可以使用如下句型:The reading proposes three arguments to support that C, all of which are questioned in the lecture. 注意,这个开头绝不能使用到其他类型文章当中。

接着,假设阅读的理由为 P(P 为句子,不是名词)。首先,假如听力的反驳策略是 P 本身,可以使用如下一系列句型:

◇ Contrary to the reading, the lecturer simply does not agree that P, because...
◇ The lecturer insists that ~P(~P 表示 P 的反面),because...
◇ The lecturer simply does not agree with the reading's claim that P, because...

我们用 TPO 47 的第一个理由段做例子,可以写为:

◇ Contrary to the reading, the lecturer insists that pterosaurs might be warm-blooded, because...
◇ Contrary to the reading, the lecturer believes that pterosaurs were not necessarily cold-blooded, because ...

若听力的反驳策略是 P 与 C 的关系,我们可用的句型就丰富多了:

◇ While the lecturer concedes that P, he/she still insists that ~C, because...
◇ While the lecturer concedes that P, he/she does not believe that C, because...

若 P 和 C 能够被名词化,则可以使用:

◇ Contrary to the reading, the lecturer does not believe that P suffices to overturn ~C/prove C.
◇ Contrary to the reading, the lecturer insists that P is compatible with ~C.

我们拿 TPO 45 的第一个理由段举例,可以写为:

◇ While the lecturer concedes that no bee fossil of 200 million years old was found, she insists that the structures could still be constructed by bees, because...

如果能够将观点和理由名词化，可以更精炼地写为：

◇ Contrary to the reading, the lecturer insists that the lack of bee fossil of 200 million years old is compatible with bee's existence at that time.

◇ The lecturer does not believe that the lack of bee fossil of 200 million years old suffices to prove that the structure was not created by bees。

在这里提醒大家注意，看后面的范文时，一定不要照搬句型本身，一定要注意句型当中对P和C的复述使用的到底是名词形式还是从句形式，注意语法准确性。在范文中，使用的句型是非常多样化的，如果有兴趣学习，请注意每种句型的语法要求以及所表现的逻辑关系，切记不要直接生搬硬套。

> **注：讨论某个事件/行为产生几个正面或负面结果的 TPO 综合写作属于观点理由型文章吗？**
>
> 如前所述，TPO 大多数文章都属于观点理由型文章，但像 TPO 2、TPO 11、TPO 16、TPO 20、TPO 21、TPO 46 等这些有点特殊的综合写作也可以被纳入观点理由型的文章当中吗？这几套 TPO 综合写作的阅读部分都是在讨论某个事件、行为将产生的正面或负面结果。我在写的时候没有直接当作观点理由型文章写，在这里解释一下。比如：TPO 21 讨论种植转基因树木会带来的好处。范文使用的句型是：The article claims that ... offers three advantages, all of which are denied by the lecturer.
>
> 在这种理解方式下，三个好处是独立的，文章没有唯一的观点。但是，这种文章其实也可以理解为"一个观点＋三个理由"，观点是种植转基因树木好，正文段落分三个方面来证明它好。如果这么理解，完全就可以在开头写："The article presents three reasons why ... is a good idea, all of which are denied by the lecturer."同理，如果某篇文章指出某个行为有三个坏处，也可以理解为本文的主旨是想说这个行为不好，用三个具体的证据来支持这个观点。大家既可以参考范文中的写法，也可以直接套用观点理由型文章的写法。

（2）现象解释型文章的备考策略

Q1：怎样辨识现象解释型文章？>>

与观点理由型文章不同，现象解释型文章的全文没有统一的观点要去支持，它的全文是由一个统一的事实所控制。现象解释型文章开头一定会抛出一个事实，或者一个对象，绝不是一个观点，所以我们看不到标志推断的那些字眼。紧接着，最明显的标志是，作者会说，人们尝试了几种不同的理论或者方式去解释这个现象。这里，有一些非常固定的标志词：theory, hypothesis, cause, explanation，表示人们在寻找这个现象的原因，即解释。一定要注意，观点理由型文章的观点本身可能是一个 theory，或是一个 hypothesis，这并不会与现象解释型文章混淆，因为观点理由型文章的观点只能是单独的一个 theory，但是现象解释型文章一定会抛出三个不同的 theory。换句话讲，观点理由型文章只有一个观点，三个理由是共同为这个观点服务的，它们可以同时成立。而现象解释型文章只有一个事实，针对这个事实抛出三个互相竞争的观点。比如 TPO 34，文章一开始就抛出了一个事实：Steller's sea cow 灭绝了。紧接着，在段尾，作者说 here are three theories about the main cause of the extinction，表明文章不会去证明 extinction，因为它是既成事实，而只会寻找造成这个现象的原因。听力也不会去否定 extinction，只会去否定这些原因。再比如，TPO 32，开篇就抛出了 strange sounds 这个现象，段尾说 there are several theories about what might have caused the odd sounds，这也非常鲜明地表明了文章是现象解释型文章。

Q2：怎样有效地阅读现象解释型文章？>>

现象解释型文章的阅读是非常简单的，开篇很容易确定我们要解释的现象是什么，我们简称为 F（fact 的缩写）。在接下来的三段中，我们的目标非常单纯，就是找到三个解释 E（explanation 的缩写）。段内一切不可能导致 F 的东西都不是重要信息，只有能够造成 F 的东西才是我们需要读出来的东西，也是听力将会反驳的东西。

以 TPO 34 为例。

> 我们已经知道要解释的 F 是 sea cows 的灭绝。看第一个正文段，发现第一句话 sea cows may have been overhunted by groups of native Siberian people，那这个段落还用仔细看吗？解释已经出现了，我们可以留下充裕的时间去预测听力可能会如何反驳。
>
> 再看第二个解释：the sea cows may have become extinct because of ecosystem disturbances that caused a decline in their main source of food, kelp。这个段落也不用再多看了，第二个解释就是"食物来源 kelp 减少"。
>
> 第三个解释是：the main cause of extinction of the sea cows could have been European fur traders who came to the island after 1741。所以很明显，fur traders 是造成灭绝的原因。这个阅读也太轻松了。

再以 TPO 32 为例。

> 开头已知要解释的 F 是奇怪的声音。第一个正文段一开始就清晰地说了，the strange noises were actually the calls of male and female orca whales during a courtship ritual，原来是鲸鱼交配，好浪漫，接下来不用细看了。
>
> 第二段，the sounds were caused by giant squid，接下来不用细看了。
>
> 第三段，Russian submarines were picking up stray sounds from some military technology, like another country's submarines that were secretly patrolling the area，说得很清楚，是敌方科技的声音。

总的来说，现象解释型文章的阅读要比观点理由型文章的阅读更简单，目的性更强。我们应该非常有自信，在读的时候，看到了那些解释，就知道接下来的内容没有必要花时间仔细读。

找到了三个解释，对听力的预测有什么帮助？现象解释型听力部分也是难度更低的一种听力，因为它只能做一件事情，否定这三个解释。即，E 不能解释 F。最常见的是两种策略：第一，E 根本就没发生；第二，E 发生了，但不可能造成 F。无论是哪一个，具体效果都是 E 并不是造成 F 的原因，所以区别不大，这个预测的价值有限，并且对写作的影响也不大，同学们没有必要非得仔细区别。

回到 TPO 34 当中，没听听力时就应该已经知道，它要说三个段落，分别是：sea cows 不是被 Siberian 捕杀没的，也不是因为缺少 kelp 而饿死的，更不是被 fur traders 杀光的。

Q3：怎样 get 到现象解释型文章的听力重点? >>

如前所说，听力时我们要减少记笔记，只记不可预测的。听力正文段如果说某个 E 不是正确的解释，这句话是绝对不需要记的，只需记之后说这个解释错误的证据或理由。其实，这种文章的听力和观点理由型文章的听力也没有特别大的区别。

Q4：怎样展开现象解释型文章的写作? >>

这一大类文章也有着统一的模型，假设要解释的现象 F 是名词，给出的解释 E 也是名词。那么，开头段最简单的写法就是：The article presents three theories/hypotheses/explanations regarding F, all of which are challenged by the lecturer.

每个正文段一开始都直接说，听力不同意某个解释，比如：

- ◇ The lecturer dismissed the possibility that E caused F, because…
- ◇ The E hypothesis is dismissed by the lecturer because…
- ◇ The lecturer does not believe that E is responsible for F, because…

回到 TPO 34，以第一个理由为例，可以写：

- ◇ The lecturer dismissed the possibility that overhunting caused the sea cows' extinction, because…
- ◇ The overhunting hypothesis is dismissed by the lecturer because…
- ◇ The lecturer does not believe that overhunting is responsible for the extinction of the Steller's sea cows, because…

但是，名词化不是一项容易的工作，如果 E 和 F 是句子，而不是名词怎么办？可以使用以下句型：

◇ The lecturer does not agree that the reason why F is that E, because…
◇ The lecturer does not believe that it is because E that F, because…

回到 TPO 34 的第一个理由，可以写：

◇ The lecturer does not agree that the reason why the Steller's sea cows became extinct is because they were overhunted by native Siberians.
◇ The lecturer does not believe that it is because they are overhunted by native Siberians that the Steller's sea cows became extinct.

当然，还有 E 是句子、F 是名词，或 E 是名词、F 是句子的情况，在此就不再赘述，请同学们在参考范文时留意句型的使用条件。

（3）问题解决型文章的备考策略

Q1：怎样辨识问题解决型文章？>>

问题解决型文章一开始一定会抛出一个问题（problem），肯定是个坏事，并且是个事实，不是个观点。比如，TPO 48 开篇的 many frog species around the world have declined in numbers or even gone extinct, TPO 42 开篇的 millions of birds are harmed every year, TPO 18 开篇的 Torreya will soon become extinct, TPO 15 开篇的 a large cane toad population now threatens small native animals。然而，不是有 problem 就是 "problem + solution" 的文章，也很可能是现象解释型文章，上面提到的关于 Stellars' sea cows 灭绝的 TPO 34，文章并不是去解决这个灭绝，而是去解释这个灭绝。再比如 TPO 16，开头段最后一句话指出 the science of archaeology was faced with serious problems and limitations in Britain，但这篇文章不是问题解决型文章，而是观点理由型文章。

问题解决型文章开头段最后一句话一定要表明，本文的目的是去解决这些问题，所以会看到一些标志词，体现解决方案、手段、策略等。比如，TPO 48 的 several methods…solve the problem，比如 TPO 42 的 several solutions, TPO 18 的 three ways to address，以及 TPO 15 的 several measures have been proposed。而 TPO 16 只是抛出了这些 problems，没说要解决，说明这篇文章就是要证明 problems 的存在，所以是观点理由型文章。

Q2：怎样有效地阅读问题解决型文章？>>

既然我们已经明白问题解决型文章正文是要寻找某问题的解决方案，那三个正文段的阅读目的就是且也仅是找到那三个方案。想一想日常说话中，我们会采用什么样的语言形式来提出解决某问题的方案呢？比如，我身体不好，有人要建议我锻炼以加强身体素质，他可以怎么说？可以说：

◇ You should/must/need/ought to work out (in order) to become healthier.
◇ You'd better work out…
◇ It's good for your health to work out…
◇ If you work out, you can be healthier
◇ One way to be healthier is to work out.

我们在读正文的时候就应该专门盯着这些能够表达解决方案的信息。本章开篇已经拿TPO 48 举过例了，现在换一篇。

以 TPO 15 为例。

文章开篇声明我们要解决的 problem 是 cane toads 传播过剩。正文第一段的 one way to 已经表明接下来肯定是 solution。紧接着看到 build a national fence，那这个段落下面的信息扫过去就好了，因为肯定是对这个策略的展开，不会给我们更多重要的信息。

第二个正文段一开始的 the toads could be captured and destroyed by 提示接下来讲解决策略，紧接着 volunteers 就是具体的策略了，下面的信息就不重要了。

第三个正文段开始的 researchers are developing a disease-causing virus to control the cane toad populations，直接说出了解决方案，后面的内容不用仔细看了。

总的来说，问题解决型文章与现象解释型文章的阅读都要比观点理由型文章简单，我们很容易找到最核心的三个信息。

问题是，我们可能一分钟就能读完这些文章，那给我们三分钟干什么呢？我们可以利用充裕的时间去预测可能的反驳。而在问题解决型文章当中，反驳策略要丰富很多，通常来说，在日常生活中，我们要反驳一个解决方案，称为 S（solution 的缩写）。解决一个问题 P（problem 的缩写），可以有五种策略：

❶ S 不可行，我们根本做不了；
❷ S 无效，做了 S 也解决不了 P；
❸ P 根本不是个很大问题，不需要解决；
❹ S 的副作用太明显，虽然能解决 P，但带来的问题更大；
❺ 有比 S 更好的方案。

但是，在综合写作中，由于阅读和听力都会默认该 P 是值得解决的，所以方案 3 是不存在的；并且，听力的目的只是否定阅读的建议，所以听力并不会提出新的方案，所以方案 5 也是不存在的。所以，在综合写作中，否定阅读建议的常见方案只有：

❶ S 不可行，根本没有能力执行；

❷ S 无效，不能解决 P；

❸ S 副作用明显。

回到 TPO 15 的三个策略，我们瞬间就可以想到听起来比较合理的可能策略。第一个理由：造个 fence 根本不可能，做不到；造个 fence 解决不了 toad spread；造个 fence 会产生副作用。第二个理由：volunteer 根本没法做；volunteer 无法解决 toad spread；volunteer 会带来副作用。第三个理由：virus 根本没法执行；virus 无法解决 toad spread；virus 会带来副作用。

Q3：怎样 get 到问题解决型文章的听力重点？>>

对于问题解型文章的听力部分我们只需注意听两个内容：第一，确定听力的反驳策略，因为这决定了我们的写作形式；第二，这个策略失败的具体原因。

以 TPO 15 为例，在听第一个理由反驳的时候，听到 won't stop toad…，就已经明白了，该策略是否定建议的有效性，这个建议不能解决 toad spread。接下来，听出具体不能解决的理由就好了，和其他类型的文章没有区别，详见解析。

Q4：怎样展开问题解决型文章的写作？>>

开头段，一般可以写：The article presents three solutions/measures/ways to…, all of which are questioned in the lecture.

正文段的形式取决于听力的反驳策略。如果是否定可行性，可以写：

> ◇ The lecturer does not believe the proposal to be practical, because…
> ◇ The lecturer claims that the solution is impractical, because…

如果是否定有效性，可以写：

> ◇ The lecturer does not believe that the proposal can effectively…, because…
> ◇ The lecturer argues that the proposal will not effectively…, because…

如果是提出副作用，可以写：

> ◇ While the proposal might effectively…, the lecturer argues that it would generate a bigger problem.

然后展开该 problem。当然，实际可以使用的句型五花八门，同学们可以参考相关章节的范文。

重要的听力论述形式

我参加 TOEFL 考试很多次，听力部分从来都是满分，即便如此，要求我什么信息都听到而不遗漏是不现实的，但我从来不会漏掉关键信息。那是如何做到的呢？除了听力应该训练的基本发音的辨识等，最重要的是学会在听力时思考。具体来说，很多论述方式中，下文会说什么，上文已经暗示得很清楚了，那么下文我只需要听到重点字眼验证自己的预期就可以了，笔记也不用记，因为都是无用信息，听起来很轻松。换句话说，就是把耳朵的任务交给脑子去完成一部分，这样耳朵的压力就小很多。本小节中，给大家介绍三种常见的听力反驳套路：对比、举例/类比、虚拟语气。这三种论证一旦出现，我们就可以很清楚地预见下文展开的策略。

(1) 对比论证的反驳套路

如果有人说："万炜是个好人。"我现在要反驳，我说了上半句："诚然，万炜以前人很好"，你觉得我后半句会说什么？是不是很明显？那一定是"他现在很不好"之类的意思。综合写作中，听力也惯常使用这样的套路：我们首先会听到让步词，接着，让步的信息肯定和阅读的信息一致，但对比阅读妥协的部分，听力妥协得并不完全，它一旦加上了定语和状语，后面的信息很可能是说，在不满足该定语或状语限制的条件下，情况不同。认识到这个模式，后面的信息基本都可以脑补出来。

以 TPO 42 为例，这是一篇问题解决型文章。

> 要解决的问题是，鸟会冲向玻璃受伤。阅读的第三个解决方案是：制造磁场来影响鸟的运动，听力肯定要否定。我们看看听力是怎么说的。The third solution... won't work 体现作者是要否定该建议的有效性。it's true 体现让步；birds use Earth's magnetic field to help them navigate 和阅读一致；only when ... travelling long distances，怎么多了个状语？这说明只承认远距离飞行用磁场。那下面要说什么呢？肯定是：我们现在面对的问题是城市里鸟都是近距离飞行，所以这个策略没用。接着听下文，文章说"For example, if a bird is migrating from a cold country to a warm one"，这没意义，这是展开刚才的远距离飞行。"But this ability isn't used to go over short distance, such as going from one side of the city to another..."这些是不用听就知道要说的内容。

复述这种反驳的时候，句型选择也不难，简单的 while 让步就好了，比如，在刚才那个例子中，可以写：

◇ The lecturer does not believe that using a magnetic field would help, because while birds do use magnetic field to navigate when they travel long distances, they rely on other instruments when travelling short trip...

(2) 类比/举例论证的反驳套路

如果有人说："万炜，你努力了一定会考好的，你看张炜……"那他估计要说张炜发生了什么？很显然，张炜应该努力过，后来考好了；当然，有较小的可能性是张炜没努力，后来没考好。总的来说，如果某人要借用别人/某地的例子，来支持对另一个人/另一个地方的看法，显然，双方一定有相似性。在综合写作中，听力的立场已经确定，接下来如果明说"让我们来看看……"的例子，那这个例子不用听，其特点一定和我们需要的立场相符。

以 TPO 41 为例，这是一篇观点理由型文章。

观点是：不该对 coal ash 制定更严格的规则，其第二个理由是：会让人们影响 coal ash recycling，进而让人们不愿意购买 coal ash product。

下面来看一下听力是怎么反驳这一点的，首先明确，听力肯定支持更严格的规则。段首的...won't ... mean that consumers will stop using coal ash products，直接否定了阅读的理由。接着，Let's look at how people responded to ... other...Take mercury for example 这样的信息，说明她要借用 mercury 的例子。不听这个例子，你期望这个例子包含什么信息呢？显然，应该是政府制定了更严格的 mercury 的规则，但是 recycle 没有受到影响，并且人们仍然购买 mercury product。... subject to strict ... rules ... Yet ... successfully and safely recycled for over 50 years ... consumers have ...few concerns，是不是全是我们早已经预见到的事情了呢？

(3) 虚拟语气的反驳套路

这是英文会使用的论证方式，中文不存在这种概念。假想阅读的观点是：万炜很努力。现在听力要反驳，听力说："假如万炜努力了，他后来的成绩理应很高。但是……"后面会说什么呢？是不是应该是"他成绩低"之类的内容？

这是第一种常见形式。第二种是，听力说："可是，万炜成绩很差啊。假如他努力过……"请问后面应该说什么？也很明显吧，应该说"他成绩理应好才对"之类的信息。

假设阅读的观点是 X，听力用证据 Y 来否定，使用虚拟语气论证的方式就是：❶ 假如 X，理应 ~Y，可是 Y。❷ Y。假如 X，理应 ~Y 才对。

以 TPO 47 为例，阅读要证明 pterosaurs 不能进行 powered flight。阅读的第三点理由是：

pterosaurs 不能 take off。听力说："...takeoff would be a problem ... if they took off the way birds do."那下面会说什么呢？显然会说："但是它们和 birds take off 的方式不同，所以 take off 不是个问题。"

再以 TPO 32 为例，阅读想要解释海底怪声。阅读的第二点说可能是 squid 的声音。听力肯定要否定，听力说："...first detected ... in the 1960s and reports ... continued for about two decades ... But the sounds disappeared by the 1980s. However, squids have always lived in the ocean... and continue to live today."其实这个逻辑已经清楚了，怪声持续了几十年后停止，但是 squid 一直存在。接着，听力说 If they were squid sounds，假如是 squid 的声音，那后面应该说什么？是不是显然应该是"不应该先有后无"这样的内容啊？

听出虚拟语气是很困难的，因为虚拟语气的表达很隐蔽。请同学们一定要学会听 should have/could have/would have/might have 的组合，因为连读会使得 have 的音被吞掉，使得实际效果变成 should've/could've/would've/might've，容易使我们放松警惕。

综合写作听力的记笔记原则

刚才的虚拟语气论证形式已经涉及听力和记笔记的原则了。高分考生会始终在听听力时进行思考，会非常谨慎地花时间记笔记。逻辑上蕴含的东西是一定不需要记的。逻辑上，如果已知听力要证明~X，且听力说因为~Y，那听力必然默认"假如 X，理应 Y"。同理，如果已知听力要证明~X，且听力说"假如 X，理应 Y"，那自然，听力必须默认~Y。下文对这些逻辑进行补足的部分是不需要记录的。

这里必须首先明确的是，综合写作永远没有要求大家必须使用原文用过的词。需要复述的是原文逻辑，而不是背诵原文。所以，记笔记关注的是忠诚于原文的关系，并不是拼命花时间原封不动地照搬。

下面总结一下记笔记的原则。

❶ 首段一般不记笔记，因为首段几乎是对阅读首段目标的否定，属于已经可以推断的内容。

❷ 每段段首用符号记录反驳大策略，而尽量不记录精确的词语。比如：阅读是观点理由型，观点是"万炜会成功"，理由是"万炜很努力"。那么听力只有两种策略，否定努力，或否定努力与成功的关系。则一般会直接在阅读笔记上标注，在"努力"上画"×"或在"努力"与"成功"之间的箭头上画"×"。现象解释与问题解决型文章同理。

❸ 所有逻辑蕴含的内容不记。比如，听力说了 X，接着说，因为 Y 发生了。这些需要记。假如他说，"因为 Y 会导致 X"，这肯定不需要记。或者假如他说，"如果不是 X，理应不是 Y"，这肯定也不需要记。这些都是上文逻辑已经蕴含的信息。

❹ 每个分论点内部的核心理由要记，展开的例子要记，但是没有展开的例子的列举不需要记，也不需要写。比如：万炜喜欢吃苹果、西瓜、桃子等水果。这种并列的例子是不用理睬的，写的时候，写"万炜喜欢吃一系列水果"就可以了。

❺ 符合基本常识的信息不需要记。比如，听力说 CO_2 的增高会带来温室效应，这是不需要记的。但每个人的常识水准不同，所以这个必须结合自己的知识面来决定。

常用的笔记符号

本书将常用以下一些符号来表达逻辑关系，同学们不需要照搬，请选择自己习惯的符号笔记方式。

符号	意义	英文案例	笔记案例
√	肯定	Working hard is a good thing.	work hard √
×或~	否定	Working hard is a bad idea.	work hard ×
→或←	导致	Carbon Oxide can lead to global warming.	$CO_2 \rightarrow$ 温 ↑
↑或↓	增/减	Employee performance has improved.	员工表现 ↑
>或<	支持	The fossil is probably fake since it is too dark.	化石 × < dark
vs.	对立	Birds are different from mammals.	birds vs. mammals

怎样选择综合写作的写作信息？

综合写作允许的词数有限，信息选择成为关键。选择信息的原则如下：

❶ 开头只复述阅读观点，并说，听力不同意。

❷ 正文段不复述阅读（阅读是可以复述的，但为了节省词数，就可以不复述），但对听力的复述一定要保证读者能直接看出阅读被反驳的内容。比如，写 The lecturer simply does not agree that X can lead to Y 时，很显然，阅读说的就是 X can lead to Y。

❸ 听力中每个段落的核心理由必须复述，且有几个就要复述几个；核心的被展开的例子也必须复述。

❹ 听力中逻辑蕴含的内容根据篇幅选择性复述或省去，不影响大局。

❺ 听力中列举的例子不复述。

❻ 听力使用的词语、句型，是否照搬完全没有影响，但是得保证和原文逻辑关系一致。

Part 2

落笔生花——
新托福综合写作高分范文精讲

综合写作高分范文精讲

阅读解析与听力预测
⇩
听力解析
⇩
满分范文

TPO 1

阅读解析与听力预测

总 论：
公司应该提供员工每周工作4天的选择。[1] 阅读接下来肯定会给三个理由支持这个建议，所以这是典型的"观点+三个理由"的文章。听听力时应该注意到底是在否定前提还是在否定逻辑。

理由1：
这会让公司利润增加，因为员工工作状态会更好；并且，公司支出不会增多，因为虽然员工多了，但每个人的工资都少了。[2]

理由2：
这会降低失业率。[3]

理由3：
提高员工生活水平，因为有更多可自由支配的时间。[4]

[1] 5 = > 4-day week

➡ 听力肯定不支持这个选择。

[2] $↑ ← rested, alert, error↓, more staff, less pay

➡ 这个理由很有意思，分为两个部分，所以理论上都可以讨论。

[3] unemployment↓

➡ 可能会直接否定前提，说并不能减少失业；或者否定逻辑，说就算减少失业，这个变化也不好。当然，这个说法听起来有点不符合常理。

[4] life quality↑ ← family, leisure

➡ 最可能说的是，就算有更多闲暇时间，也不见得会提高生活质量；理论上可以否定前提，但鉴于这个前提看起来是事实，估计很难否定。

[5] 无需笔记

[6] spend more, new workers → training, medical benefits; cost the same 4 or 5; more office space, computers

听 力 解 析

Offering ... a 4-day workweek won't affect company profits, economic conditions, or the lives of employees in the ways the reading suggests，直接与阅读对抗，我们已经预见到了，不需记录。[5]

First，准备听公司利润。spend more，导致支出增加。...more money... training, and medical benefits... costs... the same whether ... works 4 days or 5，这里解释了增加的点。因为根据阅读，员工人均工资是减少的，所以这里听力选择了人均不变的支出，即培训和医保，所以人数增多，自然支出增多。... more office space and more computers，继续指出增加的来源。[6]

◆ **本段逻辑梳理：**（首先注意，本段并没有真的去讨论员工工作质量是否会提高的问题，只讨论了阅读所声称的不会增加支出）4天工作日会造成公司成本增加，因为这会要求雇用更多的员工，而更多员工意味着培训、医保、工作空间、电脑等投入都增多。

TPO 1

Second，准备听就业率。... doesn't follow that... more jobs will become available，直接否定前提，并不会带来工作岗位。Hiring new workers is costly... And companies have other options，意思是公司并不需要招新人，有别的解决方法。那接下来肯定是解决方法。ask employees to work overtime，加班。raise expectations，expect ... 4-day employees... to do the same... in 5 days，这里都是在说，不用招新人，让工作 4 天的人做 5 天的事情就可以了。no additional jobs will be created 是无用信息，current jobs will become more unpleasant 是逻辑的必然结果。[7]

◆ **本段逻辑梳理**：4 天工作日并不能解决就业问题，因为公司并不需要招更多的人，只需要让现有的工作 4 天的人员加班，在 4 天内完成 5 天的工作量。这样，就业没变，现有工作还更高压。

Finally，准备听生活质量。while 表让步，offers more free time，承认有更多闲暇，接下来肯定会说这些闲暇不等于生活质量提高。risks... reducing their quality of life，是无用信息，因为我们预见到了。decrease... job stability and harm ... chances for advancing their careers，工作不稳定，没有升迁的机会。the first to lose jobs during an economic downturn，这是在展开刚才的 job stability，经济危机来了，公司肯定先开掉这些工作 4 天的员工。passed over for promotions，就是刚才的没有升迁机会，because companies ... prefer ... 5-day employees in management positions，招经理肯定得招工作 5 天的，to ensure continuous coverage and consistent supervision，因为这样才能保持随时在岗。[8]

◆ **本段逻辑梳理**：工作 4 天反而可能降低员工的生活质量，因为他们的工作会变得不稳定，也失去了升职的可能性。首先，经济危机时公司肯定会先裁掉他们。其次，公司招经理，肯定会招那些能够一周都在公司工作的人。

[7] ✎ *other options, work overtime, raise expectations, expect 4 to do 5, no additional jobs, current jobs unpleasant*

[8] ✎ *risks, reduce quality, job stability, career advance ↓, first to lose jobs during economic ↓, prefer 5 in management positions, consistent supervision*

📝 满 分 范 文

The article presents three arguments why companies should offer employees the option of a four-day work week, all of which are contested in the lecture.[9]

[9] 很鲜明的"观点 + 三个理由"的文章。这个开头明显体现的是观点理由型文章的开头形式。到了别的文章中，同学们就会学到其他文章类型的开头方式。

For starters, contrary to what the article suggests, the lecturer maintains that the change would result in a cut in company profits, because of increased expenditure.[10] The change would require the company to hire more staff. Even though the salary for employees working 4 days is only 80% of those working 5 days, the expense on medical benefits and training would be the same per person. Also, more employees entail more spending on office space and computers.[11]

Second, the lecturer does not believe that[10] the change would increase employment rate, because it is likely that the companies would adopt other options rather than hire more staff to compensate for the reduced workdays. Companies may expect the 4-day employees to complete just as much work as the 5-day employees. They may require them to work overtime. As a result, no additional jobs will be created, while the current jobs are becoming more unpleasant.

Last, according to the lecturer, the change might lower, rather than improve,[10] the employees' life quality. Their jobs will be less stable, because during economic downturn, they might be laid off first. Also, they may lose opportunity for career advancement, because the companies would prefer managers who can be there the entire work week.

---

[10] 这样的句型大家下一次可以模仿:contrary to what the article suggests, the lecturer maintains that... 可以用来表达听力直接反对阅读中的前提或理由本身。下面两段中的 "the lecturer does not believe that..." 和 "according to the lecture, ... might ... rather than..." 也都可以用来反驳阅读前提。但到了别的文章中,同学们就会学到反驳逻辑的各种表达方式。

[11] 在看段内展开时,请同学们稍加留意诸如 even though, also 之类的逻辑词,看看是如何尊重原文逻辑的。

TPO 2

1. ✎ teamwork √

   ▶ 听力肯定会说 teamwork 不怎么好。

2. ✎ wider range of knowledge; more resources → quick, creative < risky < spread responsibility

   ▶ 这很难预测，可以说很多东西，考场上肯定没有时间仔细想。也许资源多不是好事；也许资源就不多；也许责任不能均摊，或者均摊了不代表更敢冒风险，也不意味速度更快。

3. ✎ rewarding < decision-making; chance to shine < results far-reaching

   ▶ 这更难预测了，就不预测了。

4. ✎ 无需笔记

📝 阅读解析与听力预测

▶ 总 论：
teamwork 有各种好处，¹ 下文将会展开各种好处，而听力会直接说这些好处不存在，或者干脆说是坏处。

注：第一段看完，直接就看出这是一篇非常奇特的文章，和其他所有 TPO 文章都不同，它只有两个正文段，因此我们只能特别处理。

▶ 段落 1：
团队资源丰富；并且，团队效率高，敢冒风险，这是因为责任均摊。²

▶ 段落 2：
更有成就感，因为能够参与决策，并且每个人都有机会出彩，这又是因为团队的成果影响力更大。³

📝 听力解析

在听之前，我们就应该极其谨慎，因为这是百里挑一的奇葩文章，因此听力的反驳估计也不见得按套路出牌，所以几乎只能完全依靠听力实力了。

I wanna tell you what one company found when... turn over... projects to teams of people...这个开头与众不同，直接说例子——一个公司研究团队工作的结果，我们期望不是什么好结果。"After about 6 months, the company... look at how well the teams performed." 是无用信息。⁴

On virtually every team, some members ...free ride, 有很多人会吃白食。其实这条信息不好说是反驳阅读的哪一条，勉强可以和"团

TPO 2

队资源多"挂上钩，因为很多人根本不会贡献。didn't contribute much at all 是无用信息。but if their team did a good job, they nevertheless benefit...这些不贡献的人仍然能够在团队成功时坐享其成。what about group members who worked especially well... the recognition... went to the group as a whole，优秀的贡献者却得不到特别的奖励。no names were named 是无用信息；So... when the real contributors were asked how they felt... their attitude was just the opposite of what the reading predicts 也是无用信息，这些优秀的人肯定不开心。所以，这应该是和阅读中的 rewarding 形成了比对。[5]

◆ **本段逻辑梳理：** 团队合作中总有人吃白食，坐享其成，而优秀人才却得不到特殊赞誉，自然不爽。

Another finding 说明要分层了。projects just didn't move quickly 很明显是和阅读部分对立，工作开展缓慢。took so long to reach consensus，这应该不会让我们意外，达成共识很难。took many meetings to build the agreement 是无用信息。On the other hand 说明要指出相反方面了。1 or 2 people... become very influential，这时确实是相反的，不需要听所有人意见了，有一两个意见权威，后面肯定不是什么好事。Sometimes when those influencers said "That will never work" about an idea... the idea was quickly dropped instead of being further discussed，他们想否决就否决；when ...convinced ...a plan of theirs was... creative... even though some ...warn ...the group ... they were basically ignored，他们想推进就推进。这里正反两方面都在说当群体有领袖时，虽然不会进展缓慢，但导致的问题是决策专断。"When the project failed, the blame was placed on all" 是说工作失败后，所有人都要担责任。这个段落听完，总的来说在两个方面和阅读形成了对立：首先，工程运行速度不见得更快。其次，并不是每个人都能参与到决策中，甚至这些人后面还要承担责任。[6]

◆ **本段逻辑梳理：** 首先，团队不见得更快，因为要达成共识很慢。若是没有这个问题，那可能有一两个意见领袖，这时就会决策专断，导致很多人的意见被忽略，但糟糕的是，当团队决策失败后，这些被忽略的人却也要和别人平摊责任。

[5] ✏ some free ride, receive benefit; recognition to whole, no particular name; contributor: ✗

[6] ✏ ✗ move quickly; took long to consensus, how move along; 1 or 2 influential, not work → dropped, ✗ discuss; convince, some warn → ignored, blame placed on everyone

TPO 2

📝 满分范文

The article discusses several advantages of group work; however, the lecturer presents a case study done by a company that suggests otherwise.[7]

For starters, the lecturer points out that not all of the group members in the study contributed in their task. In fact, there were always some free riders who nonetheless received benefits when the projects were completed. What's worse, the recognition of success went to the team as a whole without crediting particular contributors, so the ones that actually did a lot of work did not end up feeling good.

Second, opposite to what the reading claims, the lecturer pointed out that in some group projects, things moved forward quite slowly, because it took too long for the team to reach consensus because everybody's voice had to be heard.

On the other hand, according to the lecturer, in some groups where there were one or two leading voices, things might have worked out faster, but decisions were often made arbitrarily. For example, if these leading people felt that a plan wouldn't work, the idea would immediately be dropped without being discussed further; on the contrary, when they felt positive about a decision, they would push it and ignore all opposite opinions. The problem was that, when the project failed in the end, the blame went to everybody.

> [7] 这是个特殊的开头，因为听力是直接通过一个研究调查来反对阅读的。

📝 总　结

请同学们千万不要以这篇文章为参考，因为在整个 TPO 中，只有这一套用了这种非常不规则的模式，阅读和听力之间的对应性很差，阅读、听力结构都不完全清晰。我们并不需要将这种模式应用到综合写作中，因为实际考试中并不会出现这种奇怪的情况。

TPO 3

阅读解析与听力预测

▶ 总　论：

画不是 R 的。[1] 后文肯定是三个理由支持这个观点，所以是典型的观点理由型文章，听听力时注意是反驳证据还是反驳逻辑。

▶ 理由 1：

R 很注意细节，而此画中帽子的朴实与带皮草领子的外套的奢华不搭。[2]

▶ 理由 2：

光影也不搭，脸上有下面反上来的光，但下面的毛领子不反光。[3]

▶ 理由 3：

画板是拼装的，但 R 不拼装画板。[4]

---

[1] ✎ ×R's
　🗒 听力肯定说是 R 的。

[2] ✎ dress — servant linen cap vs. lux coat, R — detail
　🗒 很难反驳事实，所以不好说画上没有这两个东西，也不好说 R 不重视细节；所以，最有可能说"画面上看到这两个东西"与"R 关注细节"不矛盾。

[3] ✎ light, shadow ×, face illuminate below, below dark
　🗒 很难反驳画上的事实，所以估计只能说"上面的亮"与"下面的暗"不矛盾。

[4] ✎ paint on panel, wood together, R — ×glue panel
　🗒 还是很难反驳事实，所以估计只能说这些不矛盾。

[5] ✎ 无需笔记

[6] ✎ fur collar ×original, 100 after painted over, increase $, aristocrat lady

---

📝 听力解析

　　Everything you just read...is true，这里其实已经暗示出了听力的反驳策略了，听力不可能攻击阅读给出的证据，只能说这些证据不充足。after … re-examination…recently concluded … indeed … Rembrandt，这是预期之中的，还是要说是 R 的，不需要记录，是无用信息。[5]

　　First，准备听朴实的帽子和昂贵的外套。X-rays… shown …collar wasn't…original painting，基本不用听了，全说清楚了，那毛领子根本就不是原画，那和原画矛盾也无所谓了。painted over the top of the original…100 years after…展开也不意外。Someone probably wanted to increase…value …by making it …a formal portrait of an aristocratic lady，继续展开，添加这个领子是为了让画增值，所以要把人画得更正式一点，贵族一点。[6]

　　◆ **本段逻辑梳理**：帽子与外套的矛盾根本不是问题，因为研究显示外套领子根本就是后来加的，为了让原画更正式，这样可以卖得更贵。

TPO 3

Second, 准备听光影。Once...collar was removed, the original could be seen...wearing a simple collar of light-colored cloth, 这下说清楚了，跟刚才一个问题，不是原画，原画中那个领子是浅色的，自然就可以反光，就不矛盾了。... reflects light that illuminates... face, 这是无用信息。That's why the face is not in partial shadow, 也是无用信息。So in the original painting, light and shadow are very realistic, and just what we would expect from Rembrandt, 也是无用信息。[7]

◆ **本段逻辑梳理**：光影的矛盾也不是问题，因为如果后加的领子被去掉，我们会发现原来的画是浅色领子，是可以反光到脸上的。

[7] ✎ remove collar → light-colored cloth, reflect light, illuminate face, original - realistic

Finally, 准备听画板拼接。when the fur collar was added, the wood panel was also enlarged with extra wood pieces, 还是一样的问题，连拼接的画板都是后来加的，基本不用说什么了。glued to the sides and the top to make...more grand and valuable, 还是为了增值。So the original...on a single piece of wood 是无用信息。And... wood in the original form ... from the very same tree as ... another painting..., his *Self-Portrait with a Hat*, 额外的证据，原来的那块板和 R 的另一幅画的木头来自同一棵树，进一步佐证这幅画是 R 的。[8]

◆ **本段逻辑梳理**：拼接画板也无法证明这不是 R 的画，因为拼接的部分是后来人加的，为了增值。而早先画板只是一块木板，并且其木头和 R 的另一幅画的画板来自同一棵树。

[8] ✎ wood — enlarged, glued, make grand, $, original — single piece; from the same tree as another, Self-Portrait with a Hat

📝 满分范文

The article presents three arguments why a painting of an old lady was not created by Rembrandt, all of which, according to the lecturer, are countered by a recent study.[9]

[9] 典型的"观点 + 三个理由"的文章开头。

First, regarding the inconsistency between the humble linen cap and the luxurious coat with the fur collar, the recent study shows that the collar was not a part of the original painting. In fact, someone perhaps added it about 100 years after to increase the painting's value by making the lady in the picture look more aristocratic.

Second, this study also helps the lecturer explain away the seemingly ill-fitted[10] light and shadow; once the fur collar was removed, the underneath painting displays a light-colored cloth reflecting light onto and thereby illuminating the face. Clearly, the original painting was done quite realistically.

[10] explain away the seemingly X 的用法理解如下：阅读认为是 X，但听力认为这只是表象，给出了更本质的解释消除（explain away）这种看法。

As for the fact that the panel of the painting was made of pieces of wood glued together, something Rembrandt wouldn't do, the study also shows that the original painting was painted on just one piece of wood. All the others were later glued onto the original to enlarge the frame and thus to make the painting more grand and more valuable. In fact, studies have shown that the original piece of wood was cut from the same tree as the panel of another of Rembrandt's painting, his *Self-Portrait with a Hat*.

TPO 4

阅读解析与听力预测

总　论：
恐龙是 endotherms。[1] 正文将用三个理由支持这个观点，所以是典型的观点理由型文章，听听力时应该注意是反驳理由还是反驳逻辑。

理由 1：
在极地发现恐龙化石，只有恒温动物才应该能生活在极地。[2]

理由 2：
腿长在身下，而不是两侧，说明腿是恒温动物用来跑步的。[3]

理由 3：
有 Haversian canals，而只有恒温动物才有。[4]

---

[1] 恐龙 — endo
听力肯定说恐龙不见得是 endotherm。

[2] polar fossil
肯定不可能否定这些化石本身，这是事实；所以只能否定关系，就算有化石，也不代表恒温。

[3] leg-under body vs. side
肯定不可能否认腿的位置的事实；所以只能否定关系，就算长在下面，也不代表恒温。

[4] H canal
还是无法否认这个事实；所以只能说，就算有，也不代表恒温。

[5] 无需笔记

[6] polar warmer, enough to live, cold → migrate to warmer, hibernate

听力解析

don't...prove...endotherms 是无用信息，不需要记。[5]

polar dinosaur argument，说明进入第一点。polar... warmer than today，已经把反驳说清楚了，那会儿极地暖和，不恒温也能住。warm enough... part of the year for... not endotherms... 这是无用信息。During months cold, migrate or hibernate，完美解决了恐龙当年的生存。doesn't prove...endotherms 是无用信息。[6]

◆ **本段逻辑梳理**：就算有极地恐龙，也不需要恒温，因为当年极地暖和，一年里某些时候恐龙就可以生存在那儿，冷了迁徙或冬眠就可以了。

what about...legs placed under...，进入第二点。doesn't...mean ...high-energy endotherms built for running，是无用信息。another explanation 是空话。supports more weight, so...can grow to a very large size，解释清楚了，腿在下面，不是为了跑得快，而是因为体积大。Being large had advantages，体积大就是好处。so we don't need…endotherm or running to explain，这是无用信息。[7]

◆ **本段逻辑梳理**：腿长在下面也不代表是需要长时间跑步的恒温动物，因为腿在下面可以支撑大的身体，这对恐龙就足够有益。

[7] ✕ run, support more weight, grow large, advantage

how about bone structure，提示进入第三点。do have Haversian canals，让步，接下来肯定反驳。also have growth rings，这个 growth rings 不用听肯定知道不符合 endotherms，而符合 non-endotherms。…thickening of the bone that indicates periods of time when the dinosaurs were not rapidly growing，这个 rings 体现了恐龙停止生长的时期。evidence that dinosaurs stopped growing or grew more slowly during cooler periods. This pattern of periodic growth… characteristic of…not endotherms，说得非常清楚了，这个 rings 表明恐龙生长有周期性，冷天长得慢，热天长得快，而只有 non-endotherms 才这样。Animals…maintain a constant body temperature …grow rapidly even when…cool，恒温动物什么时候都长，这是无用信息。[8]

◆ **本段逻辑梳理**：就算恐龙有 H canals，恐龙还有 growth rings，说明它们冷天不长，热天长，而只有非恒温动物才这样。

[8] growth ring, thick ＞ not growing period, stop growing in cool, cycle — ~ endo, endo — grow when cool

📝 满分范文

The article presents three arguments why dinosaurs were endotherms, all of which are questioned by the lecturer.[9]

For starters, the lecturer believes that the discovery of dinosaur fossils in polar regions does not entail that[10] dinosaurs were endotherms. Because polar regions back at that time were much warmer than they are today, for some period of the year, the temperature could be warm enough for dinosaurs to survive there even if they were not able to adjust their body temperature. For the cooler time, dinosaurs could simply migrate or hibernate.

[9] 典型的"观点+三个理由"的文章的开头。

[10] X does not entail Y 体现了听力是在否定 X 与 Y 之间的逻辑关系。

TPO 4

[11] X while still Y 表明听力认为 X 和 Y 是可以共存的，而听力认为 Y 足以证明 X 是错的（或者 X 足以证明 Y 是错的）。

Second, the lecturer argues that dinosaurs could well be non-endotherms while still[11] having legs growing underneath their bodies. The leg position does not have to be explained by intense running, as in the case of endotherms; instead, it could alternatively help sustain a larger and heavier body, which could provide survival advantage for dinosaurs.

Last, even though dinosaurs do have Haversian canals, which typically belong to endotherms, the lecturer points to the discovery of growth rings in dinosaur fossils that suggest a similarity between dinosaurs and non-endotherms. The rings indicate a cycle of fast growth in warm periods followed by little growth during cool periods, a cycle that typically belongs to non-endotherms.

TPO 5

📝 阅读解析与听力预测

> ● 总　论：
>
> great houses 是用来干什么的，有三个猜测。[1] 典型的现象解释型文章，下文肯定是三个解释，来讨论 great houses 的功能。
>
> ● 解释 1：
>
> 住人的，因为像后来的 apartment。[2]
>
> ● 解释 2：
>
> 储存 maize 的。[3]
>
> ● 解释 3：
>
> ceremony center，证据是 pots。[4]

[1] ✏️ great houses?
　　🐾 听力肯定是否定每一个可能的猜测。

[2] ✏️ resident ≈ apartment
　　🐾 否定 resident。

[3] ✏️ store food (maize)
　　🐾 否定储存食物。

[4] ✏️ ceremony center < pots
　　🐾 否定 ceremony center。

📝 听力解析

[5] ✏️ 无需笔记

none…is convincing，符合预期，是无用信息。[5]

First，准备听关于住人的内容。sure，估计是让步；from the outside…look like…apartment，承认从外面看像住人，接下来肯定反驳说内部怎么不像住人的，典型的对比论述形式。but the inside…casts…doubt 是无用信息。If hundreds of people were living…there would have to be many fireplaces, where each family did…cooking，这个虚拟语气的出现直接暗示下文肯定说发现的 fireplaces 很少或根本没有。but…few fireplaces 是无用信息。In one of the largest houses, there were fireplaces for only around ten families, yet…enough rooms …for more than 100 families，这是例子，表明 fireplaces 很少，不是很重要。so…couldn't have been residential 是无用信息。[6]

◆ **本段逻辑梳理**：不是住人的，假如是住人的，理应有很多壁炉，但实际上发现的壁炉很少。

[6] ✏️ <out ≈ apartment > inside ✗, 100 → fireplace, cook; ↓ fire, large 10 family fire places, rooms for 100 families

Part 2 | 039
综合写作高分范文精讲

TPO 5

Second, 准备听与储存食物有关的内容。store grain maize is unsupported by evidence 是无用信息，不需记录。may sound plausible, 表让步, 什么都没有说。but ... not uncovered many traces of maize or maize containers, 这个反驳很直接, 就是没发现谷物和谷物容器。If...were used for storage, why isn't there more spilled maize ... 这个虚拟语气又是无用信息。Why aren't there more...containers 是无用信息。[7]

◆ **本段逻辑梳理**：也不是储存玉米的，因为在地上没有发现溅落的玉米痕迹，也没有发现玉米容器。

Third, 准备听仪式。ceremonial center isn't well supported either 是无用信息。mound...contains...other materials besides...pots, stuff you wouldn't expect from ceremonies ... building materials, sand, stone, even construction tools, 发现了很多不属于仪式的东西。suggests...the mound is just a trash heap of construction material, 说明其实是垃圾堆。stuff ... thrown away or not used up ... pots ... be regular trash too, left over from the meals of the construction workers, 说明 pots 也只是垃圾。[8]

◆ **本段逻辑梳理**：也不是仪式场所，因为发现了很多不属于仪式场所的东西，说明这其实是个垃圾堆，包括那些 pots 其实是工人留下来的垃圾。

[7] ✗ uncover traces of maize and containers

[8] mound, other stuff, building materials, sand, stone, construction tool, trash heap, thrown away, pots — left from meals of workers

📝 满分范文

The article presents three potential theories regarding the function of the "great houses", all of which are challenged by the lecturer.[9]

For starters, the lecturer does not consider the main function of the houses to be residential, because although the outside of the houses looks like the later apartment buildings, the inside tells a different story. Such a large residential house would require plenty of fireplaces for cooking and yet very few fireplaces were discovered. For example, in the largest house, fireplaces enough for only 10

[9] 典型的现象解释型文章开头。

families were excavated, yet the rooms in the houses were able to support over 100 families.

Second, the lecturer does not believe that the houses were mainly used to store maize either, because archaeological excavations had revealed extremely few traces of maize spilled on the ground as well as very few maize containers.

Last, the ceremonial center hypothesis is challenged as well, because in the mound near Pueblo Alto, more than just the pots were discovered. Materials revealed also include large building materials like sand, stone, and construction tools, which wouldn't belong to a ceremonial center, suggesting that the site was probably just a trash heap. The pots were probably just among things thrown away by construction workers after meals as well.

TPO 6

📝 阅读解析与听力预测

⚪ 总 论：
网络百科不如纸质百科。[1] 接下来肯定是提供三个理由论述为什么网络不如纸质，典型的观点理由型文章。

⚪ 理由 1：
网络百科不如纸质百科可靠，撰写人缺乏水准。[2]

⚪ 理由 2：
网络容易受到攻击。[3]

⚪ 理由 3：
网络太关注大众流行的不重要的问题，而纸质能够挑选真正重要的问题。[4]

---

[1] ✏️ communal online 百科 < traditional

🔸 听力肯定是说网络和纸质一样好，甚至更好。

[2] ✏️ contributor ✕ academic credential → ✕ accurate

🔸 说网络的撰写人水平一样好，甚至更好；或者说，网络和纸质一样准确，甚至更准确；或者说，就算网络不准确，网络也和纸质一样好，甚至更好（这个有点不现实）。

[3] ✏️ fabricate, delete, corrupt information

🔸 要么说网络并不比纸质更容易受到攻击；要么说，就算受到攻击，网络也不比纸质差。

[4] ✏️ focus on trivial and popular topics

🔸 要么说网络和纸质一样能关注重要问题，甚至更好；要么说，就算网络更关注流行问题，网络也不比纸质差，甚至更好。

[5] ✏️ 无需笔记

[6] ✏️ traditional ✕, easy to correct online, print — remain decades

📝 听力解析

The criticism ... result of prejudice ... ignorance about how far online... have come 说明听力要捍卫 COE（communal online encyclopedia），这是无用信息。[5]

First，准备听错误。Traditional ... never ... perfectly ... 看来反驳策略是传统百科一样有缺陷。if you are looking for ... without any mistakes ... not going to find it，这是无用信息。easy ... to be corrected...online...第二个策略，网上的错误好修正，那肯定是说纸质错误不好修正。But...printed...errors remain for decades，是无用信息。[6]

◆ **本段逻辑梳理**：首先，纸质百科一样有错误；而且，网上错误好改，纸质的错误一旦犯了几十年不变。

TPO 6

Second,准备听黑客。One strategy...is to put the crucial facts... that nobody disputes in a read-only format... no one can make changes to,解决方案是只读化。Another strategy...is...editors...monitor all changes...and eliminate...malicious,雇用编辑监控。[7]

◆ **本段逻辑梳理**：面对黑客，网络百科第一会将大家都接受的核心信息只读化；第二，雇用编辑来监控一切改动，把有害改动删除。

[7] strategy: crucial — read-only format; editors, monitor change, eliminate malicious

Third,准备听内容大众化。what's worth knowing about 不知道要说什么。The problem for traditional... is that they have limited space, so they have to decide what's important and what's not,这一下子说清楚了策略，很显然，可能会说网络百科不需要决定重要不重要，因为网络没有空间问题。in practice, the judgments...do not reflect...range of interests,而且纸质百科所决定的重要问题并不能体现人们的需要。space...not an issue for online...是无用信息。The academic articles are still represented in online...过去重要的问题在网上也能呈现。but...greater variety of...topics...reflect the greater diversity of user interest,基本也是无用信息。strongest advantages,这恰恰是网络的优势。[8]

◆ **本段逻辑梳理**：传统百科之所以需要选择重要内容，因为传统百科有空间限制，更何况它们所选的所谓重要内容并不见得反映大众真实的多种需求；相反，网络百科没有空间限制，不需要挑选所谓的重要内容，网络百科能把那些学术内容包含在内，还能更好地表现多种多样的大众实际需求，这恰恰是网络的好处。

[8] traditional, limited space, has to decide importance, judgments don't reflect range; space, not an issue for online, academic still represented, great variety of topics, advantages

满分范文

The article presents three arguments why communal online encyclopedias (COEs) are less valuable than traditional, printed encyclopedias, all of which are dismissed by the lecturer.[9]

[9] 典型的"观点+三个理由"的文章开头。

For starters, even though the lecturer admits that COEs are fallible, she insists that traditional ones are just as prone to errors. What's worse, while the errors on COEs are easy to detect and

TPO 6

correct, those on printed pages often remain for decades before they are corrected.

As for hacking, the lecturer argues that COEs have adopted several strategies to address this problem. [10] First, COEs use a read-only format for all those crucial materials already accepted by everybody. Second, editors are hired to monitor and recognize all changes made to the online materials, and are ready to delete all the malicious ones.

Third, contrary to the article, the lecturer considers the diversity of topics on COEs their main strength rather than weakness. [11] The reason why traditional encyclopedias have to decide what is important is that they have limited space; consequently, their judgments often fail to represent a diverse range of interest. On the contrary, space is not an issue online, so while academic interest is still represented, there is a greater variety of topics that suit a much more diverse audience.

[10] 相当于否认了网络黑客会对COEs产生不良影响，因为网络能处理黑客问题。

[11] Contrary to/Unlike the article, the lecturer considers XXX strength rather than weakness, 暗示阅读认为XXX是缺陷，而听力认为是优势。

TPO 7

📝 阅读解析与听力预测

▶ 总 论：
美国木材厂不会寻求 ecocertification。[1] 本文会用三个理由来证明为什么美国工厂不会寻求 ecocertification，因此是典型的观点理由型文章，听听力时注意是反驳理由本身还是反驳逻辑。

▶ 理由 1：
customers 不 care 这个 label。[2]

▶ 理由 2：
ecocertification 会让产品变贵，贵了反而不好卖。[3]

▶ 理由 3：
只关注国内市场就可以了，国内消费者对现有产品是满意的。[4]

[1] ✎ VS wood company — × eco
▶ 听力会说美国工厂会寻求 ecocertification。

[2] ✎ customers × trust label
▶ 要么说 customers trust，要么说就算 customers 不 trust，工厂也会去追求 ecocertification（这个听起来有点不靠谱）。

[3] ✎ $ (examine)
▶ 要么说不会贵，要么说就算贵了也会 ecocertify。

[4] ✎ cater to domestic, satisfied
▶ 可以说不仅仅要关注国内市场；或者说国内消费者并不会满意；或者说就算关注国内市场，而国内消费者很满意，但还要追求 ecocertification。

[5] ✎ 无需笔记

[6] ✎ treat × same, own products vs. independent agencies (confidence)

📝 听力解析

will...seek ecocertification 是无用信息，符合预期，不需记录。[5]

First，准备听人们不 care 这个 label。companies...don't treat all advertising the same，这句话一出现，接下来肯定要对比，当然我们并不知道他要具体对比什么。distinguish between ... claims that companies make about their own products and claims made by independent...agencies，这句话一出现，本段已经彻底清楚了。肯定是说人们不在意的只是商家的自吹自擂，而这种 ecocertification 是第三方评估，人们是在意的。have ... confidence in independent agencies 是无用信息。Thus ... react very favorably ... 也是无用信息。[6]

◆ **本段逻辑梳理**：美国人会 care 这个 label 的，他们只是不

TPO 7

care 商家的王婆卖瓜，但这种第三方权威机构给的评定，美国人是买账的。

　　Second，准备听价钱。of course，让步；care…about price…But…price alone determines…decisions only when…听到这个 only when，就知道这个句子其实是要否定价钱的重要性了，继续听 when the price…much higher or lower。接下来肯定要对比说：price 区别不大时，就不会是决定因素，而 ecocertification 的问题带来的 price 差别肯定不大。When the difference…small, say, less than 5%, as is the case with certified wood, Americans often do choose on factors other than price, 这几乎都是无用信息。convinced of the value of…environment，指出人们如果真正在这个情况下可能更关心 factor。[7]

　　◆ **本段逻辑梳理**：这个价钱增高对消费者影响并不会很大，因为在价钱差别 5% 以内时，他们对价钱并不敏感，而 ecocertification 造成的差别就在这个区间内，美国人现在更在意环保，所以 ecocertification 肯定是个好事。

　　Third，准备听国外市场。should…pay attention…internationally，看起来和阅读直接对着干了。Not because of foreign consumers… but because of foreign competitors，这下反驳策略已经确定了，虽然不用管国外用户，但是要关注国外竞争者，国外竞争者会用 ecocertification 的产品来战胜美国工厂。good chance that many American consumers…interested in ecocertified products, and…If American companies are slow, foreign companies will…crowding into…这只是把刚才预见到的东西说出来了而已，基本是无用信息。[8]

　　◆ **本段逻辑梳理**：确实不用考虑国外用户，但得考虑国外竞争者，如果不生产 ecocertified products，国内用户还想要这些 products，那国外产品肯定就涌进来占据市场。

[7] ✏ < care $ >, much higher / lower, × 5% ↓, value of environment

[8] ✏ × foreign customers, √ competition, slow → foreign companies crowd in

📝 满分范文

　　The article presents three arguments to support its prediction that wood companies in the United States will probably not try to receive ecocertification for their products. However, all the arguments are questioned by the lecturer.[9]

[9] 典型的观点理由型文章的开头。

[10] 这里体现了听力与阅读争论的是阅读的前提本身，即消费者不 care 这种 label。

[11] 这里体现了听力与阅读争论的是阅读的逻辑：价钱确实高了，但这个价钱高并不会影响消费者。

First, the lecturer does not believe that American consumers will be indifferent to the eco-friendly label[10], because even though they tend to ignore a label a company uses to promote its own products, they do have confidence in labels that an independent agency issues. Therefore, it is very likely that American consumers will react favorably to this trustworthy ecocertification.

Second, the lecturer does not believe that the higher price generated by the ecocertification will stop consumers from purchasing the products[11], because even though consumers can be sensitive to prices, they do not have a clear preference when the price difference is smaller than 5%, as is in the case between other wood products and the ecocertified ones. Therefore, given Americans' raised awareness of environmental protection, it makes sense for wood companies to get their products ecocertified.

Last, while the lecturer concedes that American wood companies do not need to worry about foreign customers, he argues that they still need to watch out for foreign competitors. If American companies are slow to catch the ecocertification trend, companies from other countries will potentially crowd in to provide products that better satisfy American consumers.

TPO 8

1. C ×
   听力肯定说可靠。

2. wealthy vs. 借钱
   直接否定他借了钱这一点比较难，因为是否定事实；或者说，借了钱不证明他说了假话。

3. capture conversation accurately
   他并没有记录下来（这是不可能的，这等于承认他在瞎编）；所以只能说，记下来是很正常的。

4. escape from a prison with a knife vs. bribe (friends)
   肯定说他就是用刀子脱狱的，不是贿赂。

5. 无需笔记

6. spent money on parties, gambling; sell property to convert money, take time

阅读解析与听力预测

▶ **总　论：**
C 的文字不可靠。[1] 接下来肯定分三点来论证不可靠，典型的观点理由型文章，反驳时注意反驳对象是理由本身还是逻辑。

▶ **理由 1：**
C 声称自己有钱，但他借了很多钱。[2]

▶ **理由 2：**
他竟然能将和伏尔泰对话的细节记录下来。[3]

▶ **理由 3：**
说自己脱狱靠刀子，但更可能是靠朋友贿赂。[4]

听力解析

accurate, reliable, 完美符合预期，不需记录。[5]

First，准备听借钱。doesn't mean…poor, 反驳策略出现了，要说借钱和有钱不矛盾，接下来肯定详细解释。Chevalier spent…money on parties and gambling, 不知道要说什么，继续听。he had wealth, 听不懂，继续听。But…property you have to sell first to get money, 大概听明白了，很富有，但财富是要变现的。took…days to convert…into…money, 这下彻底听清楚了，得花好多天才能变现，那变现之前肯定要借钱。borrow some while…waiting for his money to arrive, 是无用信息，不用记录。[6]

◆ **本段逻辑梳理：** 有钱时借钱很正常，就算他财产很多，但这些财产得先变现才能用来开派对和赌博，而变现需要花时间，变现之前他得先借钱。

TPO 8

Second，准备听和 V 的对话。Chevalier states in his memoir that each night...after conversing with Voltaire, he wrote down，基本不用听了，策略已经很明显，对话完都记下来，以后看笔记就行了。Chevalier kept his notes...for many years, and referred to them when writing the memoir，这是必需的，是无用信息。Witnesses...confirmed that he regularly consulted notes，这在额外补充证据，方向也一致。[7]

◆ **本段逻辑梳理**：他将细节记下来很正常，因为当年对话完他每天都会回忆之前的对话并记下来，之后他写 memoir 的时候参考了这些笔记，别人也证明了这一点。

Third，准备听逃狱。Others...had ever more powerful friends，这个对比一出现，后文基本肯定会说，朋友更厉害，贿赂更多，但没能脱狱，所以通过贿赂脱狱不可能。none...able to bribe...to freedom，是无用信息；So bribery hardly seems likely in his case 也无用信息。best evidence, though, comes from some old Venetian...documents，准备听是什么证据。soon after Chevalier escaped prison, the ceiling of his...room...repaired，这说得很清楚了，他的牢房屋顶之后被修缮了，说明他之前脱狱是弄坏了牢房屋顶。[8]

◆ **本段逻辑梳理**：他肯定是那么逃走的，不是通过贿赂。首先，通过贿赂不可能，因为别的狱友有更厉害的朋友，也没能通过贿赂逃走；其次，文件显示，他逃走之后，牢房屋顶就被修缮了。

[7] wrote down everything he could remember after each night, kept many years, referred, witnesses confirm

[8] other had powerful friends, no bribe, old V document, soon after, ceiling repaired

满分范文

The article points to three controversial pieces of information in Chevalier's memoir to demonstrate the memoir's unreliability. However, the lecturer insists that the memoir, including these three segments, is generally historically accurate.[9]

First, the lecturer does not believe that borrowing money entails that Chevalier was not as wealthy as he claimed[10]. Though Chevalier had a lot of properties, it would still take days to convert his property into real cash for his gambling and party activities. During the interval, he would need to borrow money.

[9] 典型的"观点+三个理由"的文章开头。

[10] "The lecturer does not believe/mean that X entails that not Y."这个结构中，X 是阅读的证据，Y 是听力的观点，典型的否定逻辑的写法，阅读的证据并不足以证明听力的观点是错的。

TPO 8

Second, the lecturer believes that it is not surprising that Chevalier could recapitulate the details during the conversation with Voltaire, because after each night conversing with Voltaire, Chevalier would write down everything he could remember. When he wrote the memoir, he referred to those notes, which he had kept for many years. In fact, witnesses confirmed that he consulted notes frequently.

Last, the lecturer insists that Chevalier escaped from the prison in the way he described, not by bribery.[11] She points to other people held in that jail who had more powerful friends and still did not manage to get out through bribery. Also, based on an old Venetian document, soon after Chevalier left the prison, the ceiling of his former prison cell was repaired, which fit his account perfectly.

[11] "..., not .../Not ... but ..." 的结构直接暗示了双方的立场。

TPO 9

📝 阅读解析与听力预测

▶ 总 论：
FC 引擎会更好，会替换掉 IC 引擎。[1] 很显然，将会有三个理由支持这个观点，典型的观点理由型文章，听听力时注意是反驳证据还是反驳逻辑。

▶ 理由 1：
IC 靠 petro，而 petro 有限；FC 靠 H，H 无限。[2]

▶ 理由 2：
FC 产生的污染少，因为氢燃烧产生的是水，而油燃烧产生的是二氧化碳。[3]

▶ 理由 3：
便宜，能耗低。[4]

[1] ✍ FC > IC, replace
🔸 不见得更好，不能替换。

[2] ✍ IC: petro, finite; FC: H, × deplete
🔸 petro 有限基本是事实，可以反驳 H 无限，或者可以说就算 H 无限，也替换不了。

[3] ✍ × pollute, H → 水；IC → CO_2
🔸 无法否定 IC 产生 CO_2，H 产生水；估计只能说，就算燃烧 H 产生水，最后还是会有很多污染；或者说，就算产生的污染少，也替代不了。

[4] ✍ eco competitive, less money, energy efficient
🔸 能耗不低；就算能耗低，也不便宜；就算便宜，也替代不了。

[5] ✍ 无需笔记

[6] ✍ × available, <present, common > × usable, pure liquid H (artificial), difficult to produce and store, cold, elaborate cooling tech

📝 听力解析

开头让步了很久，都不重要，听到 reading is way too optimistic... Hydrogen is not the solution，确定预期正确，没有必要记录。[5]

First，准备听与"取之不尽"相关的内容。hydrogen is not as easily available，原来 H 的利用也并不是随意的。Although...present in common substances，让步，承认确实 H 数量很多，很普遍。...not directly usable in that form，接下来肯定要讲用起来多麻烦。must first be obtained in a pure liquid state，开始展开为什么麻烦，首先必须是纯净的液态；highly artificial，必须人工获得；technologically very difficult to produce and store，继续说麻烦；must be kept very cold，展开 store 的麻烦；elaborate cooling technology，继续说 store 的麻烦。So...not...practical and easily available 是无用信息。[6]

TPO 9

◆ **本段逻辑梳理**：就算 H 到处都有，但 H 并不是取之即用，要用 H 必须是纯净的液态，这需要非常麻烦的人工过程，制造和存储都不方便，比如存储必须在很冷的状态下，需要用很精密的制冷工具。

Second，准备听污染。not solve the pollution，说明还是有污染，听为什么。Producing pure hydrogen creates... pollution，原来是 H 的制造产生污染。purification... requires... energy... by burning coal or oil，基本已经说清楚了，制造 H 需要一种提纯工艺，需要燃烧化石燃料，自然产生污染。creates lots of pollution，是无用信息。although the cars would not pollute，表让步，新的车不会产生污染，但后面肯定说制造燃料的过程产生污染。factories that generated the hydrogen... pollute，是无用信息。[7]

[7] pollute, create H, purification (energy, burn coal, oil), factories generate pollute <car ×>

◆ **本段逻辑梳理**：就算车不产生污染，但是新引擎还是会连带产生污染，因为制造 H 燃料需要一种提纯工艺，需要大量能量，而能量来自于燃烧化石燃料，这会产生污染。

Third，准备听价钱。won't cost savings，直接反驳这个理由，就是贵。manufacture the... engine，制造引擎很贵，那接下来肯定要讲贵在哪儿。require components made of platinum，基本已经说清楚了，需要铂金，这很贵。a very rare and expensive metal，是无用信息。Without the platinum... hydrogen doesn't... produces the electricity，解释为什么必须要用铂金，因为没有的话没法产生电力。All the efforts to replace... been unsuccessful，还是说必须要用铂金。[8]

[8] manufacture engine $, platinum component, H → 电, no cheaper replacement

◆ **本段逻辑梳理**：新引擎还是会贵，因为一个原件必须用铂金造，而铂金很贵。没有这个原件，汽车没法产生电力，而目前铂金没法被替代。

📝 满分范文

The article presents three arguments why the hydrogen-based fuel-cell engines are superior and will probably soon replace the traditional internal-combustion engines, all of which are undermined in the lecture.[9]

[9] 典型的"观点 + 三个理由"的文章开头。

For starters, although the lecturer concedes that the petroleum required by internal-combustion engines is finite, she asserts that hydrogen is far not as accessible as the article suggests, because even though it is present everywhere, the only form of hydrogen that can be used is in a pure liquid form, which is highly artificial. It is difficult to produce and has to be stored under extremely cold temperature, which again entails an elaborate cooling technology.

Second, the lecture does not believe that the fuel-cell engines would reduce the pollution problem caused by the internal-combustion engines. True, the cars with the new fuel will not directly pollute, but to generate the hydrogen, factories have to burn coal or oil to produce enough energy, which will create a significant amount of pollution.

Last, the lecturer insists that the fuel-cell engines are very pricy, because a component of the engine has to be produced by platinum, an extremely expensive metal, or else the hydrogen cannot generate electric power. Sadly, no effective and cheaper replacement for platinum has been found.

TPO 10

📝 阅读解析与听力预测

▶ 总 论：

otter 减少是因为污染，而不是因为天敌。[1] 这是观点理由型文章而不是现象解释型文章，因为本文三个理由都一定围绕着同一个解释，而现象解释型文章应该是三个不同解释。这篇文章略微的与众不同之处在于，听力将不仅仅说污染这个解释是错的，而更可能说天敌这个解释是对的。由于这两种可能性同时存在，因此将很难具体预测听力中每个理由所采取的策略。

▶ 理由 1：

确实发现污染物增多，而这可能降低 otter 的免疫力。[2]

▶ 理由 2：

seals, sea lions 都变少了，污染最能解释这一点，因为污染是对整个生态系统的伤害。虽然天敌 orca 也能使 seals 和 sea lions 数量减少，但天敌 orca 不爱吃这么小的东西。（通常阅读中我们不在意看似细节的东西，但是这篇文章所面对的听力不好说是要否定 pollution 还是支持 predation，还是两个都做，反过来，这个阅读的重点是支持 pollution 还是否定 predation，我们也不好判断，这两个功能的信息可能都是重要的）[3]

▶ 理由 3：

各地 otter 减少的程度不同，这符合 pollution 各地不同。[4]

📝 听力解析

predation is the most likely cause，完全符合预期，不需要记录。[5]
First，准备听发现污染物的问题。weakened by the fact that no one...dead sea otters washing off on...beaches，这个内容非常令人

---

[1] 🖊 pollute, × predator → otter ↓
 🦦 听力最可能说就是 predator 而不是 pollute 导致 otter 减少。

[2] 🖊 pollute↑ → resist↓
 🦦 很难说 pollution 不增多，因为这违背事实；也许会说 pollution 不会造成 resistance 下降，也并不会造成 otter 减少；但鉴于文章背景，还有可能去支持 predator 理论。在这种复杂度下预测就得不偿失了，而后面段落会面对同样的问题，于是我们就不做预测了。

[3] 🖊 seals, sea lions ↓, pollution → entire; < orca > hunt larger

[4] 🖊 uneven decline ← uneven pollutants

[5] 🖊 无需笔记

惊讶，因为它好像完全无视了阅读的理由，直接去说新发现的证据，去攻击 pollution 理论。not what you would expect if...pollution...killing ...otters，这个虚拟语气表明刚才的证据和 pollution 理论不符，是无用信息。On the other hand，...consistent with the predator，这在逻辑上是必然的。If...killed by a predator... eaten immediately, so it can't wash up on shore，都是无用信息。[6]

◆ **本段逻辑梳理**：海獭数量减少不是污染造成的，因为如果是污染造成的，理应发现岸上有死尸，但我们没发现死尸；相反，要是被吃掉，则自然不会有死尸。

[6] × dead otters in Alaska, eaten, × wash up

Second，准备听各种动物的死。although 表让步，承认阅读内容；orcas prefer...whales，确实，orcas 并没那么喜欢吃 otters，接下来肯定反驳。whales...disappeared...because of human hunters，基本把反驳策略说清楚了，没 whales 了 orcas 只能吃 otters。orcas have had to change their diet，是无用信息。since only small ... are now available, orcas have probably started hunting those，是无用信息。So it probably is the orcas...causing the decline of all the smaller...也是无用信息。[7]

◆ **本段逻辑梳理**：各种动物的死仍然可以被 orcas 解释，因为就算 orcas 喜欢吃 whales，可是 whales 被人捕没了，orcas 只能吃小动物，于是就可能吃了刚才所有那些动物。

[7] <whale > whale ↓ ← 人, change diet, eat smaller

Third，准备听 uneven decline。better explained by...predation，不用记，符合预期。depend on ... location ... accessible to orcas or not，暗示了 predation 和 location 的关系。In those locations...access easily... declined greatly，是无用信息。However, because orcas large, they cannot access shallow or rocky locations ... precisely ... where sea otter populations not decline，完全是无用信息。[8]

◆ **本段逻辑梳理**：orcas 也能完美解释 uneven decline，因为 shallow 和 rocky 区域是 otters 没减少的地方，而恰好 orcas 很难去这些地方吃 otters，因为它们太大了。

[8] accessible to orca ↑, decline ↓, large → × access shallow rocky, otter √→ × ↓

满分范文

The article presents three arguments why pollution rather than predators is responsible for the decline of sea otters off the Alaskan coast. However, the lecturer presents three counterarguments to support the predation hypothesis.

For starters, the lecturer believes that the pollution theory is inconsistent with the lack of dead otters found onshore.[9] Instead, she prefers the predation theory because if otters were killed by predators, they would be eaten and not appear on shore.

Second, the lecturer believes that the uniform decrease of seals, sea lions and sea otters can all be explained by the orca theory as well: though orcas generally target larger mammals, they would have to turn to these smaller animals, since whales, orcas' main food source, are overhunted by humans.

Last, she argues that the uneven pattern of otter decline can be more effectively explained by the predator theory[10], since otter population has remained quite stable in shallow and rocky waters. These are exactly the regions where otters are less likely to suffer from predation, because orcas are too large to access these places.

[9] 听力的主要攻击策略是用某发现来证明阅读理论不正确，这就适合使用（阅读理论）inconsistent with（听力证据）的句型。

[10] 听力的策略是，阅读给出的现象虽然与阅读理论相吻合，但与听力理论更吻合，所以自然使用了（现象）can be more effectively explained by（听力理论）的结构。

TPO 11

📝 阅读解析与听力预测

▶ 总　论：

人们很少读文学，这会造成三方面的不良影响，包括对大众、文化以及文学的未来发展。[1] 这应该是谈一个现象的三个不良后果，常见的反驳应该是说并不会造成这些不良后果，甚至会产生好处。

▶ 坏处1：

缺乏想象力、同理心和对语言的理解力。[2]

▶ 坏处2：

转向肤浅的娱乐消遣，降低文化水平。[3]

▶ 坏处3：

使得好的作品得不到重视，未来好的文学作品进一步减少。[4]

[1] 📝 read literature↓ → ✗
(public, culture, future)
▶ 并不会产生这些坏处，反而可能有好处。

[2] 📝 public ✗ imagine, empathize, understand language
▶ 并不会产生这些坏处，反而可能有好处。

[3] 📝 trivial entertainment →
✗ culture
▶ 并不会产生这些坏处，反而可能有好处。

[4] 📝 write literature↓
▶ 并不会产生这些坏处，反而可能有好处。

[5] 📝 无需笔记

[6] 📝 ✗ literature, stimulating, science, history, politics, high quality, creative, well-written, imagine, good book

📝 听力解析

"What should we make of this？"[5] 这个开头非常令人意外，完全没有评价，不同于我们大部分情况下见到的，什么都不需要记录。

　　first，准备听缺乏想象力、同理心等。Science ... history, political... aren't literature... but...of high quality, 反驳已经基本成型，就是读别的好作品也可以实现那些目标。just as creative and well-written, 基本是无用信息。can stimulate the imagination, 是无用信息。don't assume that someone who isn't reading literature isn't reading a good book，也是无用信息。[6]

　　◆ **本段逻辑梳理**：就算人们不读文学，他们仍然可以读好书，比如史书、政治、科学，它们同样是开发智力、激发想象力的好书。

　　◆ But let's say that...people...spending less time...with books in

TPO 11

general，非常隐蔽地转到第二点，人们干脆不读书，转向其他消遣。"Does that mean...cultures...decline? No..." 是无用信息，立场符合预期。plenty of culturally...that isn't written，跟上一段策略相似，有别的方式弥补。music and movies，指出弥补方式。"Are people wasting their time... Do ... lower cultural standards? Of course not." 都是无用信息。"Culture has changed... many forms of expressions available other than novels and poems." 还是与逻辑一致的内容。speak more directly to contemporary concerns than literature does，完美反驳。[7]

◆ **本段逻辑梳理**：就算人们不读书，人们仍然可以有文化，通过听音乐、看电影，这些更流行的形式，人们一样可以获得文化，当今新的文化形式可能更能满足当代人的需求。

Finally，准备听对未来的不良影响。it's...true...less support for literature，表示让步，承认人们确实不再支持文学。"But don't... blame the readers... it's authors' faults." 听到这句话，耳朵都要惊掉了。作者根本没有否定阅读文学少对未来的不良后果，准确来说，作者纠结的不是这些不良后果，而是到底是谁造成了这些不良后果。这是几十篇 TPO 几乎独一无二的意外反驳。A lot of modern literature... difficult to understand，这只是将刚才责怪作者的理由说清楚。not much reason to suppose that earlier generations of readers would have read...today's literature，变相说现在的文学不好，前几代读者一样不会读。[8]

◆ **本段逻辑梳理**：就算文学读得少导致的结果不好，这也不能怪读者，这恰恰要怪作者，是作者经常故意把书写得很难懂，就算古人来了估计也不想看。

[7] ✎ < × book > music, movie, good culture, culture changed, many forms, speak more directly to contemporary concerns

[8] ✎ < less support > × readers' fault, author's fault, intend hard, early reader's not read today's literature

📝 满分范文

The article mentions several concerns regarding the trend that young people today are reading less literature, all of which are dismissed by the lecturer.[9]

For starters, according to the lecturer, even though people are

[9] 这篇文章纠结的是文学读得少带来的不良后果，所以采取了 express several concerns 的写法。

reading less literature, it does not entail that they are not reading good books[10]. A book can still be intellectually challenging and stimulate imagination even though it is not literature. A political essay, a scientific report, and many others can be of comparable quality.

Second, from her perspective, even if people are reading less in general, the overall level of culture is not necessarily lower[11], because people can be listening to a musical masterpiece or watching a thrilling movie, both of which are alternative platforms of culture that perhaps speak better to contemporary audiences.

Finally, granted that reading less literature is regrettable, the lecturer does not believe that the readers are blameworthy[12]. Instead, she believes that the trend might be caused by the writers themselves, who sometimes intentionally make their works difficult to understand. Even readers in the past would perhaps not want to read these contemporary novels.

TPO 12

📝 阅读解析与听力预测

▶ 总 论：
画中的人物是 JA（Jane Austen）。[1] 很明显，后面将用三个理由支持这个观点，典型的观点理由型文章。则听力将可能否定每个理由，或是否定理由与观点之间的关系。

▶ 理由 1：
A 的亲属认定就是 JA。[2]

▶ 理由 2：
和大家都承认的 C 笔下的 JA 比较像。[3]

▶ 理由 3：
画的时间恰好是 JA 年轻时，画风和 OH 比较像，而 OH 恰好是那个时期的，其地位也相称。[4]

---

[1] 🖊 画：JA
　　🐾 听力肯定说并不见得是 JA。

[2] 🖊 A's family endorsed
　　🐾 听力可能说亲属并没有认可（很难，这是否定事实）；更有可能说就算亲属认可，也不见得是 JA。

[3] 🖊 ≈ C's sketch
　　🐾 并不像；或者，就算像，也不代表是 JA。

[4] 🖊 painted when teen, style ≈ OH, time ≈
　　🐾 这个预测很难，因为阅读的理由有好几个点都有可能被攻击，所以不如不预测，但这意味着听的时候需要更谨慎，注意在哪里和阅读形成了矛盾。

[5] 🖊 无需笔记

[6] 🖊 authorized, dead 70 yrs, family ✕ seen JA, ✕ certain

📝 听力解析

evidence linking...JA is not at all convincing，是无用信息，不需要记录。一直到 arguments...questionable 都是引言，各种无用信息。[5]

First，准备听家人的认可。when ... authorized ... JA had been dead for almost 70 years，这基本把反驳策略说清楚了，家人认可时 JA 早就过世了，这个认可很可能就不靠谱。family...never actually seen her themselves... couldn't have known for certain，这些在逻辑上都完美实现了我们的需要。[6]

　　◆ **本段逻辑梳理**：就算家人认可，也不代表是 JA，因为家人认可时 JA 已经过世 70 年，家人也没见过她，也可能认错。

Second，准备听像 JA 的肖像。could...be that of a relative，策

略基本上已经清楚了，可以是亲戚，亲戚长得像是正常的。would explain the resemblance，是无用信息。extended Austen family was very large and many of…cousins were teenagers… or had children who were teenagers，这都是在说她的亲戚中有很多人年龄相符。some…could have resembled JA，这必然也是无用信息。experts believe that the true subject…was…relatives… a distant niece of JA，是谁都说出来了。[7]

◆ **本段逻辑梳理**：就算和 JA 相像，可能只是 JA 的亲戚。她的亲戚那么多，有很多和她年龄相仿的女孩儿，是亲戚的可能性很大。专家就觉得像她一个远房外甥女。

[7] relative, large extended family, cousin teenage, children teenage, expert, niece

Third，准备听那个非常麻烦的东西。"…the painting has been attributed to Humphrey only because of the style, but other evidence points to a later date." 发现主要争论的是时间问题，其实这幅画的时间和 JA 年少的时间并不吻合，那么刚才阅读的其他部分就不需要在意了。我们现在肯定主要听什么证据表明了时间问题。A stamp on the back of the picture…the blank canvass…sold by a man…did not sell canvass in London when JA was a teenager，把时间为什么不符说清楚了。He only started selling…when she was 27 years old，解释很完美。the canvass was used…when JA was clearly older than…the portrait，逻辑上是无用信息。[8]

◆ **本段逻辑梳理**：尽管风格显示时间和 JA 少年时吻合，但其他证据显示画作时间要远比 JA 年幼时晚，画背面的印章显示画布是某人兜售的，而这个人售卖画布时 JA 已经 27 岁了。

[8] style → H, other → later, canvas sold by W.L, not sell in London when teenage, sell 27 yrs, older than girl

📝 满 分 范 文

The article presents three arguments why the subject of the portrait of a teenage girl is Jane Austen, all of which are questioned by the lecturer.[9]

For starters, even though it was endorsed by Austen's family, the lecturer argues that the endorsement took place almost 70 years after Austen had passed away. This means that the family members who

[9] 典型的"观点＋三个理由"的文章结构。

TPO 12

endorsed the painting had not seen Austen in person and could not be certain if the portrait was indeed of Austen herself.

Second, the lecturer believes that the semblance between Austen and the little girl in the portrait can be explained otherwise. [10] Perhaps the image is of one of her relatives, since she had a large extended family with a lot of cousins and children of cousins who were of similar age. In fact, some experts believe that the image depicts one of Austen's nieces.

Last, even though stylistic analysis suggests that the painting was finished when Austen was a teenage girl, the lecturer points to other evidence that indicates that the completion time was actually much later. The stamp behind the picture suggests that the canvas of the painting was sold by a man who did not begin selling canvasses in London when Austen was a little girl. Instead, he only started selling when Austen was 27, much older than the girl in the painting.

[10] 阅读用 semblance 做证据，但听力认为这个 semblance 有别的解释，意味着 semblance 不能证明画的是 JA。

TPO 13

阅读解析与听力预测

总 论：

private fossil collection 对 public 和 science 都会造成不良影响。[1] 下文肯定会展开分别说三个不同的坏处。

1. private collectors own fossil ✗

   听力可能说这并不会造成三个坏处，相反可能带来好处。

坏处1：

private fossil collection 使得公众没法看到重要的 fossil，进而可能造成公众对 fossil 的 interest loss。[2]

2. public ✗ see

   可能会说 public 还是能够接触的，对 public 可能有着某种价值。

坏处2：

private fossil collection 使得 science 失去了很多重要的 fossil，对研究有不良影响。[3]

3. science loses fossil

   最可能说科学家并不会损失可见的 fossil，这么做对 science 可能有好处。

坏处3：

private fossil collection 中 collecting fossil 的过程可能破坏了重要的证据。[4]

4. destroy evidence

   最可能说并不会破坏证据，这么做反而对 science 更好。

5. ✓ > ✗

听力解析

exaggerated, benefits…outweigh the disadvantages 表明了听力的策略，坏处没那么大，好处大于坏处，[5] 需记录。这预示下文肯定要谈谈 private fossil trade 的好处了。

First of all, 准备听对 public 的影响。greater exposure to fossils, 直接反驳阅读，公众反而更能看到 fossil, 那接下来应该讲为什么。not less 是无用信息。a lot of fossils available for purchase 体现了原因，更多 fossil 被购买；"…as a result, even low-level public institutions… routinely buy…fossils and display them for the public." 把这个过程讲清楚了，因为有更多的 fossil 可买卖，有更多公立机构会购买 fossil 展

TPO 13

出给大众，于是大众反而有更多机会见到 fossil。[6]

◆ **本段逻辑梳理**：private fossil collection 恰恰有利于公众接触更多 fossil，因为这个过程当中会有更多的 fossil 可以购买，于是很多低层次公立学校也开始大量购买 fossil，恰恰给了公众更多机会接触 fossil。

As for the idea that scientists will lose access to really important fossils，准备听第二点，科学家与 fossil 的关系。not realistic 直接表明听力要和阅读相反。Before anyone can put a value…it needs to be scientifically identified，其实听到这儿这段的逻辑基本已经确定：要定价，得先经过科学检验，那谁来检验，肯定是科学家，所以科学家不会丢掉鉴定 fossil 的机会。the only people who can … are scientists 是无用信息。by…examinations and tests 其实也是无用信息。pass through the hands of…experts first 还是无用信息。not…miss out on anything important 也是无用信息总结。[7]

◆ **本段逻辑梳理**：private collection 并不会让科学界损失接触 fossil 的机会，因为在私人定价之前，fossil 必须先经过科学鉴定，而鉴定者显然只能是科学家。

Finally，准备听证据丢失。"whatever damage…collectors…do, if it weren't for them, many fossils would…undiscovered" 这是令人惊讶的，她竟然承认会损失证据，说明她的策略不是否定坏处，而是说利大于弊，即发现化石的价值大于证据残缺造成的损失。because…not that many fossil collecting…run by universities 指出了为什么如果没有私人勘探，就会有很多化石不被挖掘。better for science…have more fossils…even if we don't have all the…data 已经开始总结她的观点了，这个是可以预测的，不是必须记录的。[8]

◆ **本段逻辑梳理**：确实，证据会有所丢失，但是这个过程会让更多的 fossil 被勘探出来。因为很少有公立机构组织勘探，直接导致很多 fossil 无法被发现。显然，发掘更多 fossil 的价值可以弥补某些 fossil 证据残缺的缺陷。

[6] ↑expose, ↑purchase, low-level schools buy

[7] ×, scientifically identify → place value

[8] 这篇听力听完，最后一段让我们意识到一个重要的问题——如果阅读是指出一个行为的三个坏处，听力不见得非得说这些坏处不存在，还可以说利大于弊。

满分范文

The article expresses several concerns regarding the selling of fossils to private ownership. However, the lecturer believes that the benefits far outweigh its drawbacks.⁹

To begin with, while the article worries that private ownership prevents the public from seeing certain valuable fossils, the lecturer argues that the new development has generated more exposure of fossils to the public. As a result, a lot more fossils are now available for purchase, which in turn allows even low-level public institutions and schools to buy fossils for public display.

Second, the lecturer simply does not believe that scientists are missing out on the opportunity to examine crucial fossil discovery. She points out that all fossils are placed with a commercial value only after they are scientifically evaluated, and of course the examination and test can only be done by professional scientists.

Last, although the lecturer admits that commercial fossil collectors do sometimes destroy scientific evidence, she still insists that the new development is more beneficial than harmful. According to her, in the past, many fossils were left undiscovered because there weren't many excavations run by universities. For her, the value of having more fossils found outweighs the occasional loss of some scientific data.

[9] 本结构体现了阅读指出的三个坏处，听力要说利大于弊的策略。

TPO 14

📝 阅读解析与听力预测

▶ 总 论:
salvage logging 对森林和经济有各种好处。[1] 那下文肯定是列举三方面的好处。

▶ 好处1:
SL 会清理 dead trees, 从而为 fresh trees 的生长 make room。[2]

▶ 好处2:
SL 在清理 dead trees 的时候, 就等于清理了 insect 滋生的环境, 保证了未来树木的健康。[3]

▶ 好处3:
SL 清理出的树木是有用的, 而且清理本身创造了就业岗位。[4]

[1] 📖 SL → 林√ + $√
🔥 听力肯定会说这些好处是不存在的, 甚至会带来坏处。

[2] 📖 dead 木↓, room for fresh
🔥 最有可能说, 并不能产生这种好处。

[3] 📖 insect infest↓ → 健康
🔥 会说这并不能保证树木的健康。

[4] 📖 wood + job
🔥 可能会说, 并不能带来有用的树木, 并不能帮助增加就业岗位。

📝 听力解析

environmental damage...economic benefits questionable 表明作者既不认为 SL 有助于森林恢复, 也不认为其有助于经济发展, 这是我们本来就知道会发生的, 可以不记。[5]

First, 准备听清理死树为新树的成长留空间。not...create the right conditions for tree growth, 不用记, 如我们所预料的。natural...decomposition enriches the soil 明显从反面说不清理的好处, 暗示清理肯定没这些好处。makes it more suitable for future generation of trees 继续说好处。The rapid removal of dead trees can result in soil that lacks the nutrients 明显是我们早就知道的内容, 就是刚才故事的反面, 没有必要记。[6]

◆ **本段逻辑梳理:** SL 并不能真的为新树生长提供更好的条件, 因

[5] 📖 无需笔记

[6] 📖 decompose → soil nutrient → future√

为自然降解的死树会增加土壤营养,帮助新树生长,而 SL 破坏了这个过程。

Second,准备听虫害的防治。it's true 说明让步,有与阅读一致的地方,即 rotting wood can increase insect populations。but is this really bad...不用记,但暗示了接下来的策略肯定会说,有 insect 其实可能是好事。SBB have lived in...forests...without causing major damage,表明 insect 没那么糟糕。And of course dead trees do not provide habitats only for harmful insects,接下来肯定会说 dead trees 对好的生物有利。birds and other insects...important contributors... health 表明死树其实会带来好处。In the long run, therefore, SL may end up doing more harm 明显是无用信息总结。[7]

◆ **本段逻辑梳理**:虽然 dead tree 为害虫提供了沃土,但是 SL 对森林健康的恢复弊大于利,因为 dead tree 还为益虫、益鸟提供沃土;而且害虫给森林带来的坏处本来就不是特别大,比如:beetle 和森林和平共处很久了。

And third,准备听林业、就业等经济价值。benefits...small,直接反驳;and don't last very long,再反驳。recovered only by using helicopters...expensive,表明了为什么 benefits 小,因为代价高昂。Furthermore, jobs...temporary,体现了刚才的 don't last long。filled by outsiders with more experience or training than local residents have,表明带来的就业机会跟当地无关。[8]

◆ **本段逻辑梳理**:SL 对经济和就业并没有什么用处。首先,SL 代价高昂,需要用直升机,怎么会有经济价值?其次,SL 的岗位都是临时工,而且经常照顾外地人,因为本地人没经验。

[7] < insect > beetle × damage 100 yrs, dead trees → bird, √insect

[8] 直升机, $↑, job-temp, outside exp > local

📖 满分范文

The reading passage asserts that salvage logging is beneficial for damaged forest and economy. However, all three purported benefits are dismissed in the lecture.[9]

For starters, the lecturer does not believe that salvage logging can provide a more suitable room for the growth of fresh trees.

[9] 这种结构用于阅读指出某行为的结果,听力否定这些结果。

TPO 14

Instead, she claims that the decomposition of dead trees provide soils rich with nutrients that can tremendously benefit the growth of future woods, an advantage that would be gone if the dead trees are cleared away.

Second, while the lecturer concedes that dead trees offer habitats for some harmful insects, she argues that they also provide life space for birds and insects that are crucial for trees. Therefore, she believes that, forest logging can actually be detrimental to the health of forests. From her view, the presence of some harmful insects are not all that devastating: for example, the spruce bark beetles have existed in forests for over a hundred years without doing significant damage.

Last, she does not believe salvage logging is of much help to the local economy. On the one hand, the dead trees can only be retrieved using vehicles like helicopters, making the process extremely expensive; on the other hand, the job of salvage logging is only temporary and is offered mostly to non-local labors because the local people often lack the required expertise.

TPO 15

📖 阅读解析与听力预测

总　论：

人们用了几种方法来抑制 CT 的蔓延。[1] 下文肯定会分别说三种方法，意味着段落之间是独立的。本文不是三个证据支持一个观点的结构，而是问题解决型文章。

▶ 方案 1：

造 fence 挡住 CT。[2]

▶ 方案 2：

号召人们志愿捕杀 CT。[3]

▶ 方案 3：

virus 专杀 CT。[4]

[1] ✏ stop CT
🐾 听力肯定是分别说这几种方法不合适。

[2] ✏ fence
🐾 否定 fence 这个策略有三种可能性——建 fence 太难，条件不够；建 fence 并不能阻碍 CT；建 fence 有严重的负面后果。

[3] ✏ volunteer 捕杀
🐾 理论上仍然有三种策略——太难，条件不够；这种方法无法阻碍 CT；有负面后果。

[4] ✏ virus
🐾 理论上有三种策略——virus 太难生产；这种方法无法阻碍 CT；有负面后果。

[5] ✏ 无需笔记

[6] ✏ young T and T eggs in streams and rivers, flowing →

✍ 听 力 解 析

unsuccessful，cause…damage 都体现了作者对这些方案的否定。不过这里已经暗示了，接下来的否定策略要么是该方法不能 stop CT，要么是该方法有副作用。[5]

First of all，准备听 fence。won't stop…toad，表明策略是否定方案有效性。young toads and toad eggs are found in rivers and streams，她想说什么？值得我们继续倾听。rivers or streams flowing from one side to the other (side of the fence)，这时应该已经听明白为什么无效了，因为 fence 能挡住成年 CT，但挡不住幼体。carry…to the other side 是无用信息。Since it's only necessary for a few…to get…in order to establish population on the other side，这个道理我们都懂，不用记录，the fence is unlikely to be effective 自然更是无用信息。[6]

TPO 15

♦ **本段逻辑梳理**：fence 无效，因为 fence 挡不住水流中的 young toads 和 toad eggs 从一边流到另一边，所以只要有一些过去了，CT 还是会 spread。

Secondly，准备听人工捕杀 CT。could have success in trapping and destroying toads 体现了作者的让步，认为这种方法也许是有效的。But…these untrained volunteers would inadvertently destroy many of Australia's native frogs，体现了反驳策略是指出该方案的副作用，会意外捕杀当地的 frogs。Some of which are endangered 表明这个副作用还挺严重，使濒危动物受到威胁。not always easy to tell the CT apart from native frogs，指出了为什么会有这个副作用；especially when it's young 只是补充说明在什么时候最难区分。[7]

7 < √ > untrained, × native frogs, × tell between CT & native frogs when young

♦ **本段逻辑梳理**：volunteer 也许确实可以大规模捕杀 CT，可是 volunteer 是没有受过专业训练的，他们很可能无法区分 CT 与本地 frog，造成意外捕杀很多濒危的 frog。

…virus is a bad idea…terrible consequences for CT in their original habitat in Central and South America 体现了反驳策略是指出副作用，具体是对 CT 的原生地产生不良影响。You might be wondering how a virus…in Australia cause harm in the Americas 这句话是无用信息，只是暗示下文要具体展开为什么会有这种副作用。Australian reptiles and amphibians are often transported to other continents，感觉要联系澳大利亚与拉丁美洲了。"Once the animals infected by the virus reach Central and South America, the virus will attack the native CT and devastate their populations." 这很容易理解，病毒跟着动物去了拉丁美洲，自然就会攻击当地物种。ecological disaster because in the Americas CT are a native species and a vital… 这是对前面的补充说明，把当地生物链破坏了。[8]

8 × consequences in original, Central & South America, transported to other continents, attack native CT, vital

♦ **本段逻辑梳理**：使用 virus 会对 CT 原生地（即中南美洲）的 CT 造成灾难性影响，而在那里 CT 是很重要的。因为很多澳大利亚的 reptiles 和 amphibians 会被人为迁移到美洲，而一旦携带病毒的物种被带过去，病毒就会攻击当地的 CT。

TPO 15

满分范文

The article mentions three measures to stop the spread of cane toads in Australia. However, all three measures are dismissed by the lecturer. [9]

For starters, the lecturer does not believe that building a national fence would effectively [10] reduce the spread of cane toads, because a fence would not be able to stop rivers and streams from carrying young toads or toad eggs from one side of the fence to the other. Consequently, as long as some get through, the spread would continue.

Second, while she concedes that volunteers might effectively kill toads, she claims that [11] these untrained people might inadvertently kill native Australian frogs, many of which are endangered. The reason is that the toads and the local frogs are difficult to distinguish especially when they are young.

Last, she believes that using a virus will engender disastrous consequences on [12] cane toads in their original habitat, Central and South America. The reason is that amphibians and reptiles are often transported from Australia to the Americas by people. The chances are, if some infected by the virus reach the Americas, the virus would start attacking local toads and destroy their population. It would be catastrophic because the toads are native to the Americas and are a vital part of the local ecosystem.

---

[9] 典型的三个解决方案与三个反驳的结构。

[10] "The lecturer does not believe that ... would effectively ..." 体现了否定建议有效性的策略。

[11] "While she concedes that ... might effectively ..., she claims that ..." 体现了承认建议有效性，指出建议其他问题的策略。

[12] "She believes that ... will engender disastrous consequences on ..." 体现了指出建议副作用的策略。

TPO 16

📝 阅读解析与听力预测

1 ✏️ 考古 ✗

📣 听力可能会说考古并不存在这些问题，或者这些问题是可以克服的。

2 ✏️ construct → artifacts ✗

📣 建筑工程并不会损毁大量 artifacts，这个问题可以克服。

3 ✏️ $↓

📣 资助不少，或资助少可以弥补。

4 ✏️ jobs↓

📣 就业岗位不少；或就算岗位少，也可以弥补。

> 🔘 **总　论**：
> archaeology 面对很多困难和局限。下文肯定会分别展开三个困难和局限。[1]
>
> 🔘 **困难1**：
> 建筑工程毁掉了很多 artifacts。[2]
>
> 🔘 **困难2**：
> 考古的资金支持少。[3]
>
> 🔘 **困难3**：
> 考古就业机会少，人们只得转投其他行业。[4]

📝 听力解析

5 ✏️ new guidelines

6 ✏️ examine → start, value → preserving plan, build around/excavate + document → proceed

new guidelines were adopted, improved ... in all three areas 体现了听力的反驳策略，接下来指出 new guidelines 中具体如何解决之前阅读提到的三个问题。这篇开头比较意外，因为 new guidelines 的存在是我们没法预期的，所以是需要记下来的。[5]

First，准备听 construction 对考古的影响。before any construction project can start, must be examined 这几个词已经表明 new guidelines 的应对策略了，那就是开工之前，必须先让专家考察考古价值。那我们自然会知道，接下来会说一旦有价值，怎么避免工程带来损害。If...of archaeological interest...make a plan for preserving，是无用信息。either by building around them or by excavating and documenting in them properly 具体指出了两种 preserve 的方式。before the construction...proceed，这是预料之中的。[6]

TPO 16

◆ **本段逻辑梳理**：新规则要求建筑开工之前必须先 examine 工地，如果发现有考古价值，则大家会制订保护方案，要么是 build around，要么是挖掘并标注，然后才能开工。这就避免了 artifacts loss。

Second，准备听资金不足的解决方案。work...paid for by the construction company not by the government 表明了资金的来源，原来工地上各种考古工作还得施工公司掏钱，好惨。initial examination...all the work...under the preservation plan 具体体现了要掏哪些钱，基本上就是全部步骤都要掏钱。new source of financial support 是无用信息，不用记录。allowed...a far great range of...sites 体现了这个措施的结果，就是现在比以前研究范围大多了。[7]

◆ **本段逻辑梳理**：新规则要求之前提到的工程中的一切工作（从开始的 examination 到后来的 preserving 过程）中的花费都由工程公司来支付，这就有了新的资金来源，导致现在考古学家研究的对象反而更丰富了。

Last，准备听就业岗位。a lot of paid work，问题解决了，新规则提供了大量新岗位。that didn't exist before，是无用信息。archaeologists...hired in all stages of the process，这是必然的。to examine... then ... draw the preservation plan to do research in a scientific manner, finally process the data and write articles，把整个过程都展开了。increased the number of professional archaeologists in Britain，这是必然的，不用记录；highest it's ever been，只是为 job 增多提供了具体证据。[8]

◆ **本段逻辑梳理**：新规则下创造了很多岗位，因为刚才所谈到的所有过程都需要专业人员参与，从一开始的 examine，到后来的 draw the preservation plan，到后来的研究，到最后的数据处理和写报告、文章。于是，现在考古学家数量达到了英国历史新高。

[7] paid by company, examine → preservation plan, greater range of site

[8] paid work, ✗ exist, all stages, examine → raw plan → research → process data → report, highest

📝 满分范文

The reading expresses three concerns regarding the status of archaeology in Britain. However, the lecturer claims that the new guidelines have successfully dealt with all three issues.[9]

[9] 典型的困难和解决方案式的开头。

TPO 16

For starters, the lecturer believes that the new guidelines can reduce the potential damage and loss of artifacts caused by construction work. Specifically, the guidelines require that no construction work should start unless its archaeological value is examined beforehand. If a site is of archaeological interest, then a preservation plan should be drawn. Before construction proceeds, the company would either build around the site, or artifacts should be excavated and documented properly.

Second, the lecturer argues that the new guidelines also offer a remedy to the lack of funding. The guidelines require that all aforementioned work, the examination and everything related to the preservation process, be paid for by the construction company. As a result, the new source of funding has allowed archeologists to research on a wider range of topics than before.

Last, the lecturer also believes that the new guidelines have addressed the issue of job shortage. According to the new rule, every stage of the aforementioned process, the initial examination, the latter preservation, the research afterwards, and the final data processing and report writing, would all call for expert advice. As it turns out, today the number of professional archaeologists is higher than ever in Britain.

TPO 17

📝 阅读解析与听力预测

▶ 总 论：
文章预测，在人类农业、杀虫剂等的威胁下，鸟类数量将持续下降。[1] 本文很可能是"观点+三个理由"的结构，用三个理由支持鸟的数量为什么会下降。

▶ 理由1：
人类的入侵使得鸟的栖息地减少。[2]

▶ 理由2：
农业也会占据鸟的栖息地，进一步缩小鸟的生存空间。注意，这一点和第一点有区别，回过头去看，第一点应该是人类的 settlements 占据了鸟的地盘。[3]

▶ 理由3：
pesticides 的使用增多造成鸟类直接死亡或不孕不育。[4]

1. 🖉 鸟↓

   ▶ 很可能要论证鸟的数量不会下降。

2. 🖉 habitats↓

   ▶ 两种反驳可能：鸟的栖息地不会减少；或者就算栖息地减少，鸟的数量不会受到显著影响。

3. 🖉 第一点笔记：人 settlement → habitats↓

   ▶ 第一点听力预测修正：两种可能性：人的 settlement 并不会造成鸟栖息地减少；就算如此，鸟的数量不会受到显著影响。

   🖉 第二点笔记：人 agri → habitats↓

   ▶ 两种可能性：人类的农业并不会影响鸟的栖息地；就算如此，鸟的数量不会受到显著影响。

4. 🖉 pesticides

   ▶ 两种可能性：pesticides 的使用并不会增多；就算如此，不会使鸟的数量减少。

5. 🖉 无需笔记

📝 听 力 解 析

unconvincing 表明作者立场，我们本来就知道，不需要记录。[5]
First，准备讨论人类 settlement 对鸟的影响。it's true 表明让步，urban growth... bad for some types of birds 体现了作者的妥协。provides better and larger habitats for other types，体现了作者的反驳策略，指出城市给某些鸟类带来了新的好的栖息环境，典型的对比论证模式（some 与 other 对比）。dwellers often complain about increased birds' populations 佐证了作者的立场，鸟反而增多了。seagulls, pigeons 等都是并列的细节例子，不需要记录。hawks, falcons 和前面一样，不需要记录。not...a story of uniform decline 总

TPO 17

结这一点，没有意义，不用记录。Some...shrink... others will grow 完全是无用信息。[6]

◆ **本段逻辑梳理**：确实，人类的城市化造成了某些鸟领地的丧失。但它为其他一些种类的鸟提供了新的领地，以至于现在城市居民经常抱怨鸟的数量增长。我们经常在街道等地见到各种不同的鸟。

As for agriculture, 提示我们进入第二点，讨论农业对鸟类的影响。it's true 表明让步, it too will increase in the future 承认农业会增长。but 接下来肯定反驳。less land is being used for agriculture every year, 反驳策略是指出农业根本就不会入侵鸟类领地，因为农业用地会减少。Increases... production have resulted from... more productive varieties of crops 体现了理由，因为我们开始种植更高效的作物，产率提高，使得农业用地会减少。new crops produce more food per unit of land 是在总结刚才的理由，把可能没听懂的东西说清楚。no need to destroy wilderness areas 是我们可以预期的，没有必要记录。[7]

◆ **本段逻辑梳理**：确实，农业会持续增长。但是，农业用地会减少。因为我们现在研究出了各种产率更高的作物，意味着我们可以用更少的土地种出更多的食物，所以我们不再需要扩张农业用地侵犯 wilderness areas 了。

And third, 准备讨论 pesticides。it's certainly true 表明让步, traditional pesticides... destructive 体现了作者对对立面的妥协，承认过去的 pesticides 对鸟类有害。it's incorrect to project this theory into the future 直接表现了作者的反驳策略，肯定会对比说未来的 pesticides 不会有害。Now that people are aware of the possible consequences... two changes have occurred, 肯定要说两种变化意味着 pesticides 不会害死鸟。new and much less toxic pesticides, 对鸟无害的 pesticides 出现。trend to develop more pest-resistant crops, 指出直接不用 pesticides 了；crops... genetically designed to be unattractive to pests 展开说明这种 crops 是什么；reduce the need for chemical pesticides 体现了反驳策略，指出这下不用 pesticides 了；don't harm birds at all 肯定是作者必然要说的。[8]

◆ **本段逻辑梳理**：确实，过去的 pesticides 害死了很多鸟。但是，现在了解了这种危害后，我们开始进行两种变革。第一，发展了无害的 pesticides；第二，种植了 pest-resistant crops, 它们天然不

[6] ✏ < some birds ↓ > better habitats for other, complain about increased birds

[7] ✏ < 农 ↑ > less land, more productive crops, more food, no need to destroy wild

[8] ✏ < traditional pesti > aware → changes, less toxic pesti, pest-resistant crops, reduce pesti, ✗ harm birds

TPO 17

吸引 pests，则不需要用 pesticides，而这种作物是绝对不会坑害鸟的。

满分范文

The article projects that bird population is likely to shrink in the future. However, the lecturer claims that the three arguments that are used to support the prediction are all unsound.[9]

First of all, while the lecturer accepts that human settlement has infringed the homeland of some bird species, she argues that it offers better habitats for other species. In fact, she points out that many city and suburban dwellers are complaining about the increasing number of birds in their neighborhood.

Second, while the lecturer concedes that agriculture will continue to expand, she does not believe that agricultural land use will take up more wilderness areas. Her reason is that, with the development in agricultural technology, we are able to produce a variety or more productive crops, meaning that we can increase food yield by using less land.

Last, while she acknowledges the negative effects of traditional pesticides, she holds that with the growing awareness of the harm pesticides have done, we are now embracing two changes that are going to benefit the birds. On the one hand, we are developing less toxic pesticides that will do less harm to birds. On the other hand, we are planting pest-resistant crops that are unattractive to pests, crops that eliminate the needs for pesticide use. What's great is that these crops are not harmful to birds at all.

[9] 典型的"观点 + 三个理由"式文章的开头。

TPO 18

1. 📝 3 ways → T ↑
   🔊 听力肯定会分别否定三种策略。

2. 📝 reestablish in the same location
   🔊 对三种常见建议的否定：代价高昂做不到；并不能实现复兴 T 的目标；严重的副作用。

3. 📝 移植到 north
   🔊 同上，三种可能性。

4. 📝 research centers
   🔊 同上，三种可能性。

5. 📝 无需笔记

6. 📝 × success, affect by climate, T ↑, wetland drain, dry ↑

📝 阅读解析与听力预测

▶ **总　论：**
专家们考虑了三种方法来解决 Torreya 的减少。[1] 非常明显的问题解决型文章。

▶ **方案 1：**
把 Torreya 重新种植在以前它们繁盛的地方。[2]

▶ **方案 2：**
把 Torreya 移植到更北边更适合它们生长的地方。[3]

▶ **方案 3：**
保存在 research centers。[4]

📝 听力解析

none...provides a satisfactory solution 明显要说三个方案失败，我们早就知道，是无用信息，不用记录。[5]

About the first solution，准备听本地重建。that's unlikely to be successful，说明可能采取的策略是，指出这么做不能救活 T。because of what's happening to the coolest, dampest areas，肯定是给出理由，说当地的环境发生了什么不好的改变。affected by changes in...the larger region，指出受到了别的地区的影响。global warming has contributed to an increase...temperatures，指出了一种变化——温度增高；or...wetlands...been drained，指出另一种变化。areas...becoming drier，总结刚才提到的变化结果。unlikely that...Torreya...survive 说明了结果，这是我们知道的，不用记录。[6]

◆ **本段逻辑梳理：** 本地重建不能恢复 T 的数量，因为本地那些冷

TPO 18

湿地已经发生了改变，使得不利于 T 生长。比如，气候变暖以及湿地被 drain 都造成了气候变干。

About the second，准备听移植。let's look at what happened when humans helped another tree 直接暗示作者的反驳策略是类比，指出另一个物种移植的失败经历。spread so quickly，其实已经感觉到是常见话题，外来物种入侵了。killed off many plants and trees in the new environment，明显是说杀死了当地物种。some … already in danger，杀死的是濒危物种。So…can have unpredicted outcomes 是在总结无用信息。所以这个段落的策略是指出移植的负面影响。[7]

◆ **本段逻辑梳理**：assisted migration 会造成副作用，比如之前移植另一种树到北方，结果它传播太快，毁掉了当地很多植被，而且还是濒危植被。

[7] another tree, spread quickly, kill new environment, endanger

Third，准备听研究中心。the population of Torreya trees that can be kept in the centers will probably not be able to resist diseases，暗示研究所能装的树少，不够抵抗疾病，说明需要抵抗疾病的树的数量多。For a population of trees to survive diseases, it needs to be relatively large and…genetically diverse，就是刚才我们已经暗示的需要抵抗疾病的树的数量多，种类多。Tree populations in the wild usually satisfy，这没有什么用处，说的是自然界的树可以抵抗疾病，只是辅助对比。research centers would simply not…large and diverse population，听到这些就知道这也是我们已经暗示过的东西。not be capable of surviving diseases 是无用信息总结。显然，本段的策略也是说研究所不能恢复 Torreya 的数量。[8]

◆ **本段逻辑梳理**：研究所也不能恢复 T 的数量，因为研究所能够承载的树的数量少，diversity 低，因此面对疾病很可能不能抵抗，与自然界不同。

[8] pop 少，× resist disease, need large, diverse

📝 满 分 范 文

The article cites three potential solutions to revive the population of Torreya. Unfortunately, the lecturer dismisses all the three approaches.[9]

[9] 典型的三种解决方案型文章的开头方式。

To begin with, the lecturer does not believe that reestablishing Torreya in its original microclimate could bring Torreya back to its former glory, because the local environment is changing, more specifically, becoming drier as a result of global warming and because the surrounding wetland is drained.

Furthermore, concerned about its potential negative impact, she does not regard assisted migration as a viable solution. She points to the relocation of another tree species as an example: they spread wildly and killed off local plants and trees, many of which were themselves endangered species in the first place.

Last, she does not consider research centers as the solution, either, because research centers could only accommodate a relatively small number of Torreya trees. If the tree population is too small and not diverse enough, she suggests, the species might not be able to survive under the threat of diseases. Unfortunately, in her view, a large and diverse Torreya population can only be kept in the wild.

TPO 19

阅读解析与听力预测

▶ 总　论：
critics 认为 buzzing 应该被禁止，这估计就是阅读要展开的观点了。接下来可能提供理由支持 buzzing 该被禁止，观点理由型文章。[1]

▶ 理由1：
consumers 并不知道这个人其实是被 paid 来宣传产品的，他们很可能会收到假信息。[2]

▶ 理由2：
由于 consumers 以为 buzzers 是普通人，所以很可能 uncritically 听从他们的意见。[3]

▶ 理由3：
buzzing 会毁掉 social relationship，会导致人与人之间失去信任。[4]

---

1 ✎ *buzz* ×

　👉 听力最可能说 buzzing 不该被禁止，值得提倡。

2 ✎ × *know paid*, × *info*

　👉 也许会说，consumers 知道 buzzers 是被 paid（这可能否定了事实）；更有可能会说，尽管是被 paid，不见得会给假信息。

3 ✎ *private* 个人 → *uncritical*

　👉 鉴于无法否定他们看似是 private individuals，估计听力会说，就算不知道他们被 paid，consumers 也仍然会 critical。

4 ✎ *trust* ×

　👉 听力估计很难去辩论说毁掉了 trust 不是什么坏事，估计听力只能说 buzzing 并不会毁掉 trust。

5 ✎ 无需笔记

6 ✎ *tell truth, use* → *good,* × *actor*

🖉 听力解析

　　一堆无用信息，听到 really misleading，终于要开始正题了。gives the wrong impression 继续是无用信息。[5]

　　First，准备讨论假信息。it makes it sound like buzzers don't tell the true 暗示接下来听力要说其实 buzzers 给的是真信息。That's not true 是无用信息。Companies find people who use their products and...think the product is good，估计要展开为什么是真话了。not like ordinary advertisements where an actress is paid to read some lines 体现了和虚假广告的区别。yes 体现让步；get paid 具体说明让步的地方。but you get the truth 再次强调他的观点，不用记录。[6]

Part 2　081
综合写作高分范文精讲

TPO 19

◆ **本段逻辑梳理**：buzzers 并不会给出虚假信息。因为，他们不像 paid actors 那样纯粹念稿，不知道产品好坏。他们是因为使用了产品觉得好，才被公司雇来做 buzzers。

Second，准备讨论 uncritical。Not true，说明要直接否定这一点，观众是会 critical 的。In fact, the opposite is true 是无用信息。People …ask a lot of questions 体现了 critical。price, service 等都是展开的 questions，这种细节并列并不需要全部记下来，能写则写，不能写也不影响段落逻辑。If I don't have good answers, they won't buy 显然没有什么新意，顺着上文逻辑的发展。[7]

◆ **本段逻辑梳理**：本段非常直白，顾客是 critical 的，面对 buzzers，他们会问很多问题，各种各样的问题。

[7] ✎ ask questions, × answer → ×buy

Finally，准备讨论 trust。that's stupid，看来是要直接否定 destroy trust 了。If a product is bad, the company can't recruit buzzers, so what you get from a buzzer is not only sincere but…about a good product，直接表明听了 buzzers 的建议会买到好东西。If you try the phone service I use, you are gonna love it 明显是他用个人的例子展开刚才的观点，属于无用信息。good experience, end up…trustful and open up to people 落到了反驳点上，显然最后不会 distrustful，而会更 trustful。[8]

◆ **本段逻辑梳理**：buzzing 反而会加固 trust。因为，不好的产品找不到 buzzers，所以如果你听了 buzzers 的话，很可能会买到好的产品，有了好的体验，最后你会更相信他人，人际关系反而更可靠。

[8] ✎ bad → × buzzers, sincere, try a good product → good exp → trust

📖 满分范文

The article mentions critics' three reasons to argue for the ban on buzzing. However, the buzzer in the lecture denied each of these three reasons.[9]

For starters, the buzzer claims that information from the buzzer is in fact reliable, in contrast to what the article says. Buzzers are not paid actors who just read the lines, he reasoned, but are

[9] 显然，这是"观点+三个理由"式的文章开头。

instead ones who first experienced satisfactory products and then were hired to buzz.

Second, opposite to the article's point of view, the buzzer insists that the consumers are quite critical when they listen to buzzers. In fact, he points out that consumers tend to ask tons of detailed questions, and if they do not receive good answers, they will simply not buy the product.

Last, the buzzer considers it ridiculous that the article thinks buzzing is going to destroy interpersonal trust. On the contrary, he argues that, because bad products won't find buzzers, consumers who listen to buzzers' sincere advice will probably end up enjoying a good product and hence have more faith in other people.

TPO 20

📝 阅读解析与听力预测

▶ 总　论：
critics 认为"let it burn"的 policy 会产生 3 种 damage。[1] 下文肯定会具体展开这些 damage。

▶ 危害 1：
火灾对树木和其他植被产生了灾难性的影响。[2]

▶ 危害 2：
毁掉了 wildlife，而且还破坏了栖息地，让它们无法迁回。[3]

▶ 危害 3：
毁掉了旅游价值，影响了经济。[4]

[1] ✏ let — 3×
🔥 听力最有可能否认这三个危害。

[2] ✏ × vege
🔥 听力可能会说 let it burn 并不会必然造成这种影响。

[3] ✏ × wildlife + habitat
🔥 听力可能会说 let it burn 并不会必然造成这种永久的对 wildlife 的损害。

[4] ✏ × tour, ↓ $
🔥 听力可能会说 let it burn 并不会必然造成对 tourism 的破坏。

[5] ✏ 无需笔记

📝 听力解析

not just destructive but also creative 已经表明本文是要说"let it burn"的好处，不用记录。fundamentally a good one 是无用信息。[5]

First, 准备讨论对植被的破坏。in time colonized by new plants, 指出烧光之后有新植被出现，became more diverse 表明对植被的好处——多样化。the fire created an opportunity for certain plants that couldn't grow otherwise 给出了为什么产生多样化的理由，要是没有火，有些植物在这里就活不了。For example, 接下来一定是说某种植物有了新的机会成活。smaller plants that needed open, unshaded space 体现了新的物种能存活，因为有了适合它们存活的区域。another example, 应该和前面需要听到的结构差不多。seeds...won't germinate unless...heat 反映火给某些物种带来了高温，使得它们发芽。So those plants started appearing 体现了这一点，是无用信息，如果刚才没听懂 germinate, 则这里可以弥补。[6]

[6] ✏ new plants → diverse, 机会 small plants, open space, heat → start to grow

TPO 20

◆ **本段逻辑梳理**: 大火其实对森林的植被有好处，给新的树种提供了成活的机会，使树种更 diverse。一个例子是 small plants 有了 open space 可以生长；另一个例子是，heat 为某些高温发芽的物种提供了机会。

It's a similar story with the animals 隐蔽地转向了第二点，要讨论大火对动物的影响。"…not only did their population recover, but the fire also created new opportunities." 已经实现了否定阅读的作用。For instance 肯定要体现如何 recover 或 new opportunity。small plants … created … habitat for certain small animals 感觉已经体现了 opportunity。predators that depended on them for food 说明进一步被影响的生物。certain food chains actually became stronger 这显然总结了刚才的例子。[7]

[7] animals recover, new 机会, small plants → small animals → predator, food chain strong

◆ **本段逻辑梳理**: 大火其实帮助了动物的生长，动物的数量恢复了，且为新的物种提供了生长的机会。比如，大火所催生的 small plants 为一些 small animals 提供了栖息地，而相应地它们的捕食者有了生存的条件，于是这种 food chain 反而更加稳固。

last, 准备听旅游业。would be a problem … if they happened every year, 虚拟语气已经表明反驳策略。肯定会说，鉴于大火不会每年发生，所以影响不会大。But they don't 是无用信息。unusual combination of factors 也是无用信息。各种 rainfall, strong wind 等都只是展开 unusual factors, 是无用信息。This combination has not occurred since 继续是无用信息，体现 unusual。not seen such a fire since… 继续是无用信息。Visitors came back to the park next year and each year after that 才是关键反击，旅游业没有受损。[8]

[8] not every year, unusual combination, visitors came back

◆ **本段逻辑梳理**: 旅游业并不会受损，游客自大火后每年都还会来。因为这种大火并不是每年发生，当年是特殊情况，是一系列偶然因素碰巧组成的结果。

📝 满分范文

This passage points out three negative impacts caused by the "let it burn" policy. However, the lecturer denies each of these three points and argues that the fire might actually bring positive results. [9]

For starters, according to the lecturer, the fire was actually beneficial rather than harmful to the local vegetation, because it provided new opportunity for a more diverse range of plant species to grow. For instance, the open habitat created after the fire facilitated small plants; likewise, seeds of some species started growing thanks to the heat of the fire.

As for the animal species, while the article suggests that wildlife might have been permanently damaged, the lecturer points out that their population has recovered. Further, she believes that new species have an opportunity to flourish. For instance, the new, small plants allowed certain small animals to appear, which in turn benefited their predator species. Consequently, certain food chains became stronger.

Last, the lecturer insists that tourism has not suffered from the fire. The reason is that the fire in 1988 was a rare event which could take place only because the coincidental combination of several factors. Since 1988, no such fire happened, and tourists returned each year after the fire.

---

[9] 听力不仅说 fire 没产生阅读所说的坏处，反而指出了一些好处，所以用了这个结构。

TPO 21

阅读解析与听力预测

> **总 论**：
> 文章说得非常清楚：Planting genetically modified trees...to bring ...benefits. 下文肯定会展开各种 benefits。[1]

> **好处 1**：
> 基因改良后，树 hardier，更容易成活。列举了一个改良后的 papaya 抵御某 virus 的例子。[2]

> **好处 2**：
> 基因改良让农户受益更大，原因是基因改良后的树生长快，产量高，成活率高。[3]

> **好处 3**：
> 基因改良提供充足树木供人类使用，间接保护 wild trees。[4]

[1] ✎ genetically modified trees √

🥜 听力可能是说这些 benefits 不存在。

[2] ✎ hardy↑, survive↑ < papaya, ×virus

🥜 两种反驳策略：抗性本身；抗性高了，但是不足以 survive。

[3] ✎ $↑ < grow↑, produce↑, hardy↑

🥜 可以否定前提或否定逻辑。首先，grow, produce, hardy 这些维度上的优势可能不存在。其次，即便这些优势存在，不见得真的会带来更多受益。

[4] ✎ 保护 wild

🥜 仍然可以否定前提或否定逻辑。首先，基因改良的树木为人们提供所需的木材也许不够。其次，就算基因改良的树木带来了很多木材，人们仍然会去采集 wild trees。

[5] ✎ 无需笔记

听力解析

Sure, there are some benefits 说明文章一开始竟然是个让步。这并不重要，接下来肯定会反驳。but are these trees as really great as they first sound 表明作者要质疑了。可是我们早就知道了，所以这是无用信息，不需要记录。there are some problems 继续是无用信息。反正听力是要否定这些 benefits 的。[5]

First, 准备考虑 hardy 的问题。may be resistant to one particular condition, 体现了让步。does not...ensure their survival, 听力的策略是承认一定程度上的 hardy, 但不认为 hardy 可以决定 survival。那接下来肯定要说还有什么原因阻碍了 survival, 这肯定是 modify 不能解决

TPO 21

的。a typical non-modified trees' population is genetically diverse, 不确定要说什么，得记下来。for most threatening... there will be at least some...trees...that are resistant, 好像是在说非改良的树本来就有 resistance。So even if most...are killed, those few resistant trees will survive and ensure the survival of that species, 是无用信息。但还没明白这和 modify 有什么关系。But...modified trees are genetically much more uniform, 这里肯定是关键了，改良的树不够 diverse，那肯定暗示 survival rate 反而会下降。So if they are exposed to an environmental challenge they haven't been designed for, 我们知道接下来肯定要说，这些树要死了。they'll all die, 果然如此。So if the climate changes... 这里肯定是举例了，是要说这些情况可能会让 modified trees 死掉。likely to be completely wiped out, 这已经是我们知道的了，不需要记录。[6]

◆ **本段逻辑梳理**：确实，modification 能让树在某些情况下 resistant，但并不见得增加 survival。因为没 modify 的树更 diverse，面对 threats 时总会有某些树活下来，保存整个物种。但 modify 的树更 uniform，面对意外的 threats 时很可能全部死掉。

as to the second point, 准备听与农户受益相关的问题。hidden costs associated with growing genetically modified trees, 其实听到这儿的时候确定不了是 cost, clause 还是 cause, 所以得听下文来确定。company...charge...more, 原来是说那些种子公司会向农户收更多钱，那反驳策略基本清楚了，就是指出其实种改良种子反而代价更高。"...as you've grown the tree, you can't just collect the seeds and plant the new trees for free." 种完后长出来的树的种子还是不归农民，没有良心的资本家！这里其实还是在说代价。那肯定暗示，农户每一轮种植都要给钱。"By law, you have to pay the company every time you plant." 这是无用信息，好替农户心痛。[7]

◆ **本段逻辑梳理**：显然，本段的策略是直接否定种改良植物让农民受益更大，理由是代价更高。代价来源于，这些改良的种子本来就更贵；其次，每轮种植，法律规定都需要继续付钱给种子公司。

Finally, 提示要讨论最后一点，关于保护 wild trees。might actually cause even more damage to...wild trees, 要直接否定阅读理

[6] ~modified — diverse → (threat → some ×, some √) → species √; modified — uniform...

[7] hidden costs, company can charge seed and ↑, × collect seed and plant free, pay every time plant

由了。"…often grow more aggressively than natural trees… planted among natural trees. As a result…outcompete…for resources…" 这些信息已经明确地说明为什么改良植物对当地植物有危害。因为改良植物疯长，会彻底战胜当地植物。nutrients and water 这些都只是例子，说明改良植物战胜当地植物体现在哪些维度上。[8]

◆ **本段逻辑梳理**：改良植物反而更可能会伤害当地野生植被。因为改良植物长得更快，加之它们通常种植在当地植物中，所以改良植物会吸取更多的各种资源，比如水、养料，于是 outcompete 当地野生植被。

[8] 🌱 damage wild, grow aggressively, among natural → outcompete resource

📝 满分范文

The article claims that planting genetically modified trees offers three advantages, all of which are denied by the lecturer.[9]

To begin with, while the lecturer admits that genetic modification might render a tree species more resistant under certain conditions, she does not believe as the article does that it necessarily offers the trees more survival advantages. Her reason is that, because unmodified trees are naturally diverse, at least some will survive under external threats and guarantee the survival of the entire species. In contrast, since modified trees are genetically more uniform, when unexpected threats occur, the whole species might easily be wiped out.

Second, the lecturer simply does not believe that planting genetically modified trees are financially more profitable for farmers, because the companies selling the seeds tend to charge more for these modified species. Furthermore, she points out that the law requires the farmers to pay the company each time they plant, adding on to their expenses.

[9] 阅读谈了三个独立的好处，听力也肯定会分别否定这三个好处。所以，我们选择的文章开头形式应该是说阅读认为有三个好处，听力分别否定。

TPO 21

Finally, contrary to the article, the lecturer argues that planting genetically modified trees might actually harm local wild trees. She notes that the modified species tend to grow faster, so when planted among native species, they would outcompete local species with regard to resources, like water and nutrients.

TPO 22

📝 阅读解析与听力预测

> **总　论：**
> ethanol 并不能替代 gasoline，接下来会有三个理由。这是标准的"观点＋三个理由"的文章形式。[1]

> **理由 1：**
> 不能改善 global warming，因为 e 也会产生 CO_2。[2]

> **理由 2：**
> e 的制造消耗大量资源，影响别的行业。[3]

> **理由 3：**
> e 价钱太贵，需要政府资助。[4]

[1] ✎ e ✗
🚩 e 是可以用来代替 gas 的，阅读的三个理由要么错了要么不能支持结论。

[2] ✎ global warming ↑ ← CO_2 ← e
🚩 两种可能策略：e 产生的 CO_2 没有 gas 那么多；就算 e 产生大量 CO_2，但对于环境问题是有帮助的。

[3] ✎ cost 大， ✗ other 功能
🚩 两种可能策略：e 消耗的资源不会那么大；就算 e 消耗的资源很大，也不会影响别的行业。

[4] ✎ $ ↑
🚩 两种可能策略：e 根本不需要那么贵；就算贵，还是必须要使用。

[5] ✎ ✗ global warming ↑，< e → CO_2 >，grow corn → 吸 CO_2，counteract

📝 听力解析

Ethanol…good alternative to gasoline 明显是无用信息，我们当然知道要说这个。not one of these three reasons is convincing 继续是无用信息。

First，准备要讨论 CO_2 问题了。not add to global warming，立场已经表明了。It's true 说明要让步，承认阅读中的某些信息，准备听是什么。release CO_2，说明阅读确实没说错。but 说明要指出 CO_2 为什么不增加，要给出重点理由了。made from plants，不知道要说什么，继续听。growing plants counteracts this release of CO_2，这一下应该彻底明白了：种植物过程是吸收 CO_2 的，所以就和最后燃烧产生的 CO_2 平衡了，不会真的增加 CO_2 排放。Let me explain 说明接下来是详述刚才的内容，大方向已经确定。growing plant absorbs CO_2 已经是预见到的了。So growing plants for ethanol…removes CO_2 是无用信息，不用记。[5]

TPO 22

◆ **本段逻辑梳理**：尽管 e 的燃烧会产生 CO_2，但是制造 e 需要种植 corn，而这个过程是吸收 CO_2 的，所以最终使用 e 并不会为大气添加额外的 CO_2。

Second，准备讨论干扰其他行业的问题。doesn't...reduce the sources of food for animals，明显直接反驳阅读理由，不干扰畜牧业食物来源。produce ethanol using C（很可能大家只能听出一个音，并不能将 cellulose 写出来，这对于写作是不会有影响的）。component of plants' cell walls，听到这儿就知道可以绕过 cellulose 这个词了。但到这儿还没说清楚为什么不影响 animals' food。find most cellulose in those parts of plants...not eaten by animals，听到这一处，就知道阅读理由被否定了。我们显然可以用这些不被动物吃的部分制造 ethanol。So since we can produce ethanol from the plant parts that aren't eaten ... animal feed...available will not reduce，听出这些内容就知道肯定是无用信息总结了，不用记。[6]

◆ **本段逻辑梳理**：ethanol 的制造靠的是植物 cell walls 中的成分，而这种成分可以来自植物很多部分，并不需要是动物们吃的部分。所以，如果拿这些部分做 e 的原料，则使用 e 做 gas 的替代物不会影响动物饲料的产量。[7]

Third，准备谈论价钱。in the future, ethanol will...compete with gasoline in terms of price，明显就是要说 ethanol 价钱不贵了，后面看看是如何做到的。It's true，又要让步了，看阅读说对了什么。government subsidies make ethanol cheaper，这承认了现在 e 的价高。but...won't always be needed，基本符合预期了，未来 ethanol 肯定廉价。enough people start buying ethanol, producers will increase their production，基本已经明确低价的来源了。increased production...leads to a drop in its price 是无用信息。So the price of ethanol will go down as more of it becomes available 完全是无用信息。Studies show that if ethanol production...three times greater... the cost...drop by 40%，明显进一步说这个产量增加，价钱就可以减少，和前面一回事儿，不用记录。[8]

◆ **本段逻辑梳理**：虽然现在需要靠政府的补助来降价，但未来随着更多用户使用 e，e 的厂家就会增加 e 的产量，而 e 的成本就会下降，则价钱就可以与 gas 竞争。

[6] ✎ ✗ reduce food, cell walls, not eaten by animals, ✗ feed ↓

[7] ✎ 这一刻应该意识到，阅读中说制造 ethanol 影响其他行业，比如饲料来源。听力有可能针对其他各种行业，也可能只针对饲料来源这个例子。而现在我们应该确定，听力针对的是这个例子，则写作的时候也应该只复述这一个行业。

[8] ✎ future price, < subsidies >, won't need, 人 buy↑, produce↑, $ ↓

TPO 22

满分范文

The article offers three reasons why ethanol won't successfully replace gasoline. However, the lecturer insists on its support for ethanol, rejecting each of these three reasons.[9]

For starters, while the lecturer concedes that ethanol combustion releases CO_2, he claims that adopting ethanol would not, as the article suggests, increase the overall amount of CO_2 in the atmosphere. His reason is that ethanol is produced from crops like corn, the growing of which absorbs CO_2 and counteracts the later release of CO_2.

Second, the lecturer simply does not agree with the article that ethanol production reduces food sources for animals, because ethanol is mainly produced from a substance in cell walls and cell walls appear in many parts of plants that are not eaten by animals. From his perspective, as long as ethanol is produced from these parts, animal feeds will not be influenced.

As for the reading's concern about ethanol's excessive price, the lecturer accepts that ethanol is currently relying on government subsidies, but he insists that in the future such assistance will not be necessary. He projects that as more consumers switch to ethanol use, ethanol producers will increase its production, thereby eventually reducing its price enough to compete with gasoline.

[9] 这个结构体现了"观点+三个理由"的阅读模式与听力的反驳模式。

TPO 23

阅读解析与听力预测

▶ **总　论：**

yellow cedar 树变少了。说得很清楚，有 3 个可能的 hypotheses。典型的现象解释型文章，那不用预期就知道，下文要给出 3 个不同的解释。[1]

▶ **解释 1：**

可能是 cedar bark beetle（一种害虫）把树吃了。这个非常简单。[2]

▶ **解释 2：**

可能是 brown bears，把树的糖分吃了。[3]

▶ **解释 3：**

气候因素，气候变化导致 yc 在冬天开始生长，容易受损。[4]

[1] yc↓←？
　三个解释都是错的。

[2] cbb
　两种可能性：一种是说没有证据证明 cbb 存在；另一种是说，cbb 对树的影响不足以造成它的显著减少。

[3] bb
　同上，两种可能性：一种是否定阅读理由涉及的现象存在本身，即 bb 可能不存在，或者 bb 并不会消耗很多树的糖分；另一种是否定 bb 的影响足以造成 yc 的显著减少。

[4] 气候变化 → yc 在冬天生长 → 受损
　同上，两种可能性。一是否定阅读理由设计的现象存在本身，即气候并没有显著变化，该地的 yc 并没有在冬天开始生长。另一种是否定这些影响足以造成 yc 的显著减少。

[5] 无需笔记

听力解析

Unfortunately, we still don't know 基本可以确定是无用信息。none of the explanations...adequate 更是无用信息，不需要记录。[5]

First, 准备讨论 cbb。healthy yc（yellow cedars）are...more resistant to insect 听出来就已经确定论述方向了，肯定是说 ybb 是不足以伤害 yc 的。For example 提示接下来是展开，不会有关键性改变。bark... poisonous to insects, 具体说清楚了 cbb 为什么不会伤害 yc。这个信息能写出来是细节加分，写不出来也不影响段落论述的整体思路。healthy cedars are unlikely to suffer from insect damage 纯属无用信息，不需要记录。how can we explain those dead cedars...infested with beetles 是本段难点，这是对讲座者不利，对阅读有利的信息；相当于让步，接下来他一定要处理这个不利证据。already damaged 体现了作者的处理方式。不是因为 beetles 损坏了树，而是树已经损坏，所以 beetles 才能入侵。beetles are not the fundamental cause 开始是无用信息，不需要记录。[6]

◆ **本段逻辑梳理**：cbb 是不可能真正影响 yc 的。诚然，存在 dead yc infested with beetles，但这是因为那些 yc 已经受损，才被 yc 攻击。健康的 yc 是不受侵害的，因为体内有 poison，会毒死 beetles。

[6] ✏ healthy yc resist < chemical poison, <dead yc 有 beetle > damaged

Second, 准备讨论 bb。although bears damage some trees, 说明作者认为 bb 是有影响的，那反驳策略肯定就是否定这是关键原因。not the cause of the overall decline, 正是我们所预料的。Yc...declining all across the northwestern coast... on mainland and on islands, 这里应该是在展开 overall decline。no bears on the islands, 听到这几个词应该已经瞬间听懂论述逻辑了。这意味着 islands 上的 decline 肯定不是 bear 造成的。yet the islands cedars are still in decline 开始是无用信息，不需要记录。Since the decline occurs with and without bears, the bears cannot be responsible 完全是无用信息。[7]

◆ **本段逻辑梳理**：岛上以及陆地上的 cedars 都在减少，但 bears 只在陆地上有。所以，bears 不可能是造成 overall decline of yc 的原因。

[7] ✏ decline across coast, mainland, island, island no bear

finally, 准备考虑 climate 的影响。the reading passage forgot to take one factor into account, 这肯定是个关键的 factor, 仔细听。more trees are dying at lower elevations where it is warm, 其实听到这儿，后面的逻辑就自然可以补上了。阅读认为 yc 受气候影响，yc 在冬天开始生长，太冷，所以被冻死。而显然，应该是更冷的地方 yc 死得更多，不可能是 more trees are dying at warm places。If freezing damage were responsible... we would expect to see more trees dying ... higher elevations，这是无用信息，虚拟语气表明理论预期和现实不符，这是可以靠逻辑补上的，不用记。Instead, more trees are dying...of the lower elevations，是无用信息；So although the climate change...made...roots more sensitive 中的 although 表让步，承认气候有影响，但最终肯定要说这个因素不关键。this isn't what's killing them 纯属无用信息。[8]

◆ **本段逻辑梳理：** 尽管气候确实对树根造成了一定影响，但是如果气候是关键因素，理应在更寒冷的 high elevations 出现更多 decline，但现实相反。

[8] *more die at low elevations, warm*

📝 满分范文

The reading cites three possible explanations for the decline of yellow cedar population. Unfortunately, the lecturer dismisses all three possibilities. [9]

[9] 本结构体现了阅读给出的三个解释，然后听力一一否定。

For starters, the lecturer considers the impact of cedar bark beetles insignificant. While he accepts that dead cedars are found infested with beetles, he argues that it is because the cedars are already damaged that they become vulnerable to beetles. He believes that healthy cedars would be immune to insects because they contain chemicals poisonous to the beetles.

Second, while the lecturer concedes that bears may influence the population of cedars, they are not the overall cause. He points out that the decline of cedar population occurs both on the mainland and on islands, and yet no bears exist on the islands. It suggests that bears could not have been responsible for the overall decline of yellow cedars.

Last, although the lecturer acknowledges the possible impact of temperature on cedar roots, he once again denies the relevance of climate change. He argues that if cold weather were indeed the cause, more trees should be dying at higher elevations, where it is colder. However, in reality, more trees are spotted dying at lower, warmer places.

TPO 24

📝 阅读解析与听力预测

▶ 总　论：
发现了 T. rex 的 fossil，有可能还罕见地包含 remains of animal tissues。下文很可能要做的就是通过三个理由或证据展开这些 tissues 到底是什么，为什么是 animal tissues。[1]

▶ 发现 1：
在 leg bone 中的一些 ranching channels 中发现了一些 organic matter，说明这些 channels 是 blood vessels。[2]

▶ 发现 2：
发现了一些 spheres 有两个特点：包含 iron，有与 red cells 差不多大小的 red centers，说明这些 spheres 可能是 red blood cells。[3]

▶ 发现 3：
发现 collagen 是 living bone tissues 的重要组成，暗示发现了 bone tissues。[4]

---

[1] ✎ T. rex — tissue
🔊 听力可能指出这些所发现的东西并不是 animal tissues。

[2] ✎ ranching channel, organic ＞ blood vessels
🔊 理论上存在两种可能——这些发现并不存在（但这是事实，实际上很难去这么反驳）；这些发现是真的，但不代表是 blood vessels。

[3] ✎ red cell ＜ sphere (升 + red center — size =)
🔊 仍然是理论上有两种可能——第一，这些发现不存在（但事实仍然是很难去反驳的）；第二，这些发现不表明红细胞的发现。

[4] ✎ collagen ＞ bone tissue
🔊 很难说没有 collagen；最有可能说 collagen 不代表 bone tissue。

[5] ✎ 无需笔记

📝 听力解析

there are sound reasons for being skeptical，是无用信息，不需要记录。[5]

　　First 一出现，准备好联系第一个理由——blood vessels。the soft …inside the bone channels 明显就是证据，不用记。isn't necessarily …blood vessels，是无用信息，和我们的预测一模一样，完全不用记。likely to be something else，如果不是 blood vessels，当然只能是 something else，可以不用记。after an organism is died, bacteria sometimes colonize hollows… like the channels，我们应该意识到，可

能要说那些东西是什么，怎么来的，显然这个信息是我们不能准确预见到的，逻辑上也不是必然的，应该记录。When bacteria lived...they often leave behind traces of organic material，已经完全可以确定就是在讲那些 organic material 是从哪儿来的，lecturer 认为是从 bacteria 那儿来的。其实这个时候，反驳逻辑已经完整了。What the researchers ... identifying as blood vessels might just be ... left by bacteria，这些都是无用信息。[6]

6 organic ← bac

◆ **本段逻辑梳理**：在那些 ranching channels 中发现的 organic matter 并不能说明这些 channel 是 blood vessel。因为那些 organic matter 可能是 bacteria 曾经占据这里留下来的痕迹。

What about the iron-filled spheres 提示我们进入第二个理由。the problem 提示要开始反驳。scientists found identical ... spheres in ... other animals，不能预料这个信息，需要记下来。That includes ... primitive animals that did not have any red blood cells 这个信息实在是太关键了，应该意识到这个反驳已经完成了。在没有 red blood cells 的 animal fossils 中发现这些 spheres，表明这些 spheres 完全不能说明一定是 red blood cells。Clearly, if these spheres appear in organisms that did not have any red blood cells 已经开始总结我们刚才说的东西了，下半句几乎肯定说阅读的论证失败。then the spheres cannot be the remains of red blood cells 是无用信息，不需要记录。The spheres probably have a very different origin，如果不是 red blood cells，自然是 something different，我们就听听是什么吧。probably just pieces of reddish mineral 表明可能是什么。[7]

7 sphere — primitive fossil, × red, reddish mineral

◆ **本段逻辑梳理**：那些 iron-filled spheres 不意味着红细胞被发现。因为，在周围其他低等生物化石中也发现了类似的 spheres，而这些生物根本就没有 red cells。相反，这些东西可能只是一些 reddish mineral。

Third 是很明显的标志，我们准备听 collagen 与 bone tissue 的故事。we have never found collagen in animal remains that are older than 100,000 years，肯定要记录。Collagen probably cannot last longer than that 继续记录。Finding collagen from an animal that lived 70 millions years ago...contradict 后面都不用听了，显然这已经体现了问题所在。It's just too improbable 是无用信息，不用记录。The most

TPO 24

likely explanation 显然要指出这些 collagen 的真正意义，准备听和记。is that it doesn't come from the T. rex 是无用信息，不用记；but from ...recent source，也是无用信息，可以不记；for example, human skin contains collagen 暗示可能来自 human skin。come from the skin of the researchers who are handling the bone 进一步具体说明来自什么 human，逻辑完整。[8]

♦ **本段逻辑梳理**：那些 collagen 不见得来自 bone tissue。因为那些生物年龄有 70 millions 之久，而我们先前发现的 collagen 都来自于不超过 100,000 years 的 animal fossils，说明 collagen 不能存在更久的时间，这两组信息矛盾。因此，这些 collagen 很可能来自于年代更近的来源，比如 researcher 的 skin。

[8] ✎ not found C > 100,000 yrs, C × last long vs. 70m yrs, ← recent, human skin (researcher)

满分范文

The reading claims that the recent findings of materials within a T. rex's leg bones, suggest traces of actual animal tissues. However, the lecturer is skeptical toward each of the findings, claiming that none of the three findings necessarily comes from animal parts.[9]

[9] 该结构体现了阅读提到了某些可能的发现，但听力将每一个发现都进行了否定。

First, the reading purports that certain organic substances found within some ranching channels prove that these channels were once blood vessels. However, the lecturer argues that bacteria that occupied the bones, hollow spaces would also leave such traces of organic matter.

Second, the reading believes that the iron-filled spheres represent red blood cells. However, the lecturer points out that identical spheres were also spotted in remains of primitive animals in the same location, animals that do not have red blood cells at all. From his view, this would suggest that these spheres had alternative implications, perhaps just some reddish minerals.

Finally, the reading asserts that collagen discovered in the T. rex signifies animal bone tissues. Unfortunately, the lecturer notes that no collagen has been found in animal remains from 100,000 years ago, suggesting that collagen could not survive longer. From his perspective, since the current T. rex bone is from beyond 70 million years ago, the collagen almost certainly comes from other, more recent sources, such as the skins of researchers handling the bones.

TPO 25

阅读解析与听力预测

▶ **总 论:**

发现了一些古老的 clay jars,每个都有 copper cylinder,有些人认为每个 clay jar 是个 battery。但在作者看来,不太可能是 battery。

很明显,只有一句话是作者的立场,那就是,这些 clay jars 在古代不应该是 batteries。因此,下文最可能用三个理由来分别否认这些 clay jars 是 batteries,[1] 典型的观点理由型文章。

▶ **理由1:**

假如是 batteries,理应有 wires,但没发现 wires。省略结论,肯定不是 batteries。

很显然,作者真正的核心证据就是没发现 wires。[2]

▶ **理由2:**

核心信息是:这些 clay jars 中的 copper cylinders 和在 S 地发现的很像,而那些 copper cylinders 是用来放 scrolls 的,所以这些 clay jars 中的 copper cylinders 也是用来放 scrolls 的,不是 batteries。[3]

▶ **理由3:**

没有任何用电设备,所以如果是 batteries,则没有用。[4]

[1] clay jars— ×battery
  听力可能会指出,clay jars 仍然可能是 batteries。

[2] × wires
  A. 可能有 wires;B. 就算没有 wires,也可能是 batteries。

[3] cs ≈ S cs—scroll
  A. 两个 copper cylinders 并不像;B. 就算像,也可能是 batteries。

[4] 没用
  A. 有用;B. 就算没用,也可能是 batteries。

[5] 无需笔记

听力解析

the arguments...not convincing 表明作者立场,这是无用信息,我们早就知道。The battery explanation...correct 还是无用信息。[5]

First,我们应该准备听第一个理由。about the absence of wires or

other conductors 是无用信息，我们知道肯定要谈这个。discovered by local people not archeologists，对比出现，可能有门道，需警觉。These people might have found other material，应该怀疑可能是 wires。not trained...recognized the importance of that material 验证我们的想法。这时应该意识到，听力采取了反驳策略 A，目的是说，其实有可能有 wires，只是没发现。might have been... thrown away 是无用信息，wires 只是被无视。[6]

◆ **本段逻辑梳理**：其实很可能有 wires，只是没被发现，被无视了，因为发现者是 local people 而不是 trained archeologists。

Second 提示我们进入第二个理由。it's true 是常见的让步标志，可能采取策略 B，承认理由，否定逻辑。similar 已经是无用信息，验证刚才的猜测。does not ... prove anything 继续是无用信息。originally designed to preserve scrolls，继续妥协。later discovered ... produce electricity 表明仍然可以是 batteries，只不过是后来发现的功能。In other words，说明如果刚才没听懂，还有机会补听。originally used for...one purpose...adapted for another 再次验证刚才已经听出来的东西。[7]

◆ **本段逻辑梳理**：诚然，那些 copper cylinders 确实和承载 scrolls 的 copper cylinders 很像，但这很可能只能说明，这些玩意儿早先确实是用来承载 scrolls 的，之后被改变用来做 batteries。

Finally 提示我们进入第三个理由。possible uses of the battery 提示听力很可能采取策略 A，直接指出这些 batteries 是有用的。produce ... shock or tingling sensation，感觉已经开始说 function 了；interpreted as...invisible power，可能继续说 function；convince others that they had magical power 继续顺承说 function。Also 说明前后逻辑平行；could ... been used for healing 说明第二个功能；uses mild electric current to stimulate muscles and relieve aches and pains 能听到多少算多少，反正只是为了展开 healing 的细节。[8]

◆ **本段逻辑梳理**：其实这些 batteries 在古代也可能是有用的，可能用来产生 shock 和 tingling sensation，显得好像使用者有 magical power，或者可能用来治病，刺激肌肉、缓解疼痛等。

[6] ✏️ ✗ arche √ local ↓ wire
✗ found

[7] ✏️ <≈ scroll >早 scroll
晚 battery

[8] ✏️ shock, tingle → invisible 力 → magic
heal: 刺激 muscle, ✗ 疼

TPO 25

满分范文

The reading denies that the set of clay jars discovered could be used as electric batteries in ancient times, offering three reasons in support.[9] However, the lecturer dismisses these arguments and concludes that the battery hypothesis may still be sound.

The first piece of evidence cited by the reading is the lack of wires attached to the jars. However, the lecturer responds that there could have been wires, except that they were neglected and possibly thrown away during excavation because the conductors of the excavation were local residents rather than professional archaeologists.

Second, the reading mentions that the copper cylinders found within the jars looked like those found elsewhere that were used to hold scrolls, suggesting that the clay jars might also operate as scroll holders. While the lecturer acknowledges the similarity, it purports that it might only indicate the copper cylinders' original function whereas they could have been adapted later to function as batteries.

Last, the lecturer simply does not agree with the reading's assertion that the jars would have been useless if they were batteries. He claims that since the jars might generate shock or tingling sensation, people in the past might use them to convince an audience that they possess magical ability. Furthermore, the batteries could also serve for medical ends as they could stimulate muscles and relieve pain.

[9] "The reading ... offering three reasons in support" 的结构体现了阅读文章的类型是"观点 + 三个理由"的形式。

TPO 26

📝 阅读解析与听力预测

▶ 总　论：
ZM 的传播挡不住，且会危害当地鱼群。[1] 注意，这篇文章的观点有两个部分，属于"观点+三个理由"型的文章，听听力反驳时注意是反驳前提还是反驳逻辑。

▶ 理由1：
历史上 ZM 传播就很难阻挡。[2]

▶ 理由2：
在新环境下生存力强，迅速统治，没有天敌。[3]

▶ 理由3：
与当地鱼竞争食物，所以危害了当地鱼。[4]

---

[1] ✎ ZM, ✕ stop, threat
🔊 听力肯定会说可以挡住，危害不大。

[2] ✎ history
🔊 理论上可以反驳前提和反驳逻辑，但这个前提是事实，很难反驳，估计会说，历史上难防御，不代表现在难防御。

[3] ✎ dominate new, hardy, no predator
🔊 可以否定前提——没有天敌；可以说就算没有天敌，也不见得会统治。

[4] ✎ ✕ 鱼 < compete food
🔊 可以否定与当地鱼竞争食物；可以说就算与当地鱼竞争食物，也不见得危害当地鱼。

[5] ✎ 无需笔记

📝 听力解析

are ways to control...spread...not so clear...a serious threat, 都和阅读相反，不需要记录。[5]

True, 表让步, couldn't be controlled in the past, 没有用 first 等标志词，第一个论点就已经开始说明这种情况很少见，这个让步承认过去无法控制，那接下来肯定要说现在可以控制了，重点听如何控制。that's because people didn't have enough knowledge, 接下来肯定说现在有知识了。In fact, there are...ways to stop ships from carrying the mussels to new locations, 这是无用信息，不需要记录。The way zebra mussels...travel across ocean is that a ship takes on some fresh ...water in Europe...empties that water in North America... 接下来肯定说可以阻断这个过程。But the ship can be required to empty out the

TPO 26

fresh water and refill with ocean water while still out in the ocean. Salt water will kill the mussels，阻断了传播过程。这个点有很多细节，并且必须都记下来，因为都不是逻辑上必然的，是反驳成功所必需的。[6]

◆ **本段逻辑梳理**：诚然以前挡不住，因为知识匮乏，但现在可以阻挡。ZM 传播靠船只在欧洲装淡水，每周再把这些淡水排掉。而我们可以在进入美国之前就把水排掉，装上海水，那么 ZM 就会被盐水淹死。

Second，准备听没天敌的问题。it's true…don't have predators in their new habitats，承认了很重要的阅读前提。but that's only in the beginning，这很重要，并没有真的承认前提，只是说开始没有天敌，那后文基本不用听就知道反驳方向了，肯定是说之后就有天敌了。local…birds sooner or later notice there is a new food source around and change their habits…can eat a lot of mussels，基本就是把天敌进行了展开。So…aren't so likely to dominate，这是无用信息，不用记。[7]

◆ **本段逻辑梳理**：诚然一开始没天敌，但是之后，当地的鸟就会发现这种新的食物来源，就会开始吃它，能吃好多呢。

Finally，准备听对鱼的危害。It's true，又要让步了；negative impact on fishes that eat plankton，接下来估计要说对其他鱼没危害了。but on other fishes…positive impact，接下来肯定会展开是什么impact。generate nutrients…so bottom-feeding fish population may increase，说清楚了，mussel 能为下层鱼提供养料。[8]

◆ **本段逻辑梳理**：诚然对吃浮游生物的鱼有不良影响，但对其他鱼好，比如，它能为下层鱼提供养料。

[6] <past> × knowledge, stops ships carrying fresh water in Europe, emptying in America, refilling with salt in Ocean

[7] < × predator beginning > bird, new food, change habit, eat a lot

[8] < plankton eating > other fishes, generate nutrient, bottom-feeding fish ↑

满分范文

The article presents several arguments why the zebra mussel's invasion in North America is unstoppable and threatening the local fish populations, all of which are dismissed by the lecturer.[9]

For starters, while the lecturer concedes that the zebra mussels' spread in the past was not effectively stopped, he argues that this

[9] 典型的"观点+三个理由"的文章。

[10] 承认过去，用现在反驳。

was only because of people's limited knowledge.[10] When ships carried fresh water when they left Europe and emptied that water in North America, zebra mussel was transported. However, now that people know this process, they can empty the water before they reached America and refill the ship with salt water. Since the mussels cannot survive in salt water, they will be killed.

[11] 承认开始的情况，用之后的情况反驳。

Second, even though the lecturer acknowledges that the mussels have no predators when they just invade a new territory, he argues that this situation is not going to last.[11] What's been happening in Europe is that sooner or later local birds realize the presence of this new food source and change their habits, and birds can actually eat a lot of zebra mussels.

[12] 承认 plankton-eating fishes，用其他鱼反驳。

Last, although the lecturer agrees that the mussels' feeding behavior might threaten certain plankton-eating fishes, he argues that the mussels' existence can actually benefit certain other fish populations[12], for example, bottom-eating fishes, because the mussels can help generate nutrients in the bottom layer of the waters.

TPO 27

阅读解析与听力预测

总　论：
LIA 是怎么产生的?[1] 典型的"现象+三个解释"的文章。

解释 1：
温度上升，冰融化，导致墨西哥湾洋流扰动，产生 LIA。[2]

解释 2：
火山爆发，遮天蔽日，产生 LIA。[3]

解释 3：
人少了，树多了。[4]

1. ✎ LIA ← ?
   🖍 听力肯定是把每个解释都否定了。

2. ✎ T↑ → 冰融化 → GS
   🖍 要么是说这件事情根本没发生，要么是说这个过程无法产生 LIA。

3. ✎ volcano
   🖍 要么是说这件事情根本没发生，要么是说这个过程无法产生 LIA。

4. ✎ 人↓ → 树↑
   🖍 要么是说这件事情根本没发生，要么是说这个过程无法产生 LIA。

5. ✎ 无需笔记

6. ✎ GS → NA, 欧 vs. LIA → south 半球

听力解析

none...could account for LIA 是无用信息，不需要记录。[5]

First, 准备听洋流。disrupting the Gulf Stream...cooling only in Europe and North America, 接下来肯定是对比，说不能影响别的地方，而 LIA 肯定会影响别的地方，准备看看是哪儿。but...southern hemisphere 涉及南半球。like New Zealand and Southern Africa, 这不重要，只是例子。Gulf Stream cannot explain, 是无用信息。[6]

◆ **本段逻辑梳理**：GS 不可能是原因，因为 GS 只影响北美和欧洲，而 LIA 的影响波及南半球。

Second, 准备听火山。it's true, 表让步，承认阅读；volcano...put enough dust...results...cooler climate, 承认火山如果足够强，会造成天气变冷。接下来肯定反驳。But...volcanic dust...would have also produced striking visual effects that people would have noticed, 注意这里的几个 would, 暗示接下来肯定会反驳，并没有看到这些

visual effects。for example...colorful sunsets or snow being grey or brown，这些都是 visual effects 的例子，肯定没看到。But ... no reports，完美符合预期。So...volcanic eruptions during that period... not strong enough，不用记，逻辑符合。[7]

♦ **本段逻辑梳理**：火山不能解释，因为那会儿火山爆发的强度没有足够大，要是火山足够强，理应看到各种奇葩现象，比如彩色日落、变色的雪，但这些都没有看到。

about forests on farmland，准备听第三个点。not enough time，反驳大方向已经明确，时间不够。human population grew back... quickly，展开时间不够。meant that forests ... cut down again ... for crops，继续展开时间不够。As a result ... forests ... not there long enough to cause...cooling，逻辑符合，不用记。[8]

♦ **本段逻辑梳理**：不可能是人变少的结果，因为时间不够。人的数量增长很快，然后就开始砍树，所以森林存活的时间不会很长，不会产生持续的温度影响。

[7] volcano → visual effects (colorful sunset, grey, brown snow) ✗

[8] ✗ time, pop grew back quick, cut tree → crop

📝 满分范文

The article presents three possible explanations for the Little Ice Age (LIA), none of which were accepted by the lecturer.[9]

For starters, the lecturer does not believe that disrupting the Gulf Stream had much to do with the LIA[10], because while the Gulf Stream could only affect North America and Europe, the influence of the LIA had reached the southern hemisphere, to places like Southern Africa and New Zealand. Clearly, the change to the Gulf Stream could not explain the phenomena in these places.

Second, the lecturer rejects the volcano hypothesis as well, because if volcanic activity had been strong enough to produce dust that blocked the sun and reduced global temperature, people should have also observed other noticeable visual effects like colorful sunsets and grey or brown snow. However, there is no report documenting

[9] 典型的"现象+三个解释"的开头。

[10] The lecturer does not believe that X had much to do with Y，指出 X 不能解释 Y，或 Y 不能解释 X，都行。

anything like these. Therefore, there probably had not been such a dramatic volcanic event.

Last, the lecturer does not agree that humans played a big part in LIA[11], because the human depopulation was only a temporary period, not long enough for such an effect to take place. Population grew back quickly, and people soon began to cut down forests again to service agriculture and feed themselves. Consequently, the forests were not there long enough to make a difference.

[11] The lecturer does not agree that X played a big part in Y，指出 X 不能解释 Y。

TPO 28

阅读解析与听力预测

▶ 总 论：

RP 到了北极。[1] 这是典型的"观点＋三个理由"的文章。等会儿听听力时要注意是反驳前提还是反驳逻辑。

RP — North Pole
① NGS：R's account — consistent, persuasive
② TA reached ＜ 37 days, same method, possible
③ shadow in photo ＞ sun's position √

▶ 理由1：

NGS 组织判定 RP 的旅行笔记是一致的。[2]

▶ 理由2：

最近 TA 用了不到 37 天就去了北极，说明 RP 所做的是可能的。[3] 这是典型的类比式论证。

▶ 理由3：

根据 RP 照片上的 shadow 计算出太阳的位置，表明就是在北极照的。[4]

[1] RP — North Pole
听力肯定是说 RP 不见得到了北极。

[2] NGS, RP consistent
要么说 RP 的笔记并不 consistent；或者说就算 consistent，RP 也不见得去过北极。

[3] TA ＜ 37, possible
TA 就没能在 37 天内到达北极（这是不可能的，这是否定事实）；所以，只能说，就算 TA 用 37 天到了北极，也不能说明 RP 也可以做到。

[4] shadow ＞ sun
那个 shadow 的信息不准；就算 shadow 准确，也不能推算出 sun；就算推算出 sun，也不能说明到过北极。

[5] 无需笔记

听力解析

no...evidence...reached the North Pole. The arguments...not convincing，都是符合预期的，不需要记。[5]

First，准备听 NGS。it is true，要承认阅读的一部分，NGS declared that Peary indeed reached the North Pole，承认 NGS 发表了声明。But...not...objective，接下来可能要直接攻击 NGS 的结论了。

TPO 28

In fact, the committee was composed of Peary's close friends, 这个直接就表明 NGS 不靠谱了。who had contributed…money to fund Peary's trip, 继续表明为什么不靠谱。Moreover, 要继续说不靠谱。investigation lasted only two days, 估计要表明调查时间太短，结论不靠谱。according to Peary himself…not examine his records carefully, 果然非常不靠谱。So … conclusions seem biased and are not trustworthy, 这是无用信息结论。[6]

◆ **本段逻辑梳理**：虽然 NGS 确实做出了判断说 RP 成功了，可是 NGS 是不可信的，因为 NGS 都是 RP 的朋友，资助了他的旅行；而且，NGS 的调查只持续了两天，各种不仔细。

Second, 准备听 TA 的旅行。Tom Avery's journey was different from Robert Peary's, 已经表明了反驳策略，接下来肯定会说两者具体在哪些方面不同，所以 TA 的经历没有证明作用。Avery's sled was similar to Peary's sled, 这是没有用的，因为我们要听区别。but Avery carried much less weight than Peary did, because Avery did not transport his food… food was dropped…by airplane, 这里具体指出一个区别。Moreover, 要继续说区别了；Avery … favorable weather conditions, unlike Peary, who travelled in unfavorable conditions, 这是第二个区别。So, Avery's speedy trip was too different…to provide support for Peary's claims, 这是无用信息结论，不需要记录。[7]

◆ **本段逻辑梳理**：A 的旅行和 P 的不同，不能给出任何参考价值，因为 A 不需要负重太多，他的食物是旅行中飞机扔下来的，其次 A 旅行的天气好，不像 P。

Third, 准备听根据 photo 中的 shadow 计算 sun's position。The techniques…to determine the sun's position depend on measuring the shadows…precisely, 估计接下来要说这个 technique 怎么出问题了。without…shadows, we cannot establish…sun's position, 不用记，这是刚才句子的逆否命题重复。Photographs…100 years ago, 这个照片老，估计不靠谱。primitive camera…fuzzy…photographs, 具体说怎么不靠谱。Moreover, the photos have become faded and worn over time, 继续说不靠谱。As a result, the shadows…look blurred and

[6] ✎ < NGS declare > × objective, friends, contribute $; investigate 2 days, × careful

[7] ✎ TA ≠ RP, TA less weight, × food, dropped by plane; TA good weather

faded，明显不能用来计算了。cannot calculate...the sun，是无用信息。so we cannot be confident...taken at the North Pole，无用信息结论，不需要记录。⁸

◆ **本段逻辑梳理**：照片也没有参考价值，因为这是一百年前的照相机，照得就不清楚，而且照片时间久了也褪色了，导致上面的 shadow 不清楚，自然无法计算太阳的位置，也就无法判断是不是北极了。

[8] ✎ sun ← shadow, 100 yrs camera, photo faded → shadow faded → × calculate sun

TPO 28

满分范文

The article presents three arguments why Robert Peary did reach the North Pole, all of which are challenged by the lecturer.⁹

For starters, conceding that the National Geographic Society（NGS）confirmed Peary's success, the lecturer argues that NGS itself is potentially biased, because the society consists of Peary's friends who financially contributed to his expedition. Also, the society's investigation took only two days, too cursory to be trustworthy.

Second, the lecturer does not believe that Tom Avery's recent, and seemingly similar success lends support to the credibility of Peary's adventure¹⁰. These two journeys were too unlike with regard to two crucial aspects: for one thing, unlike Peary, Avery carried way less food and thus less weight as he travelled, since his food was dropped by airplane along the way; for another, Avery enjoyed good weather during his expedition, while Peary had to struggle through terrible weather conditions. Both factors would have made Peary's trip significantly harder.

Last, the lecturer dismisses the evidentiary value of the photo, because it has to rely on the estimation of the sun's position based on

[9] 标准的"观点+三个理由"的文章开头。

[10] The lecturer does not believe X lends support to Y 体现的是否定逻辑，承认 X 这个证据，否定其足以支持 Y 这个结论。

the shadows' look. Unfortunately, this photo was taken with a primitive camera a hundred years ago, and the photo has now become faded. Consequently, the shadows appear blurry and faded as well, so it cannot help generate a precise calculation of the sun's position, undermining the argument's cogency.

TPO 29

📝 阅读解析与听力预测

▶ **总　论：**

E 龙通过迁徙过冬。[1] 正文将提供三个理由支持这个观点，所以这是典型的观点理由型文章，听听力时注意是反驳理由本身，还是反驳逻辑。

▶ **理由1：**

植食动物，冬天需要迁徙。[2]

▶ **理由2：**

群居动物，适合迁徙。[3]

▶ **理由3：**

跑得快，能迁徙。[4]

1 ✏️ migrate in winter

📌 听力肯定说不需要迁徙。

2 ✏️ diet plant

📌 否定植食（这是事实，很难否定）；就算植食，也不需要迁徙。

3 ✏️ herd

📌 否定群居（这不是事实，可以否定，因为文章中说群居是推断出来的）；就算群居，也不见得迁徙。

4 ✏️ fast

📌 跑得并不快；就算跑得快，也可不迁徙。

5 ✏️ 无需笔记

📝 听力解析

migrated…not convincing，是无用信息，符合预期，不需要记录。[5]

First，准备听植食。summer…warmer，不知道要说什么，明明应该说 winter 才对，记下来，引起警惕。the Sun shines 24 hours a day at the peak of summer，听不懂。created incredibly…conditions for plants，还是听不懂。So much vegetation…summer，继续听不懂。when…died as the winter came…a lot of nutritious dead vegetation around in the winter…could have easily lived on the dead plant matter during the winter，没想到，竟然是因为这个原因不用迁徙。[6]

◆ **本段逻辑梳理：** 植食不代表迁徙，因为这里夏天阳光太好，植物繁盛，所以冬天地上应该到处是有营养的死植物，够该 E 龙吃。

6 ✏️ summer T↑ → 24 h sun → plant 多 → 冬天 dead plant 多

Part 2 | 115
综合写作高分范文精讲

TPO 29

Second,准备听 herd。just because... in herds doesn't mean they migrated,明显是要否定逻辑了。live in herds for many other reasons,要给出其他可能的解释了。provides...extra protection from predators,给出了一种解释。A modern example...is...elk,这个例子明显是类比,不用听了,肯定其特点是不用迁徙,但是为了预防天敌而群居。live in herds...do not migrate,是无用信息,不需要记录。[7]

◆ **本段逻辑梳理**:live in herds 不代表非要迁徙,可以有别的功能,比如预防天敌,这如同当今北美的一种 elk,就是群居但不迁徙。

Third,准备听跑得快。although adult ... were capable of migrating long distances,这个让步已经可以清晰地预见到,下面要说的是年轻的跑不远,后面都可以吊儿郎当地听了。"...what about...not yet adults?" 是无用信息。Juveniles...not...capable,也是无用信息。slowed the herd ... the herd never would have made it to its destination,都是必然结果,是无用信息。The herd could not have left the juveniles behind,符合逻辑,because the juveniles would not survive on their own,符合逻辑。So the whole herd had to stay where they were and survived on the cold North Slope,这是无用信息结论,不需要记录。[8]

◆ **本段逻辑梳理**:虽然成年的 E 龙跑得快,可是幼年的跑不快,迁徙不了,它们会拖慢队伍速度,于是队伍就到不了目的地,尤其是它们不能自力更生,必须要由团队陪着。

[7] predator < elk

[8] <adult > young × far, slow, × survive on own

满分范文

The article presents three arguments why edmontosaurs survived the winter by migrating south, all of which were questioned by the lecturer.[9]

For starters, she does not believe that edmontosaurs' exclusive diet on plants requires them to relocate in winter[10], because the 24-hour, non-stopping sunshine in summer brought abundant vegetation to where edmontosaurs lived and as a result even in winter, when those plants all died, the dead plants should have provided a sufficient food source for edmontosaurs.

[9] 标准的"观点+三个理由"模式。

[10] "She does not believe that X requires Y."里的 X 是前提,Y 是阅读结论,这个结构表示的是听力反对阅读的逻辑。

Second, the lecturer does not believe migration was the only explanation for the finding that edmontosaurs lived in herds; instead, she proposes an alternative explanation[11] that they survived in herds to combat predators, just like many modern animals, such as a kind of non-migrating elk in North America.

Finally, while the lecturer concedes that the adult edmontosaurs were physically fast enough to travel long distances, she argues that the juvenile edmontosaurs were not. In her view, since the juveniles were not able to survive on their own, the entire herd would have to slow down with them, and consequently they would not have been able to reach their destination in time.

---

[11] "She does not believe that X is the only explanation for Y; instead, she proposes an alternative explanation." 这里的 X 是结论，Y 是前提事实，文章根据 Y 这个事实推断出一种解释 X，而听力不同意，给出了另一种推论，在这里是另一种解释。

TPO 30

1. ✏️ × burning mirror
   📢 听力肯定是说希腊人可能正是用 burning mirror 消灭罗马的。

2. ✏️ × tech < × large + precise
   📢 否定各层理由或逻辑都有可能。比如，能造出如此一片形状精确的镜子；就算造不出这么一片形状精确的镜子，科技上也有办法克服；就算希腊科技不行，也可能用了镜子（这个听起来比较离谱）。

3. ✏️ × effect < long time
   📢 同理。比如，并不需要花那么久的时间；就算需要花很久时间，也是很有用的；就算没用，也用了（这个也比较滑稽）。

4. ✏️ flaming arrow > unnecessary
   📢 同理。比如，并不能用 flaming arrow；就算能用 flaming arrow，镜子也是必要的；就算镜子不必要，也用了（这个还是比较神奇）。

5. ✏️ 无需笔记

📝 阅读解析与听力预测

▶ **总 论：**
Greeks 不可能用 burning mirror 来消灭罗马舰队。[1] 这显然是一篇"观点＋三个理由"的文章，我们应该注意听力处理阅读理由时是否定理由本身还是否定理由与观点之间的关系。

burning mirror ×
① tech ×
② long time
③ < flaming arrow

▶ **理由 1：**
Greeks 科技不发达，因为需要特别大的镜子，这么大的镜子造不出合适的形状。[2]

▶ **理由 2：**
用镜子点着罗马船只耗时太久，没有什么用。[3]

▶ **理由 3：**
用火箭就可以了，镜子多余。[4]

📝 听力解析

unconvincing 是无用信息。[5]
First，准备听 tech。Greeks did not need to form a single sheet of copper to make a large burning mirror，这里应该已经感觉到可以用多块 copper 来解决科技限制了。dozens of ... copper ... form a large burning mirror，听到几个关键词再联系上文就应该明白了，希腊人可以用多块铜片组成镜子。The Greek mathematicians knew the

properties of a parabola and...could...assembly，是无用信息。[6]

◆ **本段逻辑梳理**：古希腊人可以克服科技上的困难，他们并不需要用一整块铜板做镜子，只需要把一堆铜片拼成合适的抛物形就好了，而这是当时数学家可以做到的。

Second，准备听时间问题。the reading...assumes...set the wood...on fire，接下来几乎必然说这个 assumption 不对。that's what takes ten minutes，还没开始反驳。But the...boats were not just made of wood，接下来肯定说还有什么成分，而那个成分不需要十分钟点燃。there were other materials，是无用信息。For example, to seal the spaces between wooden boards and make them waterproof...used a sticky substance called "pitch"，也许都听不出 pitch，无所谓，反正就是连接木块的一种物质。catches fire very quickly，是无用信息。can be set on fire ... in seconds，不用记录。once the pitch was burning, the fire would spread to the wood，非常好，符合预期。So a burning mirror could have worked quickly enough，不用记。[7]

◆ **本段逻辑梳理**：点着船并不需要那么久时间，阅读假设必须点着木头，可是希腊人只需要点着连接木头的物质就可以了，那些东西几秒就可以点着，而后火势自然就会蔓延到木头上。

Third，准备听 flaming arrows。Roman soldiers were familiar with arrows，全段策略基本暴露了，接下来肯定会说熟悉火箭，就能提防；而不熟悉镜子，防不胜防。... watching for them and ... put out the fires，很符合预期。But you cannot see the burning rays from a mirror ... just see the mirror... suddenly and magically, a fire starts at some unobserved place... much more surprising and therefore much more effective，基本不用解释了，太符合逻辑了。[8]

◆ **本段逻辑梳理**：罗马军队对火箭有所熟悉，能随时提防；但罗马军队并不熟悉镜子，镜子反射的光束可能会在令罗马人意外的地方点着火。

[6] ✗ single copper, 拼, math ✓

[7] assume wood ✗, material combines wood, catch fire easily, seconds, spread to wood

[8] familiar with arrows, watch for, readily put out; ✗ see ray, unobserved, more effective

满分范文

The article presents three arguments why the Greeks of Syracuse never really used a "burning mirror" to inflame the Roman ships.

However, all three arguments were contested in the lecture.[9]

For starters, the lecturer insists that[10] the Greeks could be technologically advanced enough to build such a device. Instead of using a single piece of copper, the Greeks could conjoin small copper pieces into a parabolic shape with the appropriate curvature, a precision that was attainable by Greek mathematicians.

Second, the lecturer believes that the argument that burning mirror would have taken too long to be effective rests on a crucial, yet unwarranted, assumption that it was intended to inflame wood. However[11], the Greeks, she claims, could simply aim at the waterproofing material that the Romans used to join wood, which would catch fire within seconds, much faster than would wood.

Last, the lecturer simply does not believe that[12] the flaming arrows were just as effective as the burning mirror, because unlike the burning mirror, which the Romans were unprepared for and which could set fire with unnoticeable rays to certain unexpected spots, the flaming arrows were completely predictable for the Romans, who would readily put out any fire caused by the arrows.

TPO 31

📝 阅读解析与听力预测

▶ **总　论：**
S 化石中的 fine line 不是 feather。[1] 这显然是"观点+三个理由"型的文章，我们要注意听力反驳的多种具体策略。

▶ **理由 1：**
是动物死后 skin decomposed 后的 fiber。[2]

▶ **理由 2：**
是 frill。[3]

▶ **理由 3：**
长在尾部，所以不能帮助飞行和控温。[4]

[1] ✏️ *fine line — ✗ feather*
🔶 听力肯定会说是 feather。

[2] ✏️ *death, skin fiber*
🔶 理论上，可以反驳理由或反驳逻辑。但在这里，并不可能说，诚然它是 skin fiber，但它仍然是 feather。所以，基本上只有一种可能性，就是说它并不会是 skin fiber。

[3] ✏️ *frill*
🔶 其实根本不知道 frill 是什么。但同上，这里最可能说，不是 frill。

[4] ✏️ *backbone, tail > ✗ fly, ✗ heat*
🔶 多种可能性。首先，并不长在尾部（这是反驳事实，概率很小）；就算长在尾部，也能帮助飞行和控温；就算不能帮助飞行和控温，也可以是 feather。

[5] ✏️ 无需笔记

[6] ✏️ *✗ see decomposition of other animals, skin well preserved > S 龙 well preserved*

📝 听力解析

represent feathers…strong… critics are unconvincing 都是无用信息，符合期望。[5]

First，准备听 skin fiber。unlikely…skin，是无用信息，不需要记。because we don't see any such decomposition in the fossils of other animals buried at the same sites，典型的借助其他对象来进行对比的论证，逻辑已经清晰了。其他生物化石都没有出现类似的 decomposition，所以这个 fine lines 应该也不是 decomposition 的结果。In fact, the fossils of many other animals … show … skin … beautifully preserved，继续顺承刚才的思路，其他生物的化石中 skin 都能完整保存，暗示这个恐龙的 skin 是不可能 decompose 的。The well preserved… of the other fossils makes it so likely that，说明这个恐龙的 fossil 是 well-preserved；not fibers caused by decomposition，这里基本都是无用信息。[6]

TPO 31

◆ **本段逻辑梳理**：不可能是 decomposed skin fiber，因为在同一个 site 中发现的其他生物化石都没有 decomposed。事实上，发现了保存完好的 skin tissue，因此这个恐龙的结构很可能也是 well-preserved，而不是 decomposed 后的 fiber。

Second，准备听 frill。chemical difference between feathers and frills，接下来肯定要用对比论证了，肯定是说 feather 和 frill 有什么不同，而这里发现的更符合 feather 之类的。Feathers contain... protein called...，接下来肯定说 frill 不包含这个玩意儿，而我们发现了这个玩意儿。Frills ... do not contain，是无用信息。chemical analysis suggests did contain...，是无用信息。So...feathers, not frills，也是无用信息。[7]

◆ **本段逻辑梳理**：肯定不是 frill，因为 feather 有某 protein，而 frill 没有，化学成分分析显示这个化石有这个 protein。

[7] feather—protein vs. frill ✗, chem analysis ✓

Third，准备听羽毛长的位置，或用来飞行和控温的问题。feathers ...other functions than flying and thermo，基本把反驳策略说清楚了，就是可以不能飞和控温，但可以仍然是 feather。Think of a bird, like a peacock，是典型的类比举例。这个类比肯定说有某种羽毛，不能飞不能控温，但有别的用处。long, colorful feathers in its tail, and displays its tail in order to attract mates，这都是在说羽毛有什么用。display function，是无用信息总结。Recent analysis showed 这个恐龙的 the structures were colorful, orange and white。supports the idea that they were feathers...for display，把逻辑说圆了，这个恐龙的结构是多彩的，那也可能就是用来炫耀的。[8]

◆ **本段逻辑梳理**：就算不能飞行和控温，也可以是 feather，因为 feather 可以有别的目的，比如像孔雀那样用多彩羽毛炫耀。研究表明，S 的 lines 确实是多彩的，所以可能就是用来炫耀的羽毛。

[8] other functions, peacock, colorful display, S structure—colorful, orange, white > display

📝 满分范文

The article presents three arguments why the fine line pattern in a recently discovered Sinosauropteryx fossil does not represent feathers. However, the lecturer dismisses all the three arguments and insists that Sinosauropteryx may indeed be feathered. [9]

For starters, the lecturer claims that the fine lines cannot be explained away as decomposed skin structures. She points to fossils of other animals in the same site, all of which had well-preserved skin tissues. Thus, she believes that the fine lines of Sinosauropteryx should be well-preserved tissues rather than decomposed, and hence more likely to be remains of feathers rather than skin tissues decomposed into fibers.

Second, she also dismisses the frill hypothesis, arguing that frills, unlike feathers, should not contain a particular type of protein, a type that is clearly indicated by chemical analysis to be present in the Sinosauropteryx fossil piece.

Last, she believes that the possibility of the lines to represent feathers is compatible with their limited use for flight and thermoregulation, because[10] feathers, like those of peacocks, might have alternative functions like display. In fact, she points to recent test result showing that the line structure of Sinosauropteryx could be colorful with orange and white colors, which lends support to the likelihood that they are indeed feathers used for display.

[9] 典型的"观点 + 三个理由"的开头。

[10] "She believes that the XXX is compatible with XXX, because…" 用在否定逻辑的论证方式中，指出对方的理由和己方的观点是可以共存的，相当于说，即便对方的理由是对的，己方观点也仍然可以是对的。

TPO 32

1. quacker ←?

   听力肯定是说几种 quacker 的解释都是错的。

2. orca courtship

   听力肯定否认 quacker 是 orca courtship 的结果。

3. giant squid

   听力肯定否认 quacker 是 giant squid 的结果。

4. military tech, sub

   完全否定是军事科技的结果或者否定是潜艇的结果。

5. 无需笔记

6. live near surface, sub deep, × hear; should detect if nearby

阅读解析与听力预测

总 论：
有一些理论解释 quacker 的来源。[1] 这是一个典型的"现象＋三个解释"的文章，下文用三个不同的观点来解释 quacker 的来源。

解释 1：
Orca courtship ritual。[2]

解释 2：
大 squid。[3]

解释 3：
military technology，比如别国潜艇。[4]

听力解析

problems with all of the theories，符合预期，不需要记录。[5]

First，准备听 orca。It's true，要承认阅读的某些内容了，orca populations in the…area，承认那里有 orca，接下来肯定要反驳。orca…live near the surface，下半句基本不用听就知道要说潜艇在深水区了。submarines… remain deep in the ocean，果然如此。should not …able to hear the whale sounds from near the surface，指出这个差别的问题，是听不到水面 orca 的声音。Also，可能要给出第二个反驳。would have been detected by…sonar if…nearby，继续反驳，假如真的是 orca 接近潜艇，则理应被听到。[6]

◆ **本段逻辑梳理：** 不可能是 orca，因为 orca 住在水面，而潜艇在深水处，所以听不到；其次，假如 orca 真的离潜艇近，那肯定就被声呐探测到了。

TPO 32

Giant squid，准备听第二点。first detected…in the 1960s，不知道要说什么，记下来，继续听。reports…continued for about two decades，还是听不明白。But the sounds disappeared entirely by the 1980s. However…squid have always lived in the ocean…and continue to live today，这下明白了。quacker 声音有始有终，而 squid 一直都在，这是矛盾的。If these were squid sound, there would be no reason to…start…and…stop，这个虚拟语气是大无用信息，假如是 squid，则不该有始有终，而应该一直都在，不用记。[7]

◆ **本段逻辑梳理**：不是 squid，因为 squid 一直都在，而 quacker 始于 1960s，终于 1980s，如果是 squid，quacker 不该有始有终，应该一直都存在。

Third，准备听军事设备或潜艇。caused by a secret submarine，说明是要讨论潜艇的作用，不用管其他军事设备了。The sources of the sound…move around，记下来，不知道要说什么。change direction that quickly，还是听不明白，记下来。Submarines cannot，这下明白了，说明不是 submarine。Also，要有第二个反驳。all submarines make some engine noise，那接下来肯定说没有听到 engine noise 之类的。But no such noise accompanied the quackers，是无用信息。Even today we don't have…submarines that are that fast and…that silent，是这段的总结，不用记。[8]

◆ **本段逻辑梳理**：不是 submarine，因为 quacker 源头动得快，而 submarine 不行；并且 submarine 会有 engine noise，而 quacker 非常 silent。

[7] first 1960s, two decades, disappear 1980s, squid always

[8] sources move around, change direction, sub ✗; sub engine noise, ✗

满分范文

The article presents three hypotheses regarding the source of the "quacker" sound, all of which are contested by the lecturer.[9]

For starters, the lecturer dismisses the orca theory with two arguments. First, submarines mainly stay deep under ocean surface, so they could not possibly capture the sound of orcas, who mostly

[9] 典型的"现象＋三个解释"的文章开头。

stay near ocean surface. Second, if orcas had indeed strayed nearby the submarines, they should have been detected by sonar.

As for the possibility of a giant squid emitting the "quackers", the lecturer argues that the "quackers" were first detected in the 1960s and disappeared by the 1980s, but squids always lived in the ocean. She argues that if squids were the source, there would be no explanation why the "quackers" started or ended all of a sudden.

Last, she does not believe that the "quackers" were sounds of a submarine, either. On the one hand, the "quackers" must be from a source moving around and changing directions quickly, but no submarine at that time was this agile. On the other hand, the "quackers" were quite silent sounds, but all submarines at that time would emit noisy engine sounds.

TPO 33

阅读解析与听力预测

1 ✎ carved stone balls' purpose/meaning

📣 听力肯定会说这几个 meaning 和 purpose 都不存在。

2 ✎ hunt/fight < hole

📣 大方向肯定说不是用来 hunt 或 fight 的。

3 ✎ measure weight

📣 肯定说不是用来测重量的。

4 ✎ social status

📣 肯定说并不能体现社会地位。

▶ 总 论：

关于 carved stone balls 的 purpose 和 meaning 有一些 theories。[1] 下文肯定是三个独立的段落，各自提出一个关于这个 ball 的作用的说法，之间没有任何关系，现象解释型文章。

▶ 作用1：

hunting 或 fighting weapons，证据是中间有个孔。[2]

▶ 作用2：

用来测 weight。[3]

▶ 作用3：

标志主人的社会地位。[4]

听力解析

5 ✎ 无需笔记

None...convincing，是无用信息，早预见到了。[5]

First，准备听 hunting / fighting。common...weapons...show signs of wear，下文逻辑基本已经确定了。weapons 是有 wear 的，要证明这个 ball 不是 weapon，那估计下文就说它没有 wear 了。if the stone...weapons...they too would...that use，注意这个虚拟语气，这一定是无用信息，下文一定会说没有 wear。Many...would be cracked or have pieces broken off，只是具体展开说是什么样的 wear。However, the surfaces...well preserved，这就是说没有 wear，终于如我们所预见的。showing little or no wear or damage，继续是无用信息。[6]

6 ✎ common hunt—wear (crack, broken off), ✕ wear

◆ **本段逻辑梳理**：不可能是 hunting weapons，因为没有 wear，而通常 weapon 都有 wear。

TPO 33

Second，准备听 measure weight。maybe remarkably uniform in size，体现和阅读一致的地方，让步。but their masses，后面还听不太懂。那怎么办？这靠逻辑一推断就知道了，前半句承认 size 一致，转折后说 masses，那肯定要说不一致了。我们知道这个段落的目的是要证明不能测 weight，而 weight 和 mass 显然很有联系，所以这个推测很可能是准确的。我们接着听，because…made of different types of stone，包含具体的一些石头种类。这里说由不同石材组成，那很可能就会导致质量不统一。Each…has a different density，密度不同，还是要说质量为什么不同。Some…heavier than others，这是无用信息。just as a handful of feathers weigh less than a handful of rocks，这个类比完全没有用。Two balls of the same size have different weights，还是无用信息；depending on…stone they are made of，继续是无用信息。Therefore…not…used as a…weighing system，还是无用信息。[7]

◆ **本段逻辑梳理**：不可能用来称重量，虽然大小差不多，但质量相差太多，因为材质不同、密度不同。

Third，准备听标志社会地位。unlikely…social marker，是无用信息，不用记。A couple of facts are inconsistent with the theory，不用记，是空话，但暗示下文我们将听到两种反驳。while some…carved with intricate patterns，这是让步，下文肯定反驳说 others 了。many others have markings… extremely simple, too simple … like status symbols，已经反驳清楚了，虽然有的设计图案精妙，但许多图案简单，不能标志社会地位。Furthermore，准备听第二个反驳。when someone died…buried with their possessions，一个人去世要有陪葬品，不知道要说什么。However，none of the…balls…found in tombs or graves，这下反驳清楚了，要是真的标志社会地位，理应作为陪葬品在古墓中被发现，但在古墓中没有发现。[8]

◆ **本段逻辑梳理**：不可能标志社会地位，因为首先虽然有些设计精妙，但是大部分设计普通，不能标志地位；其次，要是标志地位，人去世时应该陪葬，但是在古墓中没有发现。

[7] <size = > mas ≠ ←
different stones, different dense

[8] < some intricate > others simple; die → burry, ✗ found in tomb

TPO 33

满分范文

The article mentions three speculations regarding the purpose and meaning of the carved stone balls, all of which are challenged in the lecture.

For starters, the lecturer does not believe that the balls were used for hunting or fighting, because unlike most hunting tools that were discovered, the balls were well preserved and did not show any signs of wear. For example, nothing was cracked or broken off.

Second, the lecturer rejects the possibility that the balls were used to measure weights, because even though they do have the same size, their masses are anything but uniform. The reason is that they are made of different types of stones with completely different density.

Last, the lecturer holds that the balls probably carry no social significance, because while some balls do possess elaborate designs, many others only have extremely simple patterns, too simple to signify the owner's social status. Furthermore, she claims that an artifact marking social status would often be buried with its owner when he dies, but none of the balls were discovered in a tomb.

TPO 34

阅读解析与听力预测

总 论：
有三个原因可以解释 sea cows 的灭绝。[1] 这是典型的"现象 + 三个解释"型的文章，下文必然是三个独立的可能导致 sc 灭绝的原因。

解释 1：
西伯利亚当地居民为了食物而过度捕食。[2]

解释 2：
kelp 数量减少，导致 sc 没吃的。[3]

解释 3：
fur traders 打猎造成 sc 灭绝。[4]

[1] sea cows↓←？
肯定说这些解释都不行。

[2] overhunt, food
要么说当地人根本就不会捕食 sc；要么说就算捕食了，也不会造成 sc 灭绝。

[3] kelp↓
要么说 kelp 根本没变少；要么说就算 kelp 变少了，也不会造成 sc 灭绝。

[4] fur traders
要么说 fur traders 根本就没有捕猎 sc；要么说就算捕猎 sc，也并不会造成其灭绝。

[5] 无需笔记

[6] sc 大, 9 meter, 10 ton, 1 feed village for months, small population, × need to hunt lot

听力解析

don't know what the main cause…problems with each…theories, 已经表明立场，符合我们的预期，不用记笔记。[5]

First，准备听过度猎食。sea cows were massive…9 meters long…10 tons，都是在说特别大，不知道要干什么。A couple of sea cows could feed…village for months, 这下已经差不多能听出逻辑了，就是 sc 太大，一个就够村民吃很久，暗示捕猎不了那么多。population of the native Siberian…not very large, 进一步凸显村民不需要吃那么多 sc。while the Siberian…did hunt the sea cows, 承认打猎；didn't need to hunt a lot, 已经是无用信息了。unlikely they…brought the sea cows…extinction 是必然结论。[6]

◆ **本段逻辑梳理**：不可能是猎食造成的，因为 sc 个儿大，一个顶全村几个月的食物，不需要打那么多。

Second，准备听 kelp 减少。if something severe really happened…it would have affected not just the kelp, but also other parts of the ecosystem，这个虚拟语气一出现，我们早已经应该预料到下文要说的东西了，肯定是其他生物并没有受到影响，所以 kelp 肯定没有受打击。For example, it would have caused the decline in other marine animals like whales, 只是个例子；而且肯定没有发生。But...did not report a whale decline, 符合预期。Since...no indication of broader ecosystem problems, the kelp was probably growing just fine, 完全和预期一致。the sea cows did not experience food shortage, 肯定还是无用信息。[7]

◆ **本段逻辑梳理**：kelp 根本就没减少，因为若是 kelp 受到环境冲击而减少，其他生物理应也有连带反应，然而并没有。

Third, 准备听 fur traders。it might seem ... traders were responsible because...extinct soon after the Europeans arrive, 这里相当于在为阅读寻找理由，相当于让步。But...by the time that the Europeans arrived, the sea cow population was already small, 这将反驳基本已经讲清楚了，sc 减少肯定发生在 traders 来之前。the sea cow population was at its largest...before 1700s... decrease...long before the Europeans arrived, 这里基本都是无用信息了。[8]

◆ **本段逻辑梳理**：fur traders 也不可能是根本原因，因为虽然欧洲人来了后 sc 就没了，但是 sc 数量下降比欧洲人到来要早上百年。

[7] eco change → other parts < marine < whales, ×whale↓, kelp√

[8] <extinct after arrive> arrive 时 small population, largest hundred years before 1700s

满分范文

The article presents three hypotheses to explain the extinction of Steller's sea cows, all of which are dismissed in the lecture.[9]

For starters, the lecturer does admit that Siberian villagers hunted the sea cows for food, but he does not believe that they hunted enough to cause the sea cows' disappearance. His reason is that the sea cows were giant creatures of over 9 meters in length and 10 tons in mass, so one sea cow would have fed an entire village for months, especially given the local villages' relatively small population back then.

Second, he does not believe that ecological changes could have threatened kelp so much as to cause the sea cows' extinction. According to him, if ecological change did threaten kelp, other

[9] 典型的"现象+三个解释"的开头形式。

species like whales should have suffered as well. However, no such decline in other species was reported. Therefore, he believes that kelp probably grew just fine.

Last, even though he acknowledges that the sea cows died out soon after the Europeans came, he believes that something other than the fur traders must be the main villain. When the Europeans came, the sea cow population had already dropped vastly from its highest number hundreds of years ago.

TPO 35

阅读解析与听力预测

> **总　论：**
> 有三个理论可以解释 V 手稿的起源。这是典型的"现象＋三个解释"型的文章，则下文必然是三个独立的 V 起源的猜想。[1]
>
> **解释 1：**
> 这是一个真正的关于科学或魔法的手稿，展开部分提到可能是 AA 的创作。[2]
>
> **解释 2：**
> 这是个伪造的手稿，没什么意义，展开部分提到可能是 EK 创作的。[3]
>
> **解释 3：**
> 是 V 本人当代创作的。[4]

[1] ✎ origin of V manuscript
📣 肯定说这些理论都有错。

[2] ✎ scientific, magical, in a secret code (AA)
📣 并不是什么关于科学或魔法的记载。

[3] ✎ fake, no meaning (EK)
📣 并不是无意义的伪造品。

[4] ✎ modern fake by V
📣 并不是 V 创作的。

听 力 解 析

None of the three people, probably the author of the manuscript, 这几个词听完其实有点出乎我的意料。如果大家看我刚才记的阅读笔记，三个段落理论的核心我并没有判定为三个人名。事实上，阅读的三个段落的段首句只有第三段专门提到了人名，而第一、第二两个理论所涉及的人名是在两段中间展开部分才出现的。我在第一遍读阅读时记下的 AA 和 EK 两个人名纯粹是因为我阅读时间充分才顺手记下的，我并没有预料到听力会专门攻击每个人名。而事实上，如果我不听听力去复述阅读，我很可能并不会专门提到 AA 和 EK。这就是比对阅读和听力的意义，当听到听力这个开头时，我马上就意识到，看来刚才预测的前两段听力主题可能是有问题的，也许听力并不会盯着 science, magic 或者无意义的伪造品来反驳，可能就是想直接说不是 AA 和 EK 的作品。所以，这个听力开头句其实对我的写作过程起到了重大的修正作用。[5]

[5] ✎ None of 3 was the author

According to the first theory, conveying information so important, or so powerful, code to keep it secret, 这全是无用信息，复述第一个

TPO 35

理论而已。doesn't fit what we know about Anthony Ascham,这句很关键，已经表明了反驳策略，就是 AA 的特点肯定和手稿特点有鲜明区别，那接下来肯定要表明 AA 怎么和刚才的 powerful or important code 的感觉相冲突了，并且这也再次印证了这个段落要反驳的就是 AA 是作者这个猜想。Anthony Ascham was an ordinary physician and scientist whose books didn't contain any original ideas,这里很好地体现了他的书和手稿的区别，一定要记住。For instance,那接下来肯定是重复，herbal（书名不重要，因为说了是阅读提到的），common plants based on well-known sources,体现没有 original ideas。So given what we know about Anthony Ascham and his books,那肯定是要总结了，基本不可能有让我们意外的结论了，unlikely he was the author of such an elaborately coded, secret document,就是无用信息，再次突出 AA 的书和手稿的对比。[6]

◆ **本段逻辑梳理**：AA 是作者的猜想肯定不对，他的书和手稿的特点对立。AA 是一个普通学者，没什么原创的东西，比如他的那本书就很差劲，他是不可能写出 V 手稿这样玄妙的东西的。

Second, although Edward kelly was good at tricking people,做了个让步，承认第二个人喜欢骗人，那等会儿肯定要说这次不是他在骗人，刚才这个让步并不重要。unlikely he created,其实都是无用信息，我们已经知道要否认他了。creator took care to make the test look like code, people in the 16th century were easy to fool,其实这两点听完，这个段落的质疑策略已经非常鲜明了。创作者用心编码，但 16 世纪的人那么蠢，言下之意就是，需要费那么大劲骗这样一群蠢人吗？so it was not necessary to make sth. this complex,这已经是无用信息了。If Kelly wanted to create a fake, no reason to put so much work,这基本就是必然结论了。a simpler book could suit his purpose just as well,没什么好说的了。[7]

◆ **本段逻辑梳理**：EK 也不可能是伪造者。手稿那么精良，而 16 世纪的人那么蠢。想骗这群蠢人根本不需要 EK 做这么复杂的事情，他做个简单的东西一样就可以骗人了。

Third, able to date material, vellum pages and ink are at least 400 years old,非常关键的事实证据。That ruled out Voynich as the author,这倒是无用信息，因为我们知道要反驳 V 是作者。If Voynich wanted to create a fake, he could use vellum pages from old

[6] not fit with AA, ordinary phy and scientist, no original idea, herbal: common plants based on well-known sources, unlikely author, elaborately coded document（其实最后几个词也没必要记，我只是精力富余罢了）

[7] <good at tricking>, care to look like code, 16th century easy to fool, no need, simpler book could have suited his purpose

TPO 35

manuscript，这是让步，承认他有可能拿到 400 年前的 vellum pages，这不是关键反驳。where would he get 400-year-old ink，这是关键反驳，V 不可能拿到 400 年前的墨。这就意味着刚才找到的 400 年前的墨是关键反驳证据。So manuscript was created centuries before Voynich，这是无用信息。[8]

◆ **本段逻辑梳理：** V 不是作者，因为当代手段测定手稿的纸和墨都有 400 多年的历史了。虽然 V 有可能获得很老的纸，但他几乎不可能获得几百年前的墨。这说明，手稿真的就是几百年前的东西。

[8] date v (我听的时候不知道 vellum 怎么拼，但阅读提过我也就不慌) and ink, at least 400 yrs, rule out v <could use pages> no ink, centuries before v

[9] 典型的三个解释的开头形式。

满分范文

The article presents three hypotheses to explain the origin of the "Voynich manuscript", all of which are questioned in the lecture.[9]

First, the lecturer does not believe that Anthony Ascham's status fits the theory that he was the author of this manuscript, because Ascham was just an ordinary physician and scientist who proposed no original idea whatsoever. His book *A Little Herbal*, for example, was merely a document on common plants completely based on well-known sources. In contrast, the "Voynich manuscript" is quite an elaborately coded document.

Second, the theory that Edward Kelly forged this manuscript during the 16th century is also challenged by the lecturer. He argues that if the manuscript was in fact a forge, then its creator obviously took so much care and made it look like code in order to trick its audience. However, people in the 16th century were quite simple and easy to fool. Edward Kelly could have made a much simpler book and still had his way.

Finally, the lecturer does not accept that the manuscript is a modern fake composed by Voynich himself, because modern dating shows that the vellum and ink used by the manuscript are at least 400 years old. While Voynich could have somehow acquired paper from 400 years ago, it is almost impossible for him to get hold of ink that old.

TPO 36

阅读解析与听力预测

▶ **总 论：**
一些证据表明 cloud seeding 可以防止作物受 hail 的损坏。这是明显的"观点+三个理由"型的文章。那我们应该做好准备，听力可以有两种反驳策略，一是否定理由本身（当证据不是事实的时候），二是否定理由与观点的关系。[1]

1. cloud seeding √

2. lab exp

   ▶ 可能会说实验做错了，这个概率比较小；更有可能会说，就算实验如此，但现实不如此，指出实验和现实的差距。

▶ **理由 1：**
实验模拟表明 cloud seeding 有效。[2]

▶ **理由 2：**
亚洲的证据表明 cloud seeding 有效。[3]

3. Asian evidence

   ▶ 可能会说亚洲证据有问题，概率还是很小；更有可能会说，亚洲和美国情况不同。

▶ **理由 3：**
local studies 表明 cloud seeding 有效。[4]

4. local studies

   ▶ 可能会说 local studies 做得有问题；更有可能会说 local studies 和实际情况有什么不同。

听力解析

not clear that cloud seeding is effective, 纯无用信息。[5] First, it may be true, 直接让步，肯定对阅读有利，under laboratory conditions silver iodine creates snow instead of hail, 承认实验显示 cloud seeding 可以防 hail, 那等会儿只能质疑这和现实的关系了。However, in real life, silver iodine can prevent any precipitation, 关键反驳，现实中，cloud seeding 不仅防 hail, 还直接导致所有降水都不发生。这一听就不是什么好事了。snow, rain or hail, 包含在所有降水以内。bad thing, 很容易听出来，就算刚才没意识到是坏事现在也知道了。ran the risk of causing a drought, 这是必然结果。crops get damaged for lack of water, 无用信息。[6]

5. 无需笔记

6. ⟨lab √ snow, × hail⟩, prevent all precipitation, bad thing, ~ rain → drought, crop damage

♦ **本段逻辑梳理：** 是的，实验室确实表明 cloud seeding 可以减少 hail 的出现，但在实际生活中，cloud seeding 不仅减少了 hail, 还减少了各种降水，无论是雨还是雪。这意味着农作物虽然不会受 hail 的破坏，但会被旱死。

TPO 36

Second, it's not clear that Asia can be repeated in the United States，直接表明反驳策略是指出亚洲和美国情况的不同。...in Asia was tried in urban areas，亚洲的情况是在城市尝试，那这里暗示等会儿美国的情况肯定不是在城市，并且肯定要指出城市和非城市的关键区别，等会儿听到一边的情况自然就可以反推另一边的情况了。cities, high level of air pollution，那等会儿肯定是说美国的乡村没污染呗。from car, factory，污染源，想想也知道。pollution particles create favorable conditions for cloud seeding，关键信息，但其实逻辑上也是必需的，作者自然要说污染怎么有利于 cloud seeding，而没有 pollution 的时候 cloud seeding 就没什么用。because they interact with seeding chemicals，自然很合理。Such... may not occur in an unpolluted area，无用信息，我们早预料到了。may not work in farming regions in the United States，无用信息，也预料到了。[7]

[7] ✎ Asia ≠ US, Asia: try in urban areas, high level of air pollution → create favor conditions for cloud seeding, interact, × in unpolluted area

◆ **本段逻辑梳理**：亚洲的实验不能体现美国的实际情况，因为亚洲的实验是在城区做的，污染重，而污染物和 cloud seeding 的物质会发生反应，有利于 cloud seeding 起作用，但是在美国农耕区，没这种污染，那就不知道会有什么效果了。

Third, the local study isn't convincing，无用信息。hail damage decreased not just in the area where the cloud seeding took place, but in many neighboring areas... hail 减少不仅发生在做实验的地方，还发生在邻近地区。其实我听到这儿没完全领悟反驳策略，我还以为这说明 cloud seeding 效果绝佳呢。natural variation in local weather, has nothing to do with cloud seeding。这是关键信息，让我彻底领悟反驳策略，这隐藏的逻辑是，如果真的是 cloud seeding 起作用，则只应该是 cloud seeding 发生的地方 hail 减少，而不应该影响其他没做 cloud seeding 的地方。当然，说话者说出来的是，这现实情况（hail 减少发生在大片区域）反映这不是 cloud seeding 的作用，而只是当地区域气候自然变化的作用。[8] 听完整段后意识到，这个反驳策略居然是攻击实验本身了，等于实验根本没体现 cloud seeding 的作用。

[8] ✎ decrease not just in the area, but in neighboring areas, result of natural variation in local weather

◆ **本段逻辑梳理**：local study 做得就有问题。在这个实验当中，hail 减少不仅发生在做实验的区域，还发生在周围各邻近区域。这表明，hail 的减少并不是 cloud seeding 带来的，而很可能是整个区域气候自然变动的体现。

TPO 36

满分范文

The article presents three arguments why cloud seeding is effective in protecting crops from hail, all of which are challenged by the lecturer.[9]

The article's first piece of evidence is from laboratory simulation. However, according to the lecturer, cloud seeding is not just effective in preventing the formation of hail, but will stop all kinds of precipitation, including rain and snow. In the real world, it means that crops would not be damaged by hail, but damaged by a possible drought.

The article also mentions evidence in Asia to lend support to its claim. However, the lecturer emphasizes that the experience in Asia takes place in urban areas, where the high air pollution from traffic and industry creates a favorable condition for cloud seeding because of how silver iodine interacts with pollutants. Consequently, it is unclear whether the successful experience can be recreated in the agricultural areas in the United States, where there is no such heavy pollution.

Finally, the lecturer also questions whether the local studies mentioned by the article prove the effectiveness of cloud seeding. She specifically points out that the reduced hail appeared not just in the area where cloud seeding was conducted, but also in its neighboring areas. This result suggests that the reduced hail was not due to cloud seeding, but was the consequence of natural variation in local weather.

[9] 典型的"观点+三个理由"型文章开头。

TPO 37

📝 阅读解析与听力预测

▶ 总　论：
TEDS 被几个理由攻击。典型的"观点+三个理由"型文章，只不过观点不是支持一件事情，而是反对一件事情。那听力反驳策略只有两种：理由本身不成立，或者理由成立但不支持观点。[1]

▶ 理由 1：
有虾农抱怨说海龟被误抓的概率其实很低，而 TEDS 会使他们少捕虾。[2]

▶ 理由 2：
替代方案，限定撒网时间。[3]

▶ 理由 3：
TED 还是会抓到大海龟。[4]

1 ✏️ TEDS ×

2 ✏️ turtle catch↓, shrimp↓

　🖍 无非直接否认这两个数据，或者承认它们，但坚持使用 TEDS。

3 ✏️ alternative: limit net time underwater

　🖍 肯定是否定这个替代方案，指出其问题；不太可能是承认替代方案好，但坚持用 TEDS，这实在太自相矛盾了。

4 ✏️ × effective for large turtles

　🖍 直接否认这个，或者承认它但坚持使用 TEDS。

5 ✏️ 无需笔记

📝 听 力 解 析

experts believe... TEDs are a good way，听力如果要反驳阅读，自然要说 TEDs 好。Here are responses to criticisms，也没什么意外的。这个开头不重要。[5] First, it's true that catching a turtle is a rare thing，这已经很明显让步承认了阅读的数据，捕龟概率就是很低。for any one boat，其实我在听到这儿的时候已经知道反驳策略了：我承认每艘船捕龟少，那接下来肯定要说但挡不住船多呀。however, thousands of shrimp boats，我觉得没什么好说的，太重要了，但太可预期了。Collectively... catch thousands of turtles every year，这也是必然结果。endangered sea turtles whose population is already too small，这个只是补充说明，我们本来也知道，阅读也提到过，显得刚才提到的一年捕上千只海龟这个问题更严重而已。harming thousand is a big problem，这是必然的逻辑导向。considering ... TEDs, don't think an individual shrimper losing shrimps, sea turtle population is affected by the shrimp industry as a whole，听起来很高大上，其实就是总结告诉我们要顾全大局，海龟的灭绝问题比虾农少捕几只虾问题大多了。[6]

6 ✏️ <rare 1 boat>, thousands, collectively 1000/year, endangered, big problem, population as a whole

TPO 37

◆ **本段逻辑梳理**：是的，每艘船捕龟概率是很低，但架不住船多呀。几千艘船每年捕上千头海龟，这对本来就脆弱的海龟群落来说是致命的。总的来看，这个问题要比虾农少捕几只虾的问题大多了。

Second, sounds like a good idea, only in theory, 这已经暗示了等会儿肯定会说实操不行。time limits are impossible to enforce, 就是不可执行，很直接。thousands of boats, government patrol boats cannot monitor, 很清晰，船太多，政府管不过来，不可能一直盯着。The use of TEDs is easier to enforce, 没预料到，但听到了也觉得顺理成章，那个方案不可执行，那 TEDs 肯定可执行。checking before boats leave, nets have TEDs, 执行方案就是出海之前查一下有没有装 TEDs。[7]

◆ **本段逻辑梳理**：所谓替代方案，即规定在海面下撒网的时间，这根本不可行。几千只船，政府巡逻根本管不过来。相反，TEDs 就好操作多了，船只出海之前，只要检查一下是不是装了 TEDs 就好了。

Third, it's true that TEDs can be too small for large species, 承认阅读说的 TEDs 不够大，一些龟太大。in the area where they are needed, not a problem to create TEDs that are larger, 反驳策略很明显，虽然 TEDs 不够大，但真需要的地方也很容易把 TEDs 做大。TEDs can be modified easily without affecting function, 继续是无用信息，很容易改造。once large TEDs ... produced, no longer be a problem, 完全没有重要的新信息。[8]

◆ **本段逻辑梳理**：确实现在的 TEDs 对于一些大海龟来说太小了，但是 TEDs 是可以改造的，在需要的地方 TEDs 很容易被造得更大但效果不受影响。

[7] sounds good in theory, time limit: ✗ enforce, 1000 at sea, patrol boats cannot monitor all, TEDs easy to enforce, check before leave

[8] <small for large species of turtles> area needed, not a problem, modify TEDs easily, larger TEDs

✎ 满分范文

The lecturer defended the use of Turtle Excluder Devices (TEDs) in preventing sea turtles from being caught by nets against all three challenges presented in the article.[9]

First, while the lecturer admits that the shrimpers' data is correct, that one boat is likely to catch only one turtle per month. However, she argues that since there are thousands of fishing boats at work, collectively, losing thousands of turtles every year makes it a big

[9] 典型的"观点+三个理由"型文章开头，因为观点不是支持一件事，而是反对一件事。

problem, especially for an endangered species. The overall damage is much more significant than the few shrimps that shrimpers fail to catch.

As with the suggestion to limit the time boats can keep their nets under water as an alternative to TEDs, the lecturer considers this approach attractive in theory, but unenforceable in practice. The patrol just cannot monitor whether thousands of boats out there all bring up their nets within the required time limit. In contrast, TEDs are much more applicable, since each boat can be checked before it sails out whether it has installed a TED.

The final challenge is that TEDs are still too small for some large turtle species. However, the lecturer believes that in areas where larger turtle species are present, this wouldn't be a problem eventually because TEDs can be modified easily without sacrificing their functions.

TPO 38

1. 📝 international fund → forest✓

2. 📝 forest agriculture

   🐂 要么说根本不能帮助森林农业，要么承认可以帮助，但仍然反对international fund。

3. 📝 economies of villages and tribal communities

   🐂 与前面类似，直接否认可以帮助这些村子，或者承认能帮助，但仍然反对international fund。

4. 📝 forest biodiversity

   🐂 不能保护多样性，或者就算能，但仍然不该搞international fund。

5. 📝 无需笔记

6. 📝 agri is a destructive force itself. Farmers are under pressure to increase yields by using modern tech, fertilizer, pesticide, detrimental to surrounding, waste, water pollution worse than logging

📝 阅读解析与听力预测

▶ 总　论：
国际基金是最好的保护森林的方式。这是一个比较鲜明的观点句，"the best way" 体现这是观点，是一个主观判断，而不是一个客观事实的观察。因此，虽然没有明显的标志词，但这篇文章极有可能是 "观点＋三个理由" 的类型。[1]

▶ 理由1：
可以保护森林农业。[2]

▶ 理由2：
保护森林当中的村庄部落经济。[3]

▶ 理由3：
保护生物多样性。[4]

📝 听　力　解　析

an international protection fund... is flawed, 无用信息。[5] agriculture is itself a destructive force upon the forest, 这个句子已经把第一点反驳的核心逻辑说得极其清楚了，没有否认 fund 能帮助农业，而是在暗示不应该帮农业，因为农业本身是破坏森林的。那接下来肯定要展开农业怎么破坏森林，但刚才这一句是绝对不应该漏的观点句。With the rising populations, farmers are under pressure to increase yields by using modern technology and practices, 知道应该是在具体展开前文的危害。农民有压力要提高产量，于是用当代科技。such as fertilizer and pesticide, 这稍微有点常识就知道肯定要说这些玩意儿不好，怎么破坏森林。detrimental to the environment, create runoff waste and water pollution, leads to deforestation... worse than of logging, 产生的各种废物和污染比砍树更能毁林。not a good idea, 无用信息总结。[6]

◆ **本段逻辑梳理**：农业本身就是对森林的巨大威胁。因为为了提高产量，农民会使用先进科技，比如农药、化肥，它们产生的污染和废料对森林的威胁甚至比伐木还严重。

　　paying villagers a stipend is an inadequate solution，无用信息。money would go to forest owners，还看不出端倪，继续认真听。More often than not, owners are governments, not residents，大概应该明白反驳方向了，这些钱会给森林拥有者，而拥有者不是居民，而是政府。Therefore, a payout would not end up in the hands of forest dwellers，简单来说就是这些钱最后不会落到森林部落居民手里。这意味着阅读说的那个好处就肯定不存在了。Additionally, no guarantee that if governments received the money, it would be appropriately used to protect the forest。结合前文，一方面钱不会落到居民手上，而另一方面，既然落到了政府手里，那政府也不见得会正确使用这些钱，那结果自然不好。[7]

◆ **本段逻辑梳理**：这种国际基金的钱应该是落在森林控制者手里，然而一般来说控制者是政府，而不是森林居民。所以居民拿不到钱，自然无法直接保护森林。而落到政府手里，那就无法保证政府会把这些钱用在保护森林上了。

　　If money is spent by encouraging the planting, no doubt… plant trees which have commercial purposes，这种方式会导致人们种有商业价值的树。If people merely plant plantation forests, this will do nothing… goal of forest biodiversity。很简单，如果只种商业树种，那怎么会有多样性呢。[8]

◆ **本段逻辑梳理**：给钱鼓励种树的结果是人们会种最有经济价值的树，而如果只这么做，对森林树种多样性自然不会有任何帮助。

[7] 💰 inadequate, $ Go to forest owners, Gov, not residents, not up in their hands, no guarantee that gov rightly used money for forest

[8] 🖊 < plant trees with commercial purpose > not promote biodiversity

📝 满 分 范 文

　　The article presents three arguments why an international fund is a good way for forest conservation in developing countries, all of which are questioned by the lecturer.[9]

　　For starters, the article claims that the fund can help protect forest agriculture. Unfortunately, the lecturer points out that agriculture itself is a destructive force for the forest. Under pressure to

[9] 典型的"观点+三个理由"型文章开头。

increase yield, farmers rely on modern technology including fertilizers and pesticides that have proven to be detrimental to the surrounding forest environment. In fact, the waste and water pollution from forest farming can destroy the forest more than does logging.

Second, the article believes the fund can help develop economies of villages and tribal communities located in forest areas. Unfortunately, the lecturer believes that the money will go to forest owners, which are the governments rather than the forest residents. That means the money will probably not go into the hands of the villagers. Also, if the money is at the government's disposal, there is no guarantee that the money will be used in forest protection.

Finally, the article believes that the money can help conserve forest biodiversity. However, the lecturer argues that the money will encourage people to plant trees with commercial purposes only, so eventually it is not going to promote biodiversity.

TPO 39

📝 阅读解析与听力预测

总 论：
有一些理论可以解释T时代的大灭绝。典型的"现象+三个解释"的文章，听力反驳策略几乎一定是说这些理论不能解释大灭绝。[1]

解释 1：
海平面下降。[2]

解释 2：
全球变冷。浏览了一下展开内容发现是火山喷发产生SO_2造成变冷。[3]

解释 3：
陨石。[4]

[1] extinction at the end of T

[2] sea level ↓
   ▶ 海平面没下降，或者海平面下降并不能造成大灭绝。

[3] T ↓
   ▶ 全球没变冷，或者全球变冷也不会造成大灭绝。

[4] asteroid
   ▶ 就没有陨石，或者陨石不能造成大灭绝。

📝 听 力 解 析

none is a good explanation，无用信息。

sea level often going down，已经意识到听力承认了海平面下降，那接下来肯定要否认它和灭绝的关系。This isn't a good explanation for the extinction，无用信息。Coastal and shallow water ecosystems are usually capable of adapting to environmental changes that happen gradually，这下反驳讨论很清晰，全球海平面就算下降了，也不会对沿海生态系统有那么大的影响，因为后者能适应气候的渐变。The falling sea level was quite gradual，这就是无用信息了，那会儿的海平面下降就是渐变的。several million years，只是进一步展开。The change would have to be more sudden to have a negative impact，只是总结句，没什么意义。[5]

◆ **本段逻辑梳理**：海平面确实可能下降了，但是沿海生态系统是能应对这么缓慢的变化过程的。要真的产生大灭绝，那原因必须比这个激烈很多。

[5] <fluctuate, often ↓ > coastal systems usually adapt to gradual change, was gradual, million years, would have to be sudden to widespread impact

TPO 39

It's true SO₂ can lower global temperature, 让步，承认 SO₂ 可以降低全球气温。can only happen during a relatively short period, 这已经暗示等会儿肯定要说实际情况不是一个 short period thing。when SO₂ released by volcanoes is still present in the atmosphere, 已经暗示出等会儿肯定要说 SO₂ 之后就消失了。In a few years, SO₂ is cleared out, 这是我们预料中的。combines with water in the atmosphere, and falls back on earth as rain, 明显是解释 clear out 的过程。doesn't seem... even if there was a lot of volcanic SO₂, it stayed long enough to cause mass extinction, 只是无用信息总结。[6]

◆ **本段逻辑梳理**：SO₂ 确实可以造成全球变冷，但这是个短期事件，只发生在火山爆发产生的 SO₂ 还在空气中的时候。然而，在几年时间内，SO₂ 就会消退，它与水汽结合形成降水。所以火山喷发再多 SO₂，也不可能待足够长的时间造成这么大规模的灭绝。

few scientists believe the asteroid theory, 已经判了死刑。we haven't found any asteroid crater at the site where the asteroid hit that can be dated to... mass extinction occured, 我们没发现哪个陨石落下来的地方有任何坑属于灭绝那个年代。did find a crater, but it dates to 12 million years before the extinction, 有坑，时间也对不上。too long before the extinction to have anything to do with it, 根本不可能和灭绝有关。[7]

◆ **本段逻辑梳理**：就没人相信陨石理论。因为所谓陨石砸过的地方就找不到那个时期的陨石坑，找到的陨石坑也比灭绝早了 1200 万年，根本不可能和灭绝有关。

[6] ✎ < SO₂ → ↓ > only shorter period, when SO₂ released still present in atm, clear out, combine with water in air, fall back as rain, even if a lot of SO₂, × stay long enough

[7] ✎ × scientists believe, not find crater that can be dated to the time, a crater, 12 million before, has nothing to do

📝 满分范文

The article presents three hypotheses to explain the mass extinction at the end of the Triassic period, all of which are questioned by the lecturer.[8]

To begin with, while the lecturer concedes that the sea level at that time indeed often fell, she does not believe that it was sudden enough to disturb the coastal ecosystem so much, let alone to affect the entire food chain, because the coastal ecosystem could adapt to

[8] 典型的"现象 + 三个解释"的文章开头。

such gradual environmental change as the sea level fell at that period.

As with the theory that sulfur dioxide emitted from volcano eruptions caused the mass extinction, the lecturer counters that the effect of sulfur dioxide would only last a short period, when the sulfur dioxide released was still present in the atmosphere. In a few years, it would clear out as rainfall by combining with water in the atmosphere. Even if volcanic activities did emit a lot of sulfur dioxide, it would not stay long enough to generate the mass extinction.

Finally, the lecturer points out that few scientists accept the asteroid hypothesis, because no craters have been found at the site where the asteroid hit that can be dated to the time of the mass extinction. The only crater found was 12 million years before that period, too long to have anything to do with the extinction.

TPO 40

阅读解析与听力预测

▶ **总　论：**
Venus 几乎不可能让人生存。[1] 正文肯定会用三个理由来支持这个论断，所以这应该是"一个观点＋三个理由"形式的文章。

▶ **理由 1：**
气压太大，毁掉一切。[2]

▶ **理由 2：**
没有水和氧气，从地球进口简直不可能。[3]

▶ **理由 3：**
没有光，所以发不了电。[4]

[1] Venus—×人
　很可能说 Venus 是有可能让人生存的。

[2] 气压大
　也许会说气压没那么大，但否定事实是很困难的；更可能是承认气压确实大，但有办法解决。

[3] ×H_2O, ×O_2
　也许会说有水和氧气，但事实是很难被否定的；因此，更有可能是承认水和氧气很难获得，但是有办法解决。

[4] ×光 → ×电
　也许会说有光；也许会说就算没光，但有可能获得电；还有可能说就算没有电，但是能克服。

听力解析

possible 表明立场，不用记。"One solution…station…floating in …atmosphere…the problems the reading mentions can be solved." 这个开头非常令人意外，不是说它没有反对阅读的观点，而是不仅说了有可能在 Venus 上建立人类根据地，甚至连具体怎么做都说清楚了，所以必须记录。[5]

First，准备听压强。atmospheric pressure…fact that high up … the pressure is much lower，其实已经把反驳策略说清楚了。如果在空中建根据地，则压强肯定比金星地表小得多。while 表让步，是和阅读立场相符的信息，the pressure at…surface is too high for human，接下来肯定是无用信息，说空中的压强无害。up … pressure is equal to … on earth，是无用信息。no danger 也是无用信息。[6]

[5] station floating 50 km above surface

[6] <surface p↑ >up p = earth

◆ **本段逻辑梳理**：金星表面压强确实过大，但空中压强并不大，和地球差不多，对人类无害。

Second，准备听水和氧气。while，表示要让步了；Venus…CO_2 and SO_2，承认 Venus 有很多这些气体。There are chemical processes…to make O_2 and H_2O out of these…反驳策略已经表明，materials…可以另辟蹊径获得水和氧气。could be produced using chemical materials…easily obtained from Venus atmosphere，很自然，不需要必须记录。not be necessary to import，这是无用信息，不需要记录。[7]

◆ **本段逻辑梳理**：不需要从地球进口水和氧气就可以有足够的水和氧气，因为虽然 Venus 大气充满 CO_2 和 SO_2，但这些东西恰恰可以通过化学反应制造出足够的 H_2O 和 O_2。

Third，准备听光。it's true 表示要对阅读让步了；still clouds 50 km above，承认上方也有云挡光。However…not very thick，将反驳策略说清楚了，云层不厚，所以自然会有更多光。so…considerable… sunlight filtering through，是无用信息，不用记。Moreover，并列第二个反驳，是新的反驳。clouds reflect sunlight，不知道想说什么，继续听；The station can make use of this reflected light，听得似懂非懂。collect…sunlight…above and…reflected by the clouds below，这下彻底听懂了。上面射下来的光多，可以直接吸收，下面反射回来的光，也能吸收。[8]

◆ **本段逻辑梳理**：也能获得足够的光。首先，虽然有云，但是上层的云很少，因此可以透过并吸收更多的光；其次，下面的光还会反射回来，也可以利用。

[7] ✎ ＜大气— CO_2, SO_2＞ → O_2, H_2O

[8] ✎ ＜cloud＞ not thick, reflect light, collect above + below

满分范文

The article presents three main problems to prove that settling in Venus would be next to impossible for humans, but the lecturer believes that by setting up a station floating 50 km above Venus' surface, we can address all these problems, rendering possible human presence on Venus.[9]

[9] 这个开头体现了阅读有"一个观点＋三个理由"，听力对这个观点和理由进行反驳，并且具体指出了听力的策略是 setting up a floating station，这是和其他文章不同的地方。

For starters, while the lecturer concedes that atmospheric pressure on Venus' surface would be lethal to human equipment, the pressure higher up wouldn't pose a threat to humans at all, because it is almost equal to normal atmospheric pressure on earth.

Second, the lecturer does not believe that humans would have to import from the earth to have enough water and oxygen, because up in the clouds of Venus, there are significant amount of CO_2 and SO_2, chemicals that could be used in certain chemical reactions to generate oxygen and water.

Last, he also believes that there are ways to acquire sufficient amount of light. On the one hand, even though there are still clouds up in the sky, they are much thinner so more light from above can be received. On the other hand, clouds reflect light, so light reflected by clouds down below can also be utilized.

TPO 41

📝 阅读解析与听力预测

▶ 总 论：

不该对 coal ash 制定更严格的规则，没必要，且有害处。[1] 本文肯定是"观点 + 三个理由"的结构，共同反对一个行为，只不过阅读已经说清楚了它的论证策略将是否定 strict regulations 的必要性，并指出其坏处。

▶ 理由 1：
已有现有规则，要求使用 liner。[2]

▶ 理由 2：
会影响 coal ash recycling，进而让人们不愿购买 coal ash product。[3]

▶ 理由 3：
公司成本提高，导致电费增高。[4]

1 ✏️ × strict regu on coal ash – × nece, bad

🖍️ 听力肯定是支持 strict regulation

2 ✏️ exist, liner

🖍️ 很难去否定现有规则不存在，因此最可能的就是指出虽然已有规则存在，但是仍然需要严格规则。

3 ✏️ × recycle → × buy product

🖍️ 前提和逻辑都有可能讨论，可以指出人们仍然会 recycle，人们仍然会 buy coal ash product；或者就算人们不会购买了，但是仍然应该有更严格的规则。

4 ✏️ $↑ → 电 $↑

🖍️ 前提和逻辑都可以讨论，公司成本不会变高；就算变高，人们的电费也不会变高；或者就算电费高了，人们也要严格遵守规则。

5 ✏️ 无需笔记

6 ✏️ × sufficient, liner only new landfill and new pond, old sites → damage, ground water, drinking water

📝 听力解析

definitely be stricter，表明立场，不用记。[5]

regulations we have now...not really sufficient，这个不令人意外，可以记。那接下来肯定要讲为什么不够，还需要什么。current regulations, liner ... used only when ... builds a new landfill or new pond，这里其实已经表明问题所在了，关键词 only，暗示在非 new pond 或非 new landfill 的情况下，不需要使用 liner，会造成某些问题。not required to add liner to old ponds and landfills，是无用信息，可以不记。Cost significant damage，符合预期，可以不记。For example...leaked into groundwater and contaminated drinking water，是具体的危害。absolutely...regulations...the new sites as well as the old sites 是必然结论，不用记录。[6]

TPO 41

♦ **本段逻辑梳理**：现有规则不够，它只要求在新场所使用 liner，旧场所不用，但旧场所造成了各种危害，比如危害水资源，所以需要新旧场所都使用 liner 的规则。

not...mean...consumers will stop using...coal ash products，直接否定阅读的理由。"Let's look at how people responded to...other... Take mercury for example." 这些暗示作者要借用类比的方式来论证，肯定之前 mercury 有了严格规则，对 consumers 没有影响，后面基本不用怎么听了。hazardous material...subject to very strict...rules...Yet ...successfully...recycled for over 50 years...consumers have...few concerns，都是理所当然的。So it's unlikely ... afraid ... coal ash products，是必然结论。这个段落在听出类比之后就已经不会有什么新意了。[7]

♦ **本段逻辑梳理**：严格规则并不会使 recycle 停止，并不会让 consumers 不买 coal ash products，因为类似的例子出现在了水银上，规则严格，但 recycle 了很久，人们也一直没有担心相关产品。

it's true 准备让步；cost of...storage and handling will increase，确实公司成本要高。but...result is well worth the extra cost，意思是利大于弊。cost to the power companies...15 billion dollars...sounds like a lot，下面肯定要进行反击了。increase...household electricity bill by only 1 percent，那确实不多了。not a big price to pay for having a cleaner environment，总结利大于弊。[8]

♦ **本段逻辑梳理**：严格的规则利大于弊，虽然会让公司成本上升 15 billion dollars，但是每家电费只上涨 1%，这相比于干净的环境实在微不足道。

[7] ✎ ✗ *stop buying product, mercury, strict, recycle, 50 years,* ✗ *concern*

[8] ✎ *<$↑>result worth, 15 billion dollars, 1%*

📝 满分范文

The article offers three arguments to advocate against stricter regulations for handling and storing coal ash, all of which are countered in the lecture.[9]

For starters, the lecturer does not believe that the existing regulations cited in the article are sufficient to prevent environmental

[9] 典型的"观点 + 三个理由"的模式。

damage, because they only require companies to use liners for new landfills and new ponds. Unfortunately, the older sites, where liner usage is not demanded by the regulations, are damaging groundwater and, in turn, drinking water. Therefore, the lecturer demands extending the regulations to all sites, old or new.

Second, the lecturer does not believe that stricter regulations would deter the consumers from purchasing coal ash products. She points out that when similar regulations were implemented for mercury, another dangerous chemical, mercury was still recycled, and for decades consumers had no concerns at all for the related products.

Last, she insists that the benefits of stricter regulations far outweigh the increased costs, because although the disposal and handling costs for the companies might increase by as much as 15 billion dollars, a seemingly large number, the charge for electric bill on each individual person is only going to rise by 1 percent, a fair price to pay for all the environmental benefits people are going to receive.

TPO 42

阅读解析与听力预测

总 论：

有三种方式可以防止建筑物玻璃伤害鸟类。[1] 这个开头太明确了，典型的问题解决型文章，下文一定是三个解决方案，互相没有关系。

方案 1：
One-way glass[2]

方案 2：
Colorful designs[3]

方案 3：
Magnetic field[4]

[1] glass injures bird

　三个解决方案都不行，要么没条件执行，要么无效，要么有副作用。

[2] 1-way glass

　这个方案不行，要么没条件执行，要么无效，要么有副作用。

[3] colorful design

　这个方案不行，要么没条件执行，要么无效，要么有副作用。

[4] mag field

　这个方案不行，要么没条件执行，要么无效，要么有副作用。

[5] ×

听 力 解 析

None, effectively, 这两个关键词不仅说明了听力反对阅读，还说明了反对策略是很狭隘的，即只是否定阅读建议的有效性，下文则说先前预期的其他两种可能性是不存在的。[5]

First, 准备听 one-way glass。to the bird on the outside...reflects like a mirror, 开始描述 one-way glass 的缺陷，但到目前为止逻辑上还不完整，肯定还有重要信息说像 mirror 有什么不好。as bad, 接下来应该讲为什么 as bad。because bids don't understand the mirrors, 很重要。If they see a reflection of the sky...or tree...they'd think the reflection is the sky or is the tree, 说出了关键理由，就是它们以为镜像是实物。And they will fly right into them, 这个结果对 birds 是极其糟糕的。[6]

[6] reflect like a mirror, as bad, × understand, see sky → think sky, fly into

◆ **本段逻辑梳理：** 单向玻璃没用，因为从外面看到的会和镜子效

TPO 42

果一样，而鸟无法理解镜子。它们看到镜像天空，会以为是天空，就会冲进去。

Second，准备听 colorful designs。also has problems 是无用信息。include openings，估计这里有问题。birds will perceive ... as open holes，基本已经说清了问题，鸟肯定会冲进去。they will try to fly right through them 是我们已经知道的信息。To prevent ... the unpainted spaces...would have to be extremely small，这个假想可能性肯定会被否定。but that would then make the rooms ... dark for people，说明为什么无法这么做。这两句话防止有人可能会对听力的反驳进行否定。[7]

◆ **本段逻辑梳理**：colorful design 没用，因为 design 之间的部分会被鸟视为 open hole，鸟就会尝试冲过去。要解决这个问题，当然可以把 design 之间的部分缩小，但这又会让屋子里的人感觉到太黑。

third，准备听 magnetic field。won't work 是无用信息。it's true 体现让步；bird use...magnetic field to help them navigate，体现了让步的内容，和阅读一致；only when...travelling very long distance，暗示了接下来的反驳方向，即近距离飞行不用磁场。For example, if ... migrating from a cold country to a warm one，其实完全没有用，因为这个例子是展开用 magnetic field 的时候，而这个段落的关键一定是在我们讨论的情况中，鸟不用 magnetic field。But this ability is not used to go over short distances，符合预期。such as going from one side of the city to another，这个例子有点用，体现的是相关的场景。For short trips...use their eyes and...light，这是讲为什么磁场没用的根本原因。magnetic signals...won't have much effect 是无用信息。[8]

◆ **本段逻辑梳理**：人工磁场没用，因为虽然鸟用磁场导航，但只限于远距离迁徙，近距离城市内飞行时它们只用眼睛与光线。

[7] ✎ perceive as open holes, fly through, unpainted small → dark

[8] ✎ <navigate> only long distance, short distance ✗, eyes, light

📝 满分范文

The article offers three possible ways to prevent birds from being injured by glass in modern architecture, all of which are considered ineffective by the lecturer.[9]

[9] 这个开头是 problem 与 3 个 solution 的结构，只不过多暗示了反驳策略是否有效。

For starters, the lecturer does not believe that one-way glass would work, because when birds look at the glass from the outside, the glass would function like a mirror, and birds cannot understand how a mirror works. When the glass reflects open sky, then birds would perceive it as open sky and hence fly directly into it.

Second, the method of colorful design is dismissed as well, because even if colorful designs are painted on a piece of window glass, the space in between would still be perceived by birds as an open hole and hence invites birds to fly "through". The only way to avoid so would be to leave the unpainted area extremely small, but then it would make the rooms inside extremely dark.

Last, the lecturer does not believe that setting up an artificial magnetic field is the solution either, because although birds do use magnetic field to navigate long distances, they only use their eyes and light signals to travel short distances, for example, when they fly within the range of a city.

TPO 43

阅读解析与听力预测

总 论：

有三个理论猜测 A 的生活方式。[1] 又是一篇没有统一观点的文章，本文的三个段落肯定是独立的三个猜想，分别解释 A 的生活方式是 1，2，3，听力肯定会说 A 并不具有这些特点。

猜想1：

A 是 free-swimming predators，靠吃小动物为生。[2]

猜想2：

A 是海底 dwellers。[3]

猜想3：

A 是寄生生物。[4]

[1] how A lives

听力肯定会说几种猜测都是错的。

[2] free-swimming predators

很简单，说为什么 A 不是 free-swimming predators，虽然现在没法预测到底反驳 free 还是 swimming 还是 predators。

[3] seafloor dwellers

听力反驳说它们并不是 seafloor dwellers。

[4] para

听力还是说为什么不能寄生。

[5] 无需笔记

听力解析

each...serious weakness，已经表明立场，三个猜想都不对，不用记，符合我们的预测。[5]

First，准备听 free-swimming predators。other types of arthropods swam in the open ocean, hunting their prey...had large, well-developed eyes，听到这里应该已经知道下文要说 A 并不具有这些特点了。vision...best ways to track its prey 只是刚才内容的展开。But agnostids had tiny, poorly-developed eyes，符合我们的期望，和 predators 形成对比。sometimes...blind 增强刚才的对比。rule out...predators，是无用信息，不用记。If they did chase after prey, they would have had some other special sensory organs to help them，这

TPO 43

个虚拟语气表明，其他感官本可以替代视觉，但没有。But there is no evidence, 和虚拟语气所暗示的一样。[6]

♦ **本段逻辑梳理：** A 不是 predator，因为 predator 眼睛大，利于捕猎，而 A 的眼睛小，视力差，甚至是瞎子。而且证据显示 A 也没有其他感官可以代替视觉。

Second，准备听 seafloor dwellers。unlikely ... lived on the seafloor，符合预期，否定这个可能性，不用记。seafloor dwellers typically don't...move very fast or very far，暗示接下来肯定要说 A 能够跑得很远、很快。They move slowly across the seafloor 是无用信息。stay in localized areas rather than spreading to new areas，还是没有特别令人意外的地方。So typically we find...occupying a small geographic area, where they had originated, and nowhere else 应该也是逻辑上的必然结果，可以不记。However，估计要说 A 没有这些特点了，听起来应该非常轻松。many as species inhabited multiple geographic areas，和刚才的内容相反，符合预期。spread across large distances，是无用信息。suggests agnostids could move from one area to another pretty fast，还是无用信息。would be highly unusual for seafloor dwellers，也是无用信息。[7]

♦ **本段逻辑梳理：** A 不是 seafloor dwellers，因为通常的 seafloor dwellers 移动缓慢，不能去很远的地方，所以它们的生存范围较小，离发源地不远，而 A 占据了多个地区，并且 A 可以去很远的地方，游得比较快。

Finally，准备听 parasites。typical of parasites... populations are not very large，基本已经确定接下来要说 A 的数量太多了。limits, because if there were too many... kill off the host 解释为什么 parasites 数量少，多了会杀死寄主。But... populations of many agnostids were ... pretty large，说出了我们等待的东西。vast amounts of fossilized... 是证据。rule out... parasites 是无用信息。[8]

♦ **本段逻辑梳理：** A 也不是 parasites，因为 parasites 数量少，否则会害死寄主，而化石证据显示 A 的数量很多。

[6] *other — open, large eye, vision vs. A — small, poor eye, blind; other sense, no evidence*

[7] *other— ✗ move fast/far, local, small area of origin vs. A—multiple area, large distance, move fast*

[8] *para—pop ↓, ↑ → kill host vs. A—large, vast fossil*

TPO 43

满分范文

The article presents three hypotheses on how agnostids survived, all of which are questioned in the lecture.[9]

For starters, the lecturer does not believe agnostids could be free-swimming predators that hunted smaller creatures, because most predators would have open, large eyes that could aid them in catching preys, a feature that is lacking in agnostids. Also, there is no evidence suggesting that agnostids had other acute senses that could make up for their poor vision.

Second, the lecturer dismissed the seafloor dweller hypothesis, because, while most seafloor dwellers, as a result of their slow movement, could only occupy a small geographic area extending not too far away from their place of origin, the agnostids were present in multiple areas, suggesting that they must be able to move much faster and hence travel longer distances.

Finally, the lecturer ruled out the parasite theory as well. For most parasite species, their population must be contained within a fairly small amount, or else their hosts would be completely killed off. In contrast, fossil evidence indicates that the population of each of the agnostid species discovered seemed to be much larger.

[9] 这个开头适合三个独立的猜想被逐个击破的结构。

TPO 44

阅读解析与听力预测

▶ **总　论：**

coins 并不属于 Norse，是假的。[1] 那下面肯定用三个理由支持这个观点，所以本文是典型的"观点+三个理由"型文章。

▶ **理由 1：**

发现 coins 的地方和 Norse settlements 离得太远。[2]

▶ **理由 2：**

Norse settlements 中没有发现 coins，说明 Norse 根本就没带 coins 来北美。[3]

▶ **理由 3：**

这些 coins 对 Native Americans 没用。[4]

听力解析

not a fake，已经体现了我们期望的观点，不用记。[5]

First，准备听距离问题。many other objects ... come from faraway，已经可以感受到听力的策略了。别的东西都可以来自很远的地方，这些 coins 自然也可以。a perfectly...explanation，暗示接下来要解释怎么来的了。Native...travelled great distances，原来可能是土著人去了很远的地方。interested in obtaining objects from faraway，这里已经表明，那些 coins 可能是土著人带回部落的。could have reached the Norse...brought...coins back，这已经是无用信息了，可以不记。[6]

◆ **本段逻辑梳理：**距离远不代表 coins 不是 Norse 的，因为当时的印第安人经常去很远的地方把有意思的物品带回来，所以这些 coins

---

[1] 🐾 coin—fake, ✗ Norse

🐾 coin 真的是 Norse 的。

[2] 🐾 far from Norse sites

🐾 并不算很远（其实这是事实，很难真的这么去削弱）；或就算远，coins 仍然可能是 Norse 的。

[3] 🐾 no coins in Norse sites > ~coin

🐾 理论上可以削弱推理的前提或逻辑，因此，听力可以说 Norse sites 有 coins（但这相当于否定事实，所以很难这么削弱）；或者说就算 Norse sites 没有 coins，但 Norse 人带了 coins；最后，就算 Norse 人没带 coins，这些 coins 也是真的（这个听起来也很不切实际）。

[4] 🐾 useless to native

🐾 其实这些 coins 对 native 有用；或者，就算没用，但这些 coins 也是 Norse 的。

[5] 🐾 无需笔记

[6] 🐾 other objects from far, native travel, obtain far away, bring back

就被从 Norse 的地方带回来了，就像很多在印第安人遗址中发现的其他物品一样。

Second，准备听 Norse settlements 没有 coins 的问题。no other coins...mean that the Norse did not bring...Not necessarily，这里表明了听力的策略是否定没发现 coins 的证据和没带来 coins 之间的关系。The Norse did not create permanent settlements in North America，Norse 没在北美永久定居。they went back to Europe，进一步说没定居，还会回欧洲。When they packed for their return voyage, they packed up all their valuables...这里已经说清楚了，Norse 可能带了 coins 来，只不过后来又带走了。packed up all silver coins...as well，这里已经没必要记了，刚才其实已经暗示清楚了。So...brought the coins with them to North America...to Europe, they took the coins back...这里全是无用信息总结，不用记。[7]

◆ **本段逻辑梳理**：没在 Norse settlements 发现 coins 不代表 Norse 人没带来 coins。因为他们没在北美永久定居，后来又回到欧洲，所以可能将 coins 带来了，又带走了。

Third，准备听 useless 的问题。it's true，体现听力对阅读的让步。Native...would not have viewed coins as...we do today，承认土著人不把这些 coins 当钱，接下来肯定要攻击阅读。But the Norse...knew that the native...valued attractive...objects，这里已经表明了听力的反驳策略了，虽然 coins 不能当钱用，但对土著人仍然可以有吸引力。might have been very appealing because of their beauty，体现了具体的吸引力。For example...used in necklace or other...jewelry，不是很重要，已经是非常细节的例子了，只是体现有吸引力。As long as Native...found the coins interesting...the Norse could...trade，表明最终 coins 是可以用来 trade 的。[8]

◆ **本段逻辑梳理**：确实，土著人不会把 coins 当货币使用，但是 Norse 人应该知道土著人会喜欢有意思、有吸引力的东西，而 coins 如此漂亮、有吸引力，就有可能被土著人用来做装饰，于是就可以用来和土著人交换。

[7] ✎ < × coin >, bring, no permanent settle, go back to 欧, pack up valuables

[8] ✎ < × money today >, Native value attractive objects, beauty, appeal → trade

TPO 44

满分范文

The article mentions three arguments for the claim that the silver coins discovered in Maine did not really belong to the Norse, all of which are dismissed by the lecturer. [9]

First, the lecturer does not believe that the distance between where the coins were discovered and the Norse settlements suffices to undermine the coins' authenticity. The Native Americans travelled great distances in the past and often brought interesting things back from faraway. Therefore, the coins, as well as a lot of other objects, might have been brought back in this manner.

Second, while the lecturer admits that no other coins were discovered in Norse settlements, she insists[10] that it might still be possible that the Norse brought coins to their settlements in North America. The reason why no coins were found was probably that the Norse, who did not establish permanent settlements and went back to Europe later, might have taken all valuable things, including the silver coins, with them as they left.

Last, she does admit that Native Americans might not have viewed the coins as we view our currencies today, but she still believes that the Norse could have used it to trade with the Native people, so long as the attractive look of the coins would appeal to the native people, who often valued such attractive objects.

[9] 典型的"观点＋三个理由"型文章的开头方式。

[10] While the lecturer admits 后体现听力对阅读承认的部分，she insists that 体现听力的核心反驳。

TPO 45

阅读解析与听力预测

▶ **总　论：**
古树化石并不是蜂巢。[1] 下文肯定用三个理由来支持这个观点，所以这是典型的"观点＋三个理由"型的文章。

▶ **理由1：**
并没有发现蜜蜂化石。[2]

▶ **理由2：**
那时没有开花植物。[3]

▶ **理由3：**
古树化石中没有蜂巢中的细节结构，尤其是某个 cap 结构。[4]

[1] ✎ ✗ bee nest
📝 古树化石可能就是蜂巢。

[2] ✎ ✗ bee fossil
📝 常见的两种方案：其实发现了有蜜蜂的证据（可能性较小）；或者就算没有发现蜜蜂证据，但蜜蜂仍然有可能存在。

[3] ✎ ✗ flower
📝 可能有花；或者就算没有花，蜜蜂也仍然可能存在。

[4] ✎ ✗ detail (cap)
📝 有 cap 结构（可能性较小）；或者就算没有 cap 结构，蜜蜂仍然可能存在。

[5] ✎ 无需笔记

听力解析

possible…nests…made by bees 已经表明听力立场，我们早就可以预期，不用记。[5]

it's true 说明要对阅读内容进行让步，no fossil…bees 体现了让步的地方是确实没有蜜蜂化石，说明要采取策略2。reason…is that bees could not be preserved as fossils，反驳策略已经很清楚了，不是因为没有蜜蜂所以没有化石，而仅仅是因为那会儿的蜜蜂成不了化石。Fossil bees have typically been preserved in fossilized tree resin（这个词只是音听起来像，但听的时候我并不认识这个专业词汇，所以肯定不能写这个词汇），这里肯定是解释为什么蜜蜂成不了化石，还没解释清楚，还得认真听。a sticky liquid produced by trees，这是对刚才不认识的那个词的解释，所以得记录下来。However, trees with this…were very rare 200 million years ago，这下彻底讲清楚了。Such trees…common much later，已经不重要了。我们在意的是为什么之前没有

TPO 45

蜜蜂化石，而不是之后为什么有蜜蜂化石。So…no bee remains… does not mean… bees did not exist，这是无用信息总结，不用记。Maybe bees existed, but… no trees producing … resin, the bees could not be preserved，继续是无用信息总结，不用记。[6]

♦ **本段逻辑梳理**：确实没有 bee fossils 那么老，但可能只是因为那会儿的 bees 没法以 fossils 形式 preserve。因为要 preserve。需要处在树的 sticky liquid 中，而那会儿的树很少产生这种 liquid，后来的树才有。

[6] < × fossil > × preserve, tree sticky liquid, rare

while it's true 体现让步；close…relationship with flowering plants today，这是让步的部分，暗示下文肯定要说 in the past 没有这种 relationship 了，接下来听力应该轻松一些。quite possible that bees existed before flowering plants … early bees … fed on non-flowering plants 是逻辑上必然的结果。such as 后面的例子是并列的几个非开花植物，不重要。Later…bees…adapted 也是必然的，蜜蜂后来改了习惯而已。new relationship…remained stable ever since 也是必然的。[7]

♦ **本段逻辑梳理**：确实，现在的 bees 和开花植物有关，但早期 bees 可能出现得比开花植物早，那个时候它们存活依赖的是非开花植物，只不过后来有了开花植物，改了习惯而已。

[7] <flower past > bee < < flower, feed on ~flower, later adapt, stable

Third，准备听缺乏 details 的结构。even though 体现让步；lack spiral caps，体现了让步的点；chemical evidence that supports … bees built the chambers，说明接下来要展开有什么证据表明是蜜蜂造的那个 structure。Modern bees … using water-proof substance … fossilized chambers…contain the same kind of…material，这里体现了当代蜂巢和化石当中相似的化学成分，说明了我们需要的证据。[8]

♦ **本段逻辑梳理**：确实没有 caps，但是化学分析显示，化石中的某些化学成分恰恰就是当代蜜蜂用来使它们巢穴 water-proof 的物质，说明这化石中的东西就是蜜蜂造的。

[8] < × cap > chemical, water-proof, same material as modern

📝 满分范文

The article presents three reasons that suggest that the structures found inside the 200-million-year-old fossilized trees were not created by bees, all of which are challenged by the lecturer.[9]

[9] 典型的"观点+三个理由"式的文章开头。

For starters, while the lecturer concedes that no bee fossil of 200 million years old was found, she believes that it might simply be because bees then could hardly be fossilized. The reason is that bees could only be fossilized within sticky liquid produced by certain kinds of tree species, which, unfortunately, were quite rare back then.

Second, she does accept that modern bees survive on flowering plants, but she does not believe that this had to apply to 200 million years ago. She holds that it might be possible for bees to subsist on other kinds of plants, and that it was only after flowering plants evolved that bees began to adapt to a different way of survival.

Last, although she admits that no cap of a spiral pattern was found in the structures, she points to other evidence that links the structures to modern bee nests. For example, chemical study suggests that a type of water-proof material used in modern bee nests is also present in those structures.

TPO 46

阅读解析与听力预测

▶ **总　论**：
E-record 比 paper record 要好。[1] 阅读正文肯定是展开三个好处。

▶ **好处 1**：
storing 和 transferring medical records 的 costs 减少。[2]

▶ **好处 2**：
减少由字迹不清、誊写、文件组织中造成的 errors。[3]

▶ **好处 3**：
电子数据库辅助 research。[4]

[1] ✎ E > paper
🐂 听力会说 E 并不比 paper 好，甚至 paper 比 E 好。

[2] ✎ $↓
🐂 这些 costs 不会减少，当然还有可能会说造成其他 costs。

[3] ✎ errors↓
🐂 这些 errors 不会减少，当然还有可能会说造成其他 errors。

[4] ✎ research↑
🐂 并不会帮助 research，当然还可能会说危害了 research。

[5] ✎ 无需笔记

听力解析

benefits...uncertain，这是可以预见的，不需要记录。[5]

First，准备听 costs。cost savings are unlikely...significant，可以预见，不用记。won't be any savings...record storage，需记录，这是具体讲哪种 cost 不会被省下。don't throw out or discontinue the paper records，已经具体给出了为什么 storage costs 不会省下的原因，因为他们还继续使用 paper records。keep the paper records 跟刚才说的一样。as...backup or...for legal reasons，指出了为什么要保留 paper records。still ... pay ... costs associated with paper-based record keeping，这是必然结果，可以不记。[6]

◆ **本段逻辑梳理**：存储花费省不下来，因为医生仍然会保存纸质记录，他们需要做备份或者用来诉讼，所以他们还得花存储纸质记录的经费。

[6] ✎ × record store $↓，keep paper → backup，legal

落笔生花
新托福综合写作高分范文精讲

Second，准备听 errors。not eliminate...errors caused by poor handwriting or by mistakes in the transcription of data，这其实就是阅读的反面，不用记，打个×号就可以了。still use pen and paper while examining patients，还在使用纸和笔。take notes and write prescriptions，具体讲用纸和笔做什么，可记可不记，写的时候可以说还用纸笔看病就行了。staff...entered information...later time...into electronic systems，这里基本已经可以预见到为什么会有错误了，把这些数据录入电脑中会出错。poor...can still lead to errors...已经是必然结果了。[7]

◆ **本段逻辑梳理**：错误还是会出现，因为医生仍然用纸笔看病，是他们的工作人员日后把记录下来的内容誊入电子系统中，所以还是有可能看不清字迹或者误解了医生的意思。

Third，准备听科研。research would not...benefit 这是可以预见的，不用记。still...difficult to access and use medical information，研究者还是拿不到资料，那接下来肯定解释为什么。access...subject to strict privacy laws，很显然已经说清楚了一切，就是保护隐私。下文必然要说研究者拿不到病人数据就是因为保护隐私。allow patients to keep...private 是无用信息。researchers...follow strict and complicated procedures 具体指出为了保护隐私就拿不到数据了。permission from the patients...not granted，这里指出了最关键的问题，这个保护可以使病人本人决定是否允许研究者动用数据，那结果很可能就是研究者拿不到数据。For example...block the use，这已经是无用信息了。[8]

◆ **本段逻辑梳理**：电子系统并不见得能帮助科研，因为科研工作者拿病人数据的操作被 privacy laws 严格限制——需要通过非常复杂的流程，尤其是获得病人的许可，而病人通常不许可。

[7] ✎ use pen to examine, staff enter later

[8] ✎ × access, privacy law, follow strict procedure, patient permission, × grant

满分范文

The article presents three benefits regarding the switch from paper-based to electronic medical record systems. Unfortunately, all these benefits are questioned by the lecturer.[9]

[9] 典型的"三个独立好处+反驳"的文章的开头。

TPO 46

[10] The lecturer does not believe that 直接表明听力与阅读恰好相反的点。

For starters, the lecturer does not believe that[10] relying on an electronic system is going to help reduce costs from storage. Her reason is that doctors still keep paper-based files as a backup and also for potential legal disputes. Consequently, they still pay for the storage costs.

[11] The lecturer insists that 写的也一定是听力和阅读恰好相反的地方。

Second, the lecturer also insists that[11] errors generated from poor handwriting and improper transcription might still arise, because currently when diagnosing patients, doctors still use pens and paper to take notes and to write prescriptions. It is their staff that later enter the information into the electronic system. As a result, inevitably, they may still find doctors' handwriting illegible and misinterpret them.

Last, the lecturer does not believe that the electronic system would facilitate medical research significantly. Her main concern comes from the privacy law, which dictates that doctors must follow strict procedures and regulations in order to exploit patients' data. Under the law, patients reserve the rights to block any external access to their personal medical data if they so wish. Thus, often, researchers are not granted the use of patients' medical information.

TPO 47

1. P— ✗ powered flight
   ▶ 听力肯定会说 P 龙可能是能够进行 powered flight 的。

2. cold > ✗ energy
   ▶ 对理由的反驳通常可以否定每一步推理的前提，或者否定每一步推理前提与结论的关系。所以，听力可能会说 P 龙不是 cold blooded；或者 P 龙是 cold blooded，但有足够的 energy；或就算没有足够的 energy，也能进行 powered flight（这比较怪）。

3. heavy > ✗ flap fast
   ▶ 同上，可以说不 heavy；也可以说，就算 heavy 也能 flap fast；或者就算不能 flap fast，也能进行 powered flight（这也比较怪）。

4. Leg 肌 ✗ > ✗ run, ✗ jump > ✗ take off
   ▶ 同上，逻辑上，可以说 leg 肌肉弱；或可以说就算 leg 肌肉弱，也能 run or jump；也可以说就算不能 run or jump，也能神奇地 take off；还可以说就算不能 take off，也能进行 powered flight（这同样听起来不太可能）。

5. 无需笔记

6. hair, fur → warm-blooded → fast metabolism → energy

阅读解析与听力预测

▶ 总　论：

P 龙不能支持 powered flight。[1] 下文肯定会用三个理由支持这个观点，这是最传统的"观点＋三个理由"式的展开。

▶ 理由 1：

P 龙是 cold blooded，所以可能无法带来飞行所需要的 energy。[2]

▶ 理由 2：

P 龙太重，所以无法 flap fast。[3]

▶ 理由 3：

P 龙的肌肉弱，无法跑得快，跳得高，所以无法 take off。[4]

听　力　解　析

may…capable of powered flight，早知道会说这个，不需要记录。[5]

First，准备听能量问题。Issue of…metabolism，就是说能量。dense, hair-like covering, somewhat similar to fur，可能是证据。typical of warm-blooded animals，反驳点已经找到。如果是 warm-blooded，就有可能有足够的 energy，接下来基本就可以推断出来了。metabolism…like that of warm-blooded animals and so faster than the reading suggests…would have supplied…energy，这些都验证了我们的预测，没必要记录。[6]

◆ 本段逻辑梳理：P 龙有 hair 或 fur 一样的东西，所以更像 warm-blooded 动物，所以可以快速代谢，于是能量充足，可以进行 powered flight。

Second，准备听 P 龙太重，无法扇翅膀。anatomical features that

TPO 47

made them unusually light for their size,反驳点已经出现,下面基本就只是展开了。For example,肯定是讲具体的features。the bones…were hollow instead of solid,已经表明了 light 的来源。would have kept…weight low 是无用信息。allow them…air-borne by flapping 明显是无用信息,不用记。[7]

◆ **本段逻辑梳理**:一些解剖结构表明 P 龙很轻,比如骨头空。轻就能 flap fast。

[7] anatomy→light <bone 空

Third,准备听肌肉弱,无法起飞。takeoff would…be a problem…if they took off in the way birds do,常见的虚拟语气反驳法,下文必然说,其实它 take off 不像 birds,所以 takeoff is not a problem。there are…differences between birds and pterosaurs,是无用信息,前一句已经暗示必然不同。Birds only use…legs for walking…2 limbs to push…pterosaurs walked on all 4 limbs,这个对比已经很明显了。run fast enough or jump high enough 就是必然结果了,早就等着出现了。[8]

◆ **本段逻辑梳理**:P 龙和鸟的起飞方式不同,鸟通过双腿蹬起飞,P 龙是四肢一起发力,所以有足够力量跑得快、跳得高,所以能起飞。

[8] bird—leg, 2 limbs walk vs. p—4 limbs → run fast, jump high

📝 满分范文

The article mentions three arguments for the claim that pterosaurs were not capable of powered flight. However, the lecturer mentions three pieces of evidence that might cast doubt on the claim.[9]

[9] 典型的"观点和理由"式文章的开头。

For starters, in contrast to what the reading suggests, that pterosaurs are cold-blooded animals that cannot generate sufficient energy for powered flight, the lecturer points out evidence of hair- or fur-like structures, indicating that pterosaurs might actually be warm-blooded creatures with sufficiently fast metabolism to produce adequate energy for powered flight.

As for the reading's argument that the weight of pterosaurs might prevent them from flapping their wings fast enough, the lecturer argues that the anatomical structures of pterosaurs, for example, their hollow bones, imply that they are actually probably quite light compared to their size. Hence, she believes the light weight would probably allow pterosaurs to flap like birds.

Finally, opposite to what the reading suggests, the lecturer believes that pterosaurs were perhaps able to run fast enough or jump high enough to take off, even though their leg muscles might seem weak. The reason is that, unlike birds, which use two limbs to walk, pterosaurs probably use all four limbs to push themselves. This way, enough power could have been generated for them to take off from the ground.

TPO 48

阅读解析与听力预测

总　论：

有几种方式可以拯救 frogs。[1] 典型的"问题与解决方案"型的文章，听力将会针对每种解决方案进行反驳。注意，常见的反驳方式有三种：不可行、无效、副作用。我们在听听力时应该留意，切记不可以直接说每种方案都是无效的。

方案1：

禁止用农药。[2]

方案2：

用 anti-fungal medication 来帮助 frogs 抵抗疾病。[3]

方案3：

严格控制人们的 water use 和 development，以保护 frogs 栖息地的 lakes and marshes。[4]

---

[1] ✎ save frogs

　🐸 听力肯定会说几种方式都不行。

[2] ✎ × pesticide

　🐸 做不到禁止用农药，这个听起来比较荒谬；禁止用农药也帮不了 frogs；或者，禁止用农药会造成严重危害，这个其实想一想就会觉得符合常理，会危害农业啊。

[3] ✎ ~ fungal medication

　🐸 难以做到给 frogs 使用这些药；用了这些药也帮不了 frogs；或者，用了这些药会造成严重危害。

[4] ✎ ~ water use & development → lake & marsh↑

　🐸 根本无法控制 water use 和 development；控制了 water use 和 development 也并不能帮助 frogs；控制 water use 和 development 会造成严重危害。

[5] ✎ 无需笔记

[6] ✎ $ practical ×, pest → crop → competitive, disadvantage, lower yield than competing

听力解析

None...offers...solution，符合预期，是无用信息，不需要记。[5]

First，准备听禁止 pesticides。not economically practical or fair，基本上已经把反驳策略说出来了，和我们的预期是一致的，就是说经济上代价高昂。Farmers rely on pesticides to decrease crop losses and to stay competitive in market，基本是无用信息，用 pesticides 才能有收成啊，才能有竞争力。"If...stricter regulations...then...at a severe disadvantage compared to farmers in other areas. They would likely lose more crops and have a lower yield..." 全是无用信息。[6]

TPO 48

♦ **本段逻辑梳理**：禁止用 pesticides 对于农业代价太高，农民无法用 pesticides，自然会损失更多农作物，进而在市场上就缺乏竞争力，尤其和那些能够使用 pesticides 的农民相比。

Second，准备听防真菌药物。must be applied individually to each frog，这一刻基本已经注定这个策略的失败，基本上肯定要说这种方法不可行了，根本不可能给每只 frog 都涂药。so…large scale is extremely difficult，是无用信息。requires capturing and treating each individual，也是无用信息。Moreover，说明还有一个反驳。do not prevent the frogs from passing the fungus onto their offspring，这个药涂了竟然对后代无效，那还得对后代再涂一遍。So…have to be applied again and again to each new generation，是无用信息。So…complicated and expensive，是无用信息。[7]

♦ **本段逻辑梳理**：用药不现实，因为需要给每只 frog 都上药，那不可能大范围做；而且，用了药只管亲代，不影响子代，子代还得再涂一遍，代价太高。

Third，准备听保护湿地不被过度开发。while…good idea，表让步，承认有一定道理。not save frog populations，这直接要否定该建议的有效性了。water use and development are not the biggest threats to… habitats，接下来肯定要说真正的 threat 是什么了。The real threat is global warming，老生常谈了，是全球变暖。has contributed to the disappearance of many water and wetland habitats, causing entire species to go extinct，展开说 global warming 才是罪魁祸首。Prohibiting humans … is unlikely to prevent the … changes caused by global warming，是无用信息。[8]

♦ **本段逻辑梳理**：保护湿地不受人侵犯没有用，因为人为开发并不是湿地减少的罪魁祸首，全球变暖才是。全球变暖已经导致了很多湿地栖息地的消失，进而导致了很多物种的消失，而保护湿地解决不了全球变暖。

[7] apply individual, difficult large scale; not pass to next generation, apply each, expensive

[8] × big threat, global warming → × habitats → entire species extinct

📝 满分范文

The article offers three possible solutions to the decline of frog populations, all of which are questioned in the lecture.[9]

[9] 标准的"困难+解决方案"的文章开头。

TPO 48

[10] 指出了该建议会带来的危害。

For starters, while prohibiting pesticide use might help revive frog population, the lecturer believes that the measure is extremely unfair to farmers[10], because they rely heavily on pesticides to maintain crop yields and to stay competitive. If they are forced to stop using pesticides, their yields will dramatically reduce and they can no longer compete with those farmers who use pesticides.

[11] 指出该建议是无法执行的。

Second, the lecturer believes that the anti-fungal medication is extremely costly and impractical[11], because to make a difference people have to capture and apply the medication to each frog. Consequently, it is hard to apply the measure on a large scale. Furthermore, the effect would not pass onto the frog's offspring, meaning that for each new generation of frogs, the medication would have to be applied again individually.

[12] 指出该建议是无效的。

Last, the lecturer does not believe that stricter regulations on water use and development are going to affect frogs significantly[12], because even though frog habitats depend on wetlands, the main threat to wetlands is not human water use and development, but global warming, which is causing entire species to become extinct and cannot be dealt with by the suggested regulations.

TPO 49

📝 阅读解析与听力预测

▶ 总 论：

很显然，文章要证明 humpback whales 使用星星来导航。这将是一篇观点理由型的文章，我们在听听力时应该注意是反驳理由还是反驳逻辑。[1]

1 ✎ HW—navigate star

　🖐 听力肯定会否定靠星星导航。

▶ 理由1：

humpback whales 聪明。后文要么是展开如何聪明，要么是展开聪明和靠星星导航的联系，这些都不重要。[2]

2 ✎ intel

　🖐 要么否定聪明；要么说聪明不代表靠星星导航。

▶ 理由2：

humpback whales 直线迁徙。后文要么详细展开直线迁徙，要么展开直线迁徙和靠星星导航的联系，也不重要。[3]

3 ✎ migrate straight

　🖐 migrate straight 是事实，无法否定；只能否定直线导航有别的原因。

▶ 理由3：

humpback whales float straight up，像是在看天空。[4]

4 ✎ float straight up

　🖐 float straight up 也是事实，无法否定；只能否定它和靠星星导航的关系。

5 ✎ 无需笔记

📝 听力解析

evidence...not very convincing，符合预期，是无用信息，不记。[5]
First，准备听 intelligence。doesn't seem to be ... connection between intelligence and...stars for navigation，非常重要，表明没有否定聪明本身，否定的是聪明与靠星星导航的关系。there are other animals that use stars to navigate，简直是老掉牙的套路，明显要靠类比举例了，那这些 animals 不用听肯定知道不怎么聪明，否则无法论证作者的观点。Some birds...like ducks，这种信息可记可不记，无所谓，关键是它们的特点。cognitive ability...average，体现了我们要的东西，智商不高。not highly intelligent，重复信息，不用记。The fact

TPO 49

that the ducks ... stars ... for navigation does not ... connection to ... intelligent，听到这内容就知道是重复信息了，完全是无用信息。just an instinct ... not ... intelligence，没什么重要信息。So ... humpback whales ... intelligent does not make them ... likely ... stars for navigation，是无用信息，这个段落无用信息好多。The two things just don't ... connected，还是无用信息。⁶

◆ **本段逻辑梳理**：智商和靠星星导航没关系，看看鸭子，靠星星导航，可是一点都不聪明，纯粹是靠直觉。所以 HW 聪明并不意味着它靠星星导航。

Second，终于要开始讲直线迁徙了。different explanation，完全是意料之中的。for animals ... to do this, they have to sense some external objects or force，这是阅读说过的，需要用外物做参照。the ... force ... could be sensing is Earth's magnetic field，这段基本说完了，HW 不靠星星而靠地磁来导航。have a substance in their brains called ... 某个听不懂的专业词，也不用记，关键听它的性质。makes that animal sensitive to ... magnetic field，这在逻辑上是必需的。suggests ... orient ... by the magnetic field rather than the stars，这是无用信息总结。⁷

◆ **本段逻辑梳理**：直线迁徙可以有别的解释，这种生物脑子里有种物质，可以让它对地磁敏感，因此，影响它迁徙的外界参照力可能不是星星而是地磁。

Third，准备听 spy-hop。has nothing to do with looking at stars，和我们的预期一致，不用记。rare, but there are other animals that exhibit it，又是和第一点一样的策略，类比举例。那这个 other animals 肯定也会 spy-hop，但是不靠星星导航，往这个方向上听。sharks ... for example，是无所谓的信息。don't migrate or look at stars，符合预期。Sharks spy-hop to look for animals ... hunt，其实是讲要捕猎。And another thing，提示还有一个并列的反驳。spy-hop during the day，这简直是阅读文章的灾难，白天也 spy-hop，说明 spy-hop 肯定不是为了靠星星导航的。when no stars can be seen，这是无用信息。So to suggest that ... spy-hopping is to look at stars is pure speculation，是无所谓的总结句。⁸

◆ **本段逻辑梳理**：spy-hop 也和靠星星导航无关，看看 sharks，也 spy-hop，但不看星星也不迁徙，人家 spy-hop 只是为了捕猎。而

6. not connect, other stars, bird, duck, average cog, instinct, × intel

7. external object/force; magnetic field, sub in brain, sensitive to magnetic

8. rare, other animals, shark, don't migrate/look at star, look for hunting; during day, no star

且，HW 白天也 spy-hop，连星星都没有，那肯定不是为了靠星星导航了。

📝 满分范文

The article presents three arguments to support the claim that humpback whales navigate by the stars, all of which are questioned in the lecture.[9]

For starters, the lecturer does not believe that intelligence strongly supports navigation by the stars.[10] He points to other animals, ducks in particular, relying on stars to navigate, which only have average cognitive ability and whose navigation method is purely instinctive. Thus, he considers the strong intelligence of humpback whales an irrelevant factor.

As for the fact that humpback whales migrate in straight lines, the lecturer believes that external objects or forces other than stars might pose an alternative explanation.[11] Since the whales have a particular substance in their brain that makes them sensitive to the Earth's magnetic field, it is highly likely that the navigation is guided by the magnetic field.

Last, in his view, the whales' spy-hopping can also be attributed to other explanations.[12] The humpback whales might simply be looking for potential prey, just like sharks, which also spy-hop but do not engage in migration or star-gazing. Moreover, the humpback whales spy-hop in the day as well, when no stars can be seen.

[9] 鲜明的观点理由型文章开头。

[10] 这句话有多种写法，这里采用了 does not believe that X supports Y，就是说 X 和 Y 不相关，也可以用在下面两段中，因为本文三段都是否定证据与观点的联系。

[11] 由于阅读相当于在用 navigation by stars 去解释直线迁徙，听力就是在提出其他解释，于是我们就可以使用这个 alternative explanation 的写法。

[12] 与上段反驳思路相同。这两段的句型不能用在第一段，因为第一段不是用 navigation by stars 去解释 intelligence。但是，第一段的写法可以用在后面两段中，因为本质上都是否定理由与观点的关系。

TPO 50

📝 阅读解析与听力预测

◉ 总 论：

送人上火星需要解决一系列问题。千万不要觉得这是问题解决方案类的文章。不考虑听力部分，这个阅读只是指出有一系列问题，那么等会儿三个段落肯定只是展开这三个问题。所以，这仍然是"观点＋理由"型的文章，小小地变形了一下而已。本文的核心观点，就是送人去火星会遇到很大问题。而三个展开段落将会列举三个问题。一般的"观点＋理由"型的文章，反驳起来要么是反驳理由本身，要么是反驳理由对观点的支持。放到这里，听力理论上要么是说阅读的问题就不存在，要么是说这些问题就算存在，是可以解决的，本质上没有什么特别大的区别。[1]

◉ 问题 1：
往返火星花两年时间，需要带很多必需品。[2]

◉ 问题 2：
失重状态太久会对宇航员有害。[3]

◉ 问题 3：
太阳辐射。[4]

1 ✎ Mars problem

2 ✎ a round-trip 2 years, lack essentials
  ✎ 问题不存在，或可以应对。

3 ✎ 0-gravity many months
  ✎ 问题不存在，或可以应对。

4 ✎ solar radiation
  ✎ 问题不存在，或可以应对。

📝 听 力 解 析

proposed solutions，已经说明白反驳策略了，所有问题都会解决。astronauts can use hydroponics（实际考试中这种专业术语都会显示在屏幕上，不用担心），growing plants in water rather than in soil，其实听到这儿，反驳策略基本应该可以联想出来了，会有食物啊，自己种就是了。requires little space，自然很适合太空旅行。able to cultivate food crops in the spacecraft，没什么意外的。recycle waste water, release it as clean water vapor, collected as drinking water，这个方式还能间接形成饮用水。plants absorb CO_2 and release O_2，很好，有氧气了，问题解决了。thanks to hydroponics, astronauts have fresh air to breathe，无用信息，我肯定不会记。[5]

5 ✎ hydroponics (grow plants in water, little space) cultivate food in spacecraft, recycle waste water → release clean vapor → collect drink water, plants release O_2, fresh air

TPO 50

♦ **本段逻辑梳理**：使用无土栽培，宇航员在太空舱内就可以种植植物获取食物。这个过程中的废水通过循环利用可以带来饮用纯净水。植物的光合作用还能提供氧气。

launched several space stations, astronauts spent many months in zero gravity environment，过去我们宇航员已经能在失重下待好几个月了，估计这个问题是可以解决的。learned several techniques to manage，那接下来肯定要展开应对方案。regular exercise prevents the decrease in muscle mass，很好，多锻炼。taking vitamins and calcium slows down the decrease in bone density，骨密度也可以维持。[6]

♦ **本段逻辑梳理**：我们已经有很多宇航员在国际空间站里待了好几个月，一直处在失重环境下。他们可以用以下方法来应对失重：多运动，防止肌肉萎缩；摄入维生素和钙质以防止骨质疏松。

will be exposed to some solar radiation, but not be at dangerous levels all the time，暗示只有很少时候太阳辐射才是致命的。only occasionally, during periods when it is particularly active，继续展开很少时间致命。to avoid threat, could be equipped with special instruments, monitor solar radiation，可以装太阳辐射监控。with a small shelter that shields, but doesn't add much weight，解决方案已经出来了，不需要太大的防护区。Most of the time ... unshielded, when instruments detect increased radiation, stay in the shielded area，这个基本就是把刚才的逻辑补全，没什么意外的地方了。[7]

♦ **本段逻辑梳理**：太阳辐射并不总是致命的，只有很少时间危险性很大，即太阳活动极其活跃的时候。相应地，太空船需要的是太阳辐射的检测仪，以及很小的防护区域，当检测仪检测到太阳活动剧烈时，宇航员就在那个很小的区域中躲避就好了，这并不会给太空船增加太大的重量。

[6] ✎ 0 gravity, launched space stations, many months on 0 gravity, learn some techniques, regular exercise × mass, v, CA bone dense

[7] ✎ radiation × dangerous all the time, Sun release only occasional particular active, equipped with special instrument, small shelter not add weight, most time, unshielded, detect → stay in a small shielded area

[8] 非典型的"观点+三个理由"型文章的开头，具体来说，阅读提出的观点是去火星会有问题，三个理由是三个具体问题，那不如直接写阅读提出了三个问题，而听力逐一解决。

📝 满分范文

The article presents three problems for humans' trip to Mars, all of which are addressed by the lecturer.[8]

To begin with, the article believes that a two-year round-trip to

Mars requires too much food, water and oxygen. However, the lecturer proposes that with hydroponics, which allows plants to be grown in water instead of soil, astronauts can cultivate food in spaceships without taking up too much space. The released waste water can be recycled for drinking and the plants' photosynthesis provides oxygen.

As for the problem that astronauts have to endure a zero gravity environment, the lecturer mentions that we have already launched space stations where astronauts stayed under zero gravity environment for months. Astronauts have learned techniques to adapt, for example, by keeping regular exercises to prevent loss of muscle mass and by taking in vitamins and calcium to maintain bone density.

Finally, the article claims that it is difficult to shield a spacecraft completely from solar radiation because it adds too much weight. However, the lecturer argues that solar radiation is dangerous only occasionally, when the sun releases dangerous levels of particles. The spaceship can be equipped with instruments monitoring solar activity. Consequently, only a small shielded area is needed, which doesn't add much weight, and when strong solar radiation is detected, astronauts can stay in that area temporarily.

TPO 51

阅读解析与听力预测

> **总　论：**
> several beliefs about elephant behaviors，有几个针对大象行为的有趣想法。这个开头和我们之前见过的所有 TPO 都不同，这篇文章没有一个统一观点，而是三个独立观点，各观点之间毫无关系，并且也并不共同支持任何想法。但这并不难，听力也很好预测，自然是要一一反驳三个想法。[1]

> **观点 1：**
> aware of approaching death，知道死期将至。[2]

> **观点 2：**
> representing objects through art，会艺术表达。[3]

> **观点 3：**
> fear of mice，怕老鼠。[4]

[1] elephant behavior

[2] aware of approaching death
    并不知道死期将至。

[3] representing objects through art
    并不会艺术表达。

[4] fear of mice
    并不怕老鼠。

听力解析

beliefs... based on misunderstandings，无用信息。[5]

should not assume... aware... die soon just because they break away from their herds，这句话有一定价值。大方向上，肯定是否定大象知道自己死期将至，这是无用信息，是能够直接预见到的。但这句话具体指出了听力的攻击策略，即阅读文章中的证据（老象离群）并不代表大象知道死期将至，这句话在写作中必须准确体现。a practical reason why... leave herds，那听力接下来肯定要讲老象离群的真实原因。When... old, teeth worn down, difficulty chewing，老了牙口不好，嚼不动。那等会儿肯定要说离群和嚼东西有关系。Wander away to look for softer vegetation，应该不意外。usually found near water, old elephants graze near water, die there, an area we've come to call "elephant graveyards"，这就完全说清楚了。[6]

[5] 无需笔记

[6] old not aware just because they break away from herds, old enough → teeth worn down, no chewing → wander, look for soft vege, near water, old graze there, die, graveyard

TPO 51

◆ **本段逻辑梳理**：老象离群不是因为知道自己死期将至，而纯粹是因为老了牙口不好，需要去找软的植被吃，而通常这些软的植被在水边，于是我们就能见到很多老象在水边觅食，后来死在那里，形成了所谓的"大象墓地"。

whether elephants have artistic ability，无用信息。If you watch elephants trained to paint, you will notice that human trainers stroke elephants' ears whenever elephants move brush，其实基本可以猜到反驳策略了，就是这一切都是套路，大象动画笔，饲养员就动它耳朵，估计就是要形成条件反射呗。elephant ears are sensitive，当然，不然动它有什么意义。Touch them in certain ways can be used to train tricks，也是无用信息。teaches elephants to remember certain patterns，还是无用信息。encourages elephants to repeat by touching ears，就只是在重复总结。So… just painting lines as they are trained to paint，还是无用信息总结，大象只是重复被教的画的动作，那肯定不懂艺术呀。doesn't necessarily know the lines represent animals or flowers，就是说大象不懂它们自己画的什么，无用信息。[7]

◆ **本段逻辑梳理**：大象可没有什么艺术认知。它们纯粹是被驯养员教着去画那些它们也不知道什么意思的东西。饲养员想让大象怎么画，就在大象做动作的时候动大象敏感的耳朵，这样可以刺激大象重复先前的动作。所以，最后大象怎么画都只是机械记忆的结果。

misinterpreting the reaction to mice，无用信息。Elephants that react fearfully to mice aren't reacting to the mice themselves, but to the fact that mice are unfamiliar to them，这个"themselves"是非常关键的，意思是说，大象看起来面对老鼠有害怕的表现，不是因为大象怕老鼠本身，而是因为老鼠是陌生事物，暗示大象只是怕陌生事物。Being cautious about unfamiliar animals is a natural instinct，比较无用信息了，说大象面对陌生动物谨慎一点是很正常的表现。elephants that live… mice are common，要做对比实验了。like… in zoos, don't react fear to the mice，这是关键对比证据，决定性证明了大象并不必然害怕老鼠。once… familiar with mice, realize that they don't pose a threat, they don't mind them，无用信息总结。[8]

◆ **本段逻辑梳理**：大象怕老鼠的表现不是出于对老鼠本身的惧怕，而纯粹来自于对陌生事物的谨慎，而这是正常的动物反应。相反，如

[7] train to paint, stroke ears when move brush, ear sensitive, touch in certain ways to train tricks, teach to remember pattern, repeat, touch ear, paint lines trained to paint, ✗ know represent flowers, animals

[8] misinterpret reaction, ✗ react to mice, but react to unfamiliar, cautious, natural instinct, common mice → no fear react, familiar → realize no threat → no mind

果大象处在老鼠常见的环境中，比如动物园，大象是不会介意老鼠的存在的，它们知道老鼠不会对自己构成威胁。

满分范文

The article presents three interesting beliefs regarding elephant behaviors, all of which, unfortunately, are challenged by the lecturer.[9]

To begin with, the lecturer does not agree that old elephants stray away from the herds because they realize they are approaching death. Based on her explanation, older elephants' teeth become worn down, so they have to wander to places near water, where the vegetation is softer and easier to chew. Eventually, they die there and the places are regarded as "elephant graveyards".

Second, the lecturer does not believe that elephants possess artistic ability. Those elephants that use a paintbrush to portray natural objects are just trained to do so, and the process is based on memory. By touching elephant ears, which are quite sensitive, trainers reinforce elephant behaviors and thereby manipulate elephants to repeat certain patterns of brushstroke. The elephants have no idea that they are depicting flowers or animals.

Finally, the speculation that elephants are afraid of mice is also questioned by the lecturer. She believes that the fearful reaction toward mice is not driven by mice per se, but driven by caution toward unfamiliar objects, which is a natural animal instinct. As evidence, in places where mice are common around elephants, for example, in a zoo, elephants realize these little creatures pose no threat, so they don't really mind their presence.

[9] 并不是我们之前的三大类文章开头，这次阅读话题是三个独立观点，且既不是同一现象的三个解释，也不是同一问题的三个解决方案，就是三个普通观点（其实敏锐的同学应该意识到，以前的所谓三个解释或三个解决方案是从属于三个观点的次级概念），听力就是三个相应的反击。

TPO 52

1. ✎ colonize asteroid ✓

2. ✎ low gravity

   ➤ 重力小应该是事实，所以不好直接否定。估计反驳策略应该是，就算重力小，但去小行星殖民不好。

3. ✎ mine valuable metals

   ➤ 要么说不可以开采贵金属，要么说就算可以开采贵金属，但去小行星殖民不好。

4. ✎ easy to reach

   ➤ 要么直接说不好去，要么说就算好去，但去小行星殖民不好。

5. ✎ 无需笔记

6. ✎ <land, take off easy>, risk: lose muscle mass, bone dense↓, a few month in spaceship, suffer from health problems

📝 阅读解析与听力预测

▶ **总 论：**
去小行星是最好的殖民选择。[1] 这是典型的"观点 + 三个理由"的文章，等会儿肯定会给出三个理由说明为什么去小行星殖民很好。而听力的反驳策略会是否定理由本身，或者否定理由与观点之间的关系。

▶ **理由 1：**
重力小。[2]

▶ **理由 2：**
可以开采贵金属。[3]

▶ **理由 3：**
去小行星容易。[4]

📝 听力解析

not a practical idea，无用信息。Each of the points in the reading has a serious downside，还是无用信息。[5]

while low gravity would make landing and taking off easy，让步，承认阅读中的一些事实，重力小使起落容易，那等会儿的反击肯定还是说重力小不意味着殖民好，肯定会有一些 downside，毕竟前文总起已经暗示了。present certain risks，那接下来必然是详细说重力小有哪些问题。start losing muscle mass，肌肉流失，显然是在展开问题了。bone density becomes lower，继续展开。astronauts in spaceships suffer from health problems，具体举个失重状态下健康受损的例子，为刚才的理由提供依据，但没有特别重要的新信息。Imagine... the long-term... experience on asteroids，没什么价值的一句话。[6]

◆ **本段逻辑梳理**：虽然小行星的低重力状态让起落容易，但是它会带来严重的健康隐患。长期处在这种状态下，人的肌肉会流失，骨质也会疏松，这些都可以从在太空飞船上生活的宇航员的经历中看出来。

metals might make an asteroid colony seem like a profitable idea，只是承认第二个理由看起来有道理，接下来肯定还是要说问题。not the whole picture，自然暗示还有问题阅读没有说出来，但这其实就是大空话。have to consider additional factors，无用信息。One thing is the costs，代价高昂，没说清，接下来肯定要说什么 costs。The costs of supporting a colony and of transporting the metals are likely high，非常重要的信息，指出具体代价是"维护殖民地和运送金属代价高昂"，will reduce the profits，必然结果。furthermore，还有别的问题。no guarantee that the price… sell the metals will remain the same，未来金属售价不见得稳定。If… mined in large quantities, increase the supply, end up lowering in the market price… So… not profitable，这一串因果链很清晰，很好理解。如果开采贵金属这么容易，则供给就会增多，售价下降，利润降低。⁷

◆ **本段逻辑梳理**：在小行星上采矿听起来很赚钱，但实际上，维护殖民地以及运送金属都可能代价高昂，使得利润缩水；而且，随着开采量增大，贵金属的供给充足，就会导致贵金属贬值。所以，最后可能赚不了多少钱。

even if… easy to reach，让步，承认阅读理由，一些小行星还是比较容易到达的。not easy to return from，问题来了，容易去不容易回。那等会儿肯定要解释怎么就不容易回了。orbits, unusual，关键原因，小行星轨道奇葩。Some orbital paths come close to earth, but then move away from earth，其实听到这儿应该基本已经能猜出来了，肯定是说小行星近地的时候容易去，但回的时候就远地了，回不来了。often a great distance away from earth，说完刚才的话。"…even if… gets close to earth at one point, easy to get to, does not stay close, travel farther away from earth than Mars. Getting back… would be a challenge."这就是已经预测到的东西。⁸

◆ **本段逻辑梳理**：确实，一些小行星可能比较好去，但不见得好回。因为小行星轨道特别，具体来说，当它们近地时，我们确实容易到达，但接着它们就会离开，有可能跑到比火星还远的地方去，那想回地球就不容易了。

7　< seem profitable > × whole picture, additional factor: cost of support colony and transport metal, high, reduce $, no guarantee price to sell remain same, If mined in large quantity, supply ↑, lower market price

8　< some are easy to reach > × easy to return, orbits unusual, some close to earth then move away, great distance, one point close, easy to, × stay close, travel far away than mars, getting back would be a challenge

TPO 52

满分范文

The article presents three arguments why setting up a colony on an asteroid is a promising idea, all of which, unfortunately, are challenged by the lecturer.[9]

To begin with, while the lecturer does concede that the low gravity environment on asteroids might make landing and taking off relatively easy, he argues that people can suffer serious health problems living in that environment for long, as can be seen from astronauts living in spaceships, who often lose muscle mass and have reduced bone density.

The article's second point is the potential to mine valuable metals on asteroids. However, the lecturer raises additional points that may undermine this argument. First, the high cost of maintaining a colony and of transporting the metals could seriously reduce profits. Also, if metals are mined in large quantities, the oversupply would lower their market value. Overall, there is no guarantee that mining metals on asteroids will ultimately be lucrative.

Finally, while the lecturer does accept that some asteroids are easy to reach, he argues that the return trip will be much more challenging, because of asteroids' unusual orbits. To be more specific, even when humans can go to these asteroids when they come close, the return trip will be quite a daunting problem, since they will move very far away from earth, possibly even further away than Mars.

[9] 典型的"观点+三个理由"型文章的开头。

TPO 53

📝 阅读解析与听力预测

▶ **总　论：**
对不健康产品征重税有几个好处。[1] 可以把本文理解为观点是征税好，然后列三个理由说明好在哪儿。质疑方式自然就是否认好处，或者就算有这种好处，但征税不好。

▶ **好处1：**
减少不健康行为。[2]

▶ **好处2：**
经济上的公平。[3]

▶ **好处3：**
增加政府税收。[4]

[1] 📎 *imposing high taxes on unhealthy products* ✓

[2] 📎 *discourage from indulgence*

👉 并不会让人减少不健康行为，或者就算减少了不健康行为，但征税不好（这个听起来有点杠精）。

[3] 📎 *financially fair*

👉 并不会带来公平，或者就算公平，但不好（也挺杠精）。

[4] 📎 *gov revenue ↑*

👉 并不会带来更多政府税收，或者就算带来更多税收，但不好。

[5] 📎 无需笔记

📝 听力解析

Each of the arguments can be challenged，无用信息。[5]

don't necessarily lead to healthy behavior，反驳策略非常直接，阅读说会让人们选择健康的生活方式，听力认为不会。high taxes have led some smokers to buy cheaper, lower quality cigarettes，比如，征了重税，消费者只会去购买更便宜、质量更差的烟。typically contain more harmful substances，可想而知。present greater health risks，这是显然的。Similarly, some… continue buying unhealthy foods even if they are more expensive，有些消费者会继续购买不健康食品，as a result, have less money on healthy foods，反而没钱买健康食品。certainly wouldn't benefit health，无用信息。[6]

◆ **本段逻辑梳理**：征重税并不会让人们选择更健康的生活方式。比如，烟民会因为烟更贵了而去购买更廉价、劣质、危害更大的香烟。类似地，很多人也不会停止购买不健康食品，反而这些食品更贵会使得他们没钱去买其他健康食品。

[6] 📎 × → *healthy behavior, cigarette ↑ → cheaper, lower quality, more harmful substances, greater health risks, some react, might continue buying unhealthy foods even more expensive, less money spent on healthy food*

TPO 53

different ways of thinking about fairness, 基本暗示出来，从某种角度看起来更 fair, 但从另一种角度来看就不 fair, 那等会儿肯定要展开讨论怎么不 fair。unfair because they don't take into account people's incomes, 没考虑到人们的收入。那看看如果考虑了收入会怎么样。If a high-earning person and a lower-earning person are addicted to cigarettes, each smokes a pack of cigarettes a day, greater expense for the low earner, 这很明显了，有钱人和没钱人如果每天抽一样多的烟，那么没钱人缴的税相对于自己的收入显然比例更高。same argument applies to the food taxes, 没什么意义，食品和香烟情况一样。not fair because ... greater burden for those with smaller incomes, 就是无用信息，对低收入的人不公平。[7]

◆ **本段逻辑梳理**：从另一种角度来看这个政策并不公平，比如，一个低收入烟民和一个高收入烟民每天都抽一包烟，那么他们要交的税是一样的，这显然对低收入烟民在经济上造成更大的相对负担。

has the downside, 政府收入更多反而不好。millions and millions of dollars, 继续说钱多，等会儿肯定要说怎么不好。dependent on it, don't want to lose, 政府过分依赖这些税收。might not be forceful pursuing policies and implementing laws that eliminate unhealthy habits altogether, 这个结果顺理成章，如果政府靠这种不良习惯获得很多税收，那就没有动力制定政策来杜绝这些不良习惯。For example, unlikely to adopt measures such as not allowing smoking in public areas or in all areas, because they don't want to lose this income, 只是无用信息举例，比如，政府就不会制定严格的禁烟政策。[8]

◆ **本段逻辑梳理**：这种税收多了是有负面效应的。这成百万上千万的税收会使得政府过分依赖，从而失去了杜绝不良行为的动力。比如，政府就不会去制定严格的政策，例如禁止在任何场所吸烟之类。

[7] *different ways of thinking fair, don't take into account people's income, high income + low income a pack a day, Greater burden for low earners*

[8] *downside, income represents millions of dollars, become dependent, don't want to lose it, don't want to enforce laws that eliminate bad habits, ✗ allow in park, public place + private*

📝 满分范文

The article presents three benefits that might result from imposing high taxes on unhealthy products, all of which are challenged by the lecturer.

To begin with, the article believes that the taxes discourage people from indulging in unhealthy habits. However, when these taxes are imposed, according to the lecturer, instead of stopping smoking, smokers just turn to cheaper cigarettes, which are often of lower quality and contain more harmful substances. Also, some consumers don't react to the increased taxes, and they continue purchasing unhealthy products. Since they have become more expensive, the consumers will end up having less money to buy healthy products.

As for the argument of financial fairness, the lecturer believes that there is a different angle of thinking about fairness. The taxes don't take into consideration people's incomes. Suppose a high-income person and a low-income person each consume a pack of cigarettes. They both will have to pay the same taxes, but clearly the taxes pose a heavier burden on the person with lower incomes.

Finally, the article claims that the high taxes create increased government revenues. However, the lecturer presents a serious downside. Because the revenues are so large, governments become dependent on them and therefore don't want to lose them. Consequently, governments don't enforce radical policies that eliminate bad habits, for example, laws that forbid cigarette smoking in all areas.

TPO 54

阅读解析与听力预测

总　论：
Salton Sea 越变越咸，幸好有几种方案可以逆转。典型的问题解决型文章的开头，等会儿肯定是三种逆转方案。而听力肯定会质疑三种方案，听力的质疑方式有三种可能，分别是：①并不能解决，②不可行（没钱、没时间、没人等），③严重的副作用。[1]

▶ 方案1：
直接用特殊装置降低盐分。[2]

▶ 方案2：
用海水稀释。[3]

▶ 方案3：
建墙把湖隔成几块儿。[4]

[1] reverse Salton Sea's salinity

[2] direct removal in desalination facilities
　并不能降低盐分；这个建议无法执行；这个建议有危害。

[3] dilute with ocean water
　并不能降低盐分；这个建议无法执行；这个建议有危害。

[4] construct walls to divide the lake into several sections
　并不能降低盐分；这个建议无法执行；这个建议有危害。

[5] 无需笔记

听力解析

solutions aren't realistic or practical, 无用信息。[5]sure, desalination would reduce salinity, 让步，承认该方案有效。那反驳只能是另外两种策略了。present serious problems, 策略是说有严重副作用，下文肯定要具体说副作用。water pumped into desalination facilities, evaporates, leaves behind solid materials that would dissolve in water, solid materials… pose a health risk, 这一段还是蛮有难度的，一长串因果元素需要听清楚，湖水进入降盐分的装置，然后蒸发，留下一些固体，这些固体会对人的健康有危害。mostly salt, but include other chemicals, some… toxic, like selenium（专业名词一定会打在屏幕上，不用担心）。wind spreads… and other chemicals into the air, people breathe them in, dangerous。听到 wind spreads 之后就都可以自然预见到了，不难。[6]

[6] ＜would reduce sal＞ serious prob, leave behind solid materials dissolve in water, pose a health risk, mostly salt, but other chemicals, some toxic, selenium, wind blows, people breathe, dangerous

◆ **本段逻辑梳理：** 该方案虽然能降盐，但过程中蒸干的水留下的固体当中包含危险的物质，比如硒，风会把这些物质吹散到空气中，对周围的人带来严重的健康隐患。

would reduce salinity, 还是承认方案有效。require constructing pipelines or canals, 其实应该已经感觉到是要说代价高昂了。local government may not have enough resources to pay，很简单，没钱。nearest shoreline... is 100 km away，离海远。pipelines and canals are expensive to build over such long distances，必然结果，可以预见。[7]

◆ **本段逻辑梳理**：引入海水当然是可以降盐的，但是成本太高。这需要建造管道或运河，然而这里离海岸线最近也得 100 千米以上，意味着建造管道或运河代价高昂，超过当地政府的支付力。

unlikely to work for long，反驳策略已经很明显了，就是长期来说不能解决问题。located in a region... frequent and intense geological activity, like earthquakes，地质活动活跃。destroy the walls，这就没话说了。while... work for short while, walls would likely collapse the first time there is a major earthquake, water would mix back in，无用信息。[8]

◆ **本段逻辑梳理**：造墙长期无效，因为这个地区地质活动活跃，随便一次大地震就能把墙震垮，到时候不同区域的水还是会混在一起。

[7] <reduce sal> require to construct pipes and canals, local govern no resource to pay, nearest shore 100 km, expensive to build over long distance

[8] unlikely to work for long, experience frequent geo activity, earthquake, certainly destroy walls, work for a short time, collapse when there is major earthquake, water would mix back in

📝 满分范文

The article presents three solutions to reverse the increasing salinity in the Salton Sea, all of which are questioned by the lecturer.[9]

The first proposed solution is to directly remove salt through desalination facilities. However, while it could reduce salinity, the lecturer argues that as the water evaporates from the desalination facilities, solid materials formerly dissolved in the water would be left behind, which include dangerous chemicals like selenium. Wind would blow away these chemicals into the air, posing a serious threat to people's health.

The second possible solution is dilution with ocean water. However, the lecturer points out that this measure would require constructing pipelines and canals that deliver ocean water into the lake, which in turn requires immense resources that the local government might not be able to afford. The nearest shore is at least 100 kilometers away, meaning that the pipeline or canal would be quite long and therefore extremely costly.

The final proposal is to construct walls to separate the lake into areas with different salinity. However, the lecturer believes that this measure will not work for too long, because this region is located in an area with frequent geological activities. The next major earthquake would surely destroy the wall, and the waters would mix back together.

[9] 典型的问题解决型文章开头。

TPO 55

1. ✎ box ×
2. ✎ 贵

📣 听力大概率会说不贵或可以承担，逻辑上还存在一种可能性，就是"就算贵但是仍然会成功"，但这听起来太荒谬了。

3. ✎ × motivate under harsh condition

📣 这个段落的阅读对同学们还是有一点点挑战的，第一句话说的其实是"需要当地人去安装并维护这些设施"，如果同学们把这句话当核心内容记下来就错了。我们一定要有预期，我们所记录的东西要能够支持"为什么这种box device 会失败"，那光知道需要当地人安装显然不足以和这种失败联系起来，所以这个段落的核心理由肯定还在后面。听力大概率会说有办法 motivate people；逻辑上还存在一种可能性，不需要 local people，有别的途径去安装，但这听起来也很荒谬，这得创造什么神奇的替代方案。

4. ✎ limited ability, keep small trees

📣 听力直接对抗阅读，就可以说蓄水能力其实很强，不仅能维持 small trees；或者就算只能蓄一点水，只能维持 small trees，但仍然会是有用的，比如，可能只有 small tree 才需要借助这种外力。这两种方向乍一想都还算有合理性。

5. ✎ 无需笔记

6. ✎ once grow bigger, a new tree, reused, each 20 times or more, divide by number, cost reasonable

📝 阅读解析与听力预测

▶ **总 论：**
用 box-shaped device 围住树苗来对抗沙漠化会失败。这是文章的观点，等会儿应该有三个理由支持这个判断，[1] 典型的观点理由型文章。

▶ **理由 1：**
这个 device 很贵。[2]

▶ **理由 2：**
很难激励人们在如此恶劣的工作环境下去安装这些设施。[3]

▶ **理由 3：**
该设备蓄水能力有限，只能维持小树存活。[4]

📝 听力解析

The reasons against... box-like devices... not very convincing，无用信息。It is worthwhile to use these devices... fight against desertification，还是无用信息。[5]

First, the cost，符合预期。take into account that once a young tree growing inside the device gets bigger, the device can be removed and used to start growing a new tree，小树长大了就可以把 box 卸去以保护新树。其实我听到这儿脑子反应得不快，没意识到这怎么就反驳了阅读，估计脑子快的同学其实已经猜出来了。In other words, the devices can be reused，听到这儿我大概明白了反驳策略，就是可以重复利用，所以不贵。each can be used 20 times or more... divide the cost... by the number of trees... cost... reasonable，这基本就是基于上文完全合理的总结了。[6]

♦ **本段逻辑梳理：**当小树长大后，这些装置就可以卸去，然后重复利用去保护新的小树苗。换言之，这些装置可以反复回收达 20 次之多，所以拆卸的成本并不高。

Second, about installing and maintaining, 符合预期。It's true that people are being asked to maintain trees they cannot use for food, 让步，承认需要人来维护这些不能吃的树。But still..., possible rewards, 亮明了反驳策略，还是有动力的，那下面肯定要具体说哪里有动力。"... can be used to collect water for other plants, not just trees. If... are allowed to use some of the devices for their vegetables ... help them grow more food." 如果这些工具可以用来种蔬菜，那就有动力。Another benefit, once the trees become larger, branches... for firewood, 有生火的木头，这是第二个动力。more food more firewood should provide motivation, 无用的总结。[7]

◆ **本段逻辑梳理**：确实需要人们去保护一些看起来和食物无关的树，但还是可以有激励机制的。首先，如果可以挪用一些装置去保护蔬菜，这就直接帮助当地人获取更多食物；其次，这些树长大之后，它们的树枝可以用来生火。

[7] rewards: collect water for other plants, not just trees, vegetables, grow food, larger, branches for firewood

Third, a tree can survive very harsh conditions once it outgrows the box-like device, 其实反驳策略已经很明显了，就是树长大之后就不怕环境苛刻了，意味着不需要这些装置了。devices help young trees grow long roots, reach down to the moist soil that lies beneath the dry dessert surface, 进一步解释为什么不怕环境苛刻，因为这些装置可以让小树长出发达的根系，能够穿透沙漠抵达下层的湿润土层。Once... reach... water underground, can survive without the devices, 无用信息收尾。In a recent effort... in the Sahara Desert using the devices, 例子要来了，肯定是重复，90%... thriving 2 years after the devices had been removed, 用实例证明树长大之后没了这些 devices 也没事。[8]

◆ **本段逻辑梳理**：树长大了就不怕环境苛刻，不再需要这些装置保护了。因为这些装置可以帮助小树长出发达的根系，能够穿透沙漠抵达下层的湿润土层，此时，离开这些装置它们也能独立生存了。一个实例就是，最近在撒哈拉沙漠人们尝试用这些装置来保护树苗，树苗长大之后移除了这些装置，两年后90%的树都还能活着。

[8] can survive once outgrow, long roots, reach down moist soil beneath desert, survive without device, Sahara, 90% thrive 2 years after remove

满分范文

The article presents three arguments why using the box-shaped devices surrounding young trees will not successfully help against desertification, all of which are challenged by the lecturer.

For starters, the lecturer does not believe that the device is as costly as portrayed in the article, because the device can be reused after a young tree outgrows it. In fact, each device can be used up to 20 times, so if the cost of a device is divided by the number of trees that can use it, it would appear much less expensive.

As for the article's concern that people would not be motivated to take care of the devices, the lecturer points to two possible incentives. First, if the devices can be used to help grow vegetables, then people can generate more food. Second, once the trees protected by these devices grow larger, their branches can provide firewood for local people.

Finally, the article is correct that the device can only provide water enough to support a small tree. However, the lecturer argues that the device helps a small tree grow deep roots that penetrate the dessert surface and reach down to the moist soil beneath, so the tree can survive on its own even after the device is removed. As evidence, in a recent trial in Sahara Desert, 90% of the trees survived two years after the devices were removed.

TPO 56

阅读解析与听力预测

▶ **总 论：**
有三个理论可能解释 the 52-hertz whale 的 high pitch。现象解释型文章。

▶ **解释 1：**
hybrid[1]

▶ **解释 2：**
damaged sense of hearing[2]

▶ **解释 3：**
only known member of a rare species[3]

[1] 不可能是 hybrid，或是 hybrid 也无法产生这种 high pitch。

[2] 不可能拥有 damaged hearing，或拥有 damaged hearing 也无法产生这种 high pitch。

[3] 一个物种我们不可能只知道一个个体，或就算它是唯一已知个体，也无法产生这种 high pitch。

听力解析

each ... theories is flawed, whale's uniqueness remains a mystery，无用信息。

First, unlikely ... hybrid，无用信息。migration pattern is too unusual，准备听有多 unusual，以及为什么这就不能是 hybrid。All hybrid whales we know follow the migration patterns of non-hybrid whales，其实听到这儿已经彻底明白了，那后面自然会说这个 52-hertz whale 是不 follow 其他 whales 的。hybrids typically travel together with normal whales，无用信息。If the 52-hertz whale were a hybrid, it would likely do the same，无用信息。By listening to the locations of ... song, however, scientists ... determine that it does not migrate along side other whales，无用信息，逻辑完整了。migrates alone，无用信息，不知道为什么还在说，又臭又长。[4]

◆ **本段逻辑梳理：** the 52-hertz whale 不太可能是 hybrid 就能解释的。就算是 hybrid，它迁徙时也得和其他 non-hybrid 一起走，但

[4] migration: unusual, hybrid: follow non-h, travel together with normal, by listening to location of song, does not migrate along other, has own pattern

TPO 56

通过听声音位置，科学家测出来 the 52-hertz whale 是不和其他 whales 一起走的。

Second, deafness or poor hearing cannot explain... high pitch, 无用信息。"The pitch depends upon the physical structure of ... throat, vocal sounds originate... in its throat, in its vocal apparatus. To produce... high pitch, the throat... must be unusual." 这一堆说的都是差不多的事情，pitch 如此高，必须来源于极其特别的喉咙。cannot be caused by a damaged sense of hearing, because... no connection between hearing and throat structure, 完成了逻辑。[5]

◆ **本段逻辑梳理**：听力受损也无法解释 52-hertz whale。52-hertz whale 拥有如此特别的 high pitch，必须源于其喉咙的特殊结构，但这不可能是听力受损造成的，因为听力与喉咙结构之间并没有什么关系。

Third, ...unlikely that... only known member of a rare species, 无用信息。Even if ... rare, the whale had to have parents, parents would have also sung at the 52-hertz frequency, 如果真是这种解释，52-hertz whale 的亲代也肯定得有这种 frequency。"But the technology that detects whale sounds underwater has been in use for many decades. So if... parents... been around at... recent time, scientists would have heard them." 探测 whale sounds 的科技早就有了，要是真的有亲代出现，早就会被听到了。no... heard before this one, 无用信息，逻辑完成。[6]

本段逻辑梳理：也不可能因为它是一种罕见亚种的唯一已知成员。就算稀少，它也得有双亲，双亲的音频肯定也是 52-hertz。因此，要是它的双亲曾经生活在这片区域附近，那么科学家早就应该听到它们的声音了，因为探测鲸类声音的科技早已出现了。

[5] ✎ deaf cannot explain, high pitch, depends on physical structure of throat, originate in throat, vocal apparatus, must be unusual, cannot be caused by damaged hearing, no connection between hearing and throat structure

[6] ✎ have parents, parents would also sing at 52 hertz, technology used decades, around recent → heard, no ever heard before

📔 满分范文

The article presents three potential theories that might explain the unusual pitch of the 52-hertz whale, all of which are contested by the lecturer.

First, the lecturer does not believe that the 52-hertz whale could be a hybrid, because the migration pattern of the 52-hertz whale is too unusual. By listening to the location of the songs, scientists determine that this unusual whale does not migrate along other whales, yet hybrids would still have to travel together with normal whale groups.

Second, the lecturer does not believe that hearing problems could have explained the high pitch. The reason is that an unusual pitch can only generate from special physical structures of the throat, which cannot be caused by hearing damage, because there is no connection between throat structures and hearing ability.

Third, the lecturer does not believe that the 52-hertz whale could be the only known member of a rare whale species, because if it were, its parents would also sing at the 52-hertz frequency. However, the technology that detected the 52-hertz whale was used for decades, so had the parents been around, their songs would have been heard, yet no such sound had been detected before.

TPO 57

📝 阅读解析与听力预测

> **总　论：**
> Amtrak 应该私有化，后面会有三个理由。"观点＋三个理由"型文章。

> **理由 1：**
> 政府亏损。[1]

> **理由 2：**
> 对私人运输公司不公平。[2]

> **理由 3：**
> 希望政府支持国家交通时不要通过铁路，不如通过 highway。[3]

[1] 1) 不亏钱；2) 亏钱也应该国有。

[2] 1) 没有不公平；2) 不公平也应该国有。

[3] 1) 投入 highway 并没有更好；2) 就算投入 highway 更好，Amtrak 还是应该国有（这个听起来有点奇怪）。

🎧 听力解析

"Should the government sell Amtrak and let a private company run it instead? The answer is no." 全是无用信息。

First, losing money due to underused routes，无用信息。people who complain... fail to understand that the main purpose of Amtrak is not to make a profit，国有铁路不是为了赚钱，所以听力的反驳策略已经出来了，承认赔钱，但这不是个问题。but to provide needed transportation... to citizens of U.S.，目的是服务国民，基本可以预料的说辞。Some... live in remote areas，具体解释一下什么样的国民。it's true... underused and expensive to maintain，让步，承认确实这些铁路费钱。But... just as much right to government services as... more accessible areas do，其实就是需要地区平等。wrong to sell Amtrak to a private company that would cut these routes，将 Amtrak 卖给私企以后，私企肯定为了利益就不经营这些偏远线路了，这是不对的，基本就是把可以预见的逻辑说全了。[4]

[4] fail to understand, main purpose × profit, provide needed transport to 人, live in remote, < underused, expensive to maintain > they have rights to gov service as other areas, wrong to sell, private would cut

落笔生花

新托福综合写作高分范文精讲

TPO 57

♦ **本段逻辑梳理**：经营有些线路确实会赔钱，但政府投资 Amtrak 本来就不是为了赚钱，而是为了给国民提供应有的服务。那些住在 remote areas 的人和交通发达地区的人有着同等的基本权利享受公共服务。所以如果把铁路卖给私企，它们会把那些偏远线路服务砍掉，这是不道德的。

Second, the idea that… unfair… just silly, 第二点就是很蠢，直接反驳阅读，根本不存在 unfair。supports the airline industry in all kinds of ways, 国家不仅赞助铁路，肯定也赞助航空。pays for… air-traffic control towers and the training of the air-traffic control officers, weather satellites, 都是具体的赞助的领域。private airlines and other forms of mass transportation couldn't exist without… support from the government, 总结，其他所谓的私人交通方式没有政府支持根本不可能。[5]

♦ **本段逻辑梳理**：根本不存在什么国家支持 Amtrak 是对私有交通方式的不公平，因为政府同样也在支持其他交通方式。以航空为例，政府要负担起建造 air-traffic control towers，要培训 air-traffic control officers，要购买 weather satellites 从而保证飞行安全。没有政府支持，那些私人的交通系统根本就没有可能。

Third, … train travel is less popular than car travel, 让步，承认火车不如汽车流行。only because the Amtrak system is out of date, 只是因为火车系统老旧，暗示需要更新，肯定是为了说政府不应该转而支持汽车，还是应该支持火车。If people in the United States had trains that were affordable and fast, gladly take them, 要是火车又快又便宜，火车肯定也 popular。We know this because… Japan and Europe do, 日本和欧洲提供了证据（哼，就是不说中国么）。The governments … invested in high-speed train lines, train travel is popular, 这都是无用信息。What the U.S. government should do is invest more money in Amtrak to improve the service, 可以预见的无用信息。[6]

♦ **本段逻辑梳理**：政府恰恰更应该加大对 Amtrak 的投入。Amtrak 现在不如汽车流行，也只是因为现在的 Amtrak system 太老旧了。假如有了更多经费，把 Amtrak 造得又快又廉价，人们巴不得不开车整天坐火车呢。证据就是日本和欧洲，政府花了钱造高铁，于是人们非常乐意搭乘铁路。

[5] ✎ silly, support airway all ways, pays control tower, pays air-control officer, weather satellite, private couldn't exist without gov support

[6] ✎ < less pop train > Amtrak outdate, if trains affordable fast, glad to take, Japan & Europe do, have invested in high speed, train pop, should spend more improve service

TPO 57

满分范文

The article presents three arguments why the U.S. government should sell Amtrak to a privately owned company, all of which are rebutted by the lecturer.

First, the article argues that the government is losing money because many Amtrak routes are underused. However, the lecturer counters that Amtrak exists not to make money, but to provide affordable transportation to United States citizens, including those living in remote areas, who have just as much rights to government services as do people elsewhere. Cutting the routes from remote areas just because they are expensive to maintain is simply morally wrong.

Second, the lecturer dismisses as silly the argument that the government's support to Amtrak is unfair to privately owned transportation companies such as airlines. In fact, the U.S. government provides indispensable financial support to airlines, from the construction of control towers, to the training of officers, and to the maintenance of weather satellites.

Finally, directly against the article's message, the lecturer believes that the government should increase financial investment to upgrade the Amtrak system. The reason why currently Amtrak is less popular than cars is exactly that the system is outdated. If the U.S. citizens have access to fast and affordable railway system, they would gladly switch from cars to railway, just as the Japanese and Europeans do, who enjoy government-funded high-speed train service.

TPO 58

📝 阅读解析与听力预测

▶ **总　论**：
三个因素使得 Spartacus 特别 appealing。现象解释型文章。

▶ **因素 1**：
初心是要归家，每个人都可以产生共鸣。[1]

▶ **因素 2**：
靠 skill 以弱胜强。[2]

▶ **因素 3**：
试图解放奴隶，最早的人权斗士。[3]

[1] 否定人们喜欢他是因为这种归家的共鸣，或者这根本就不是他的初心。

[2] 否定人们喜欢他是因为以弱胜强，或者他根本没有以弱胜强。

[3] 否定人们喜欢他是因为他是人权斗士，或者他根本没有想要解放奴隶。

📝 听力解析

"… a real person … However, many stories … not historically accurate." 听力肯定是反驳，而且反驳策略基本已经明确了，刚才阅读的所有理论直接就是假的。

First, returning… homes… not the only goal, 所以肯定承认想归家，但肯定要指出其他动机。first battles… defeated the Roman army cleared a route… could have escaped the Roman… But they didn't take that opportunity, 初期战胜罗马后已经有了回家的路，但是没走，那等会儿肯定会说不跑的其他原因，会是我们要听的关键。Instead, …marching towards the city of Rome, probably wanted to conquer the city, take as many valuables, 想要攻城抢钱，反驳明晰了。So… not fighting just to get home, interested in revenge and wealth, less admirable goals, 总结了，基本是无用信息。[4]

[4] not the only goal, 1st battle defeat, clear route escape, ✗ take opportunity, march toward, conquer take valuable as they could, not just home, interested in revenge and wealth, less admirable

◆ **本段逻辑梳理**：回家可不是他唯一的目标，起初他打赢了就可以回家了，结果他偏不回，反而继续攻打罗马想要抢钱，说明他的目标其实包含复仇与发财，这可没那么高尚。

Part 2　201
综合写作高分范文精讲

TPO 58

Second, although Spartacus did win a few battles, not necessarily a military genius, 反驳策略肯定是说他没那么 skillful。Romans didn't take... seriously, 这句话一出现,策略已经很明了,他能赢只是因为对面轻敌,下面继续说下去肯定也就是展开怎么轻敌了。initially sent only poorly trained and ill-equipped army units, 罗马就没派厉害的人呗。It was these weak units that Spartacus defeated, 无用信息。When the Roman army sent their best soldiers, Spartacus was quickly defeated, 对面一派强敌,Spartacus 就输了,基本可以从逻辑上预料到。suggesting... wasn't a brilliant military leader, 无用信息总结。[5]

♦ **本段逻辑梳理**:这人也不是什么军事奇才。他最初能赢几仗是因为罗马根本不在乎他,派的都是训练无素、装备劣质的军队,等罗马派上精良部队对付他,他瞬间输了,这人根本不行。

Third, ... not backed by... evidence, 无用信息。where did the story come from, 原来解放奴隶什么的都是编的故事,下面要详细讲故事是从哪儿传出来的。we know exactly who created... and why, 没用的句子。18th century Europe, 有了时间和地点,等动机。widely practiced slavery, but... also an anti-slavery movement, 估计这就是动机来源了。thinkers and writers... strongly opposed to slavery, 有人反对奴隶制。wanted... inspirational hero from ancient times, 想要偶像人物的启发,估计就要编造 Spartacus 了呗。thought Spartacus could be that hero, 无用信息。So an 18th century playwright wrote a play... Spartacus... liberate all slaves, 来了来了。just an inspirational story in a play, not... truth, 无用信息总结。[6]

♦ **本段逻辑梳理**:说 Spartacus 是人权斗士完全是瞎编,我们甚至知道是怎么编出来的。18 世纪欧洲盛行奴隶制,于是也有很多人反对奴隶制。文学家们、思想家们想要从历史人物当中寻找偶像人物来激发人们反对奴隶制,于是就有剧作家编了 Spartacus 废奴的剧本。但只是美好的剧本,不是事实。

[5] ✎ did win, not necessary genius, didn't take seriously 1st, initially send poorly trained × equip weak units, send best soldier, quickly defeat, × good leader

[6] ✎ who create, 18th Europe practice slavery, also anti movement, thinker, writer, want inspiration from hero ancient, thought Sp could be hero, playwright wrote, inspiration story, × truth

📝 满分范文

The article presents three accounts why Spartacus became an appealing hero, all of which are dismissed in the lecture as not based on historical facts.

The article's first speculation is that Spartacus' original goal of wanting to go home speaks to everyone. However, the lecturer points to Spartacus' other motives in those fights. After hist first victory, his army already cleared escape routes, yet they didn't take the opportunity to flee home but instead march toward the city, potentially to take more valuables. This suggests that other than just going home, they were interested in revenge and wealth, clearly less admirable goals.

The article's second theory is Spartacus' military genius, which the lecturer also believes as groundless. The reason why Spartacus won the first few battles was that Romans initially didn't take him seriously. He only defeated weak units who were untrained and ill-equipped. Afterwards when encountering the best Roman soldiers, Spartacus quickly suffered defeat, suggesting that he was not an extraordinary military leader.

Finally, the lecturer regards as purely fabricated the idea that Spartacus was an early human activist against slavery. She traces source of such fabrication to the 18th Europe, when slavery was practiced and when there were also strong anti-slavery movements. Thinkers and writers sought inspiration from ancient heroes, so playwrights created Spartacus' legend to provide such an inspirational story.

TPO 59

📝 阅读解析与听力预测

> **总　论:**
> The Plain of Jars 之所以会有那么多 containers，考古学家提出了三种可能解释。典型的现象解释型文章。

> **解释 1:**
> fermentation（of food or drink）[1]

> **解释 2:**
> water storage [2]

> **解释 3:**
> Plain 是一个 burial site，jars 是 tombs。[3]

[1] 👈 不是用来发酵的。

[2] 👈 不是用来储水的。

[3] 👈 不是用作坟墓。

📝 听 力 解 析

The purpose of the jars is still uncertain，无用信息。

First, the fermentation... probably not true，无用信息。In Laos, pots... traditionally used to ferment drinks are made of clay，这种 fermentation 工具应该是 clay 做的。could use stone，让步，但等会儿肯定要怼回去。but... creating stone jars is difficult，怼回去了。much more time-consuming and expensive，展开 difficult。Why would ancient people have expended all this effort, when clay pots were easier to make, served the same purpose，这是无用信息总结。[4]

[4] 👈 pots ferment made of clay, could use stone, but creating difficult, much more time-consuming and expensive than clay, why effort when clay easier & same purpose?

◆ **本段逻辑梳理:** 不太可能是 fermentation device。老挝传统用来装 ferment drink 的 containers 都是 clay 做的，不是不能用 stone 做，只是 stone containers 做起来更费时也更贵，没必要。明明有成本更低的 clay，为啥要做 stone jars？

Second, ... unlikely ... storing water for travelers，无用信息。

204 | 落笔生花
新托福综合写作高分范文精讲

although... located near ancient trade routes，让步，等会儿肯定会处理掉。These routes were also close to rivers and streams，反驳策略已经出来了，这些古代商路本来就离水近，暗示没必要造这些储水装置。no need for an additional source of fresh water，没有出乎意料。So it's unlikely... this purpose，无用信息。[5]

◆ **本段逻辑梳理**：估计也不太可能是储水装置。确实这个地方离古代商路近，但古代商路也离水源很近啊，那旅客们没有必要寻找自然水源以外的其他水源呀。

Third，...may have been used... burying human remains，让步，等会儿肯定会否定这个可能性。one serious problem with this theory，无用信息，以至于前面的让步也是无用信息，给你点可能性，然后否定掉，还是不可能。Tombs were usually covered in order to protect the human remains and artifacts, from the weather, from thieves，墓穴都是要盖盖的呀，不然怎么保护尸骸以及那些陪葬品，估计就是要说这个 Plain 没有 cover 了。but the stone jars... do not have any covers, No one has found any type of cover either on the jars themselves，都是预料中的，没有 cover。unlikely... the jars were used as tombs，无用信息。[6]

◆ **本段逻辑梳理**：也不太可能是用作墓穴。墓穴都得盖盖，得保护尸骸以及陪葬品，免受小偷和天灾的影响。这些 stone jars 都没有发现任何盖盖子的痕迹，所以不太可能用作墓穴。

[5] \<trade route\> close to river stream, no need for an additional source

[6] tombs usually covered in order to protect human & artifact from weather & thief, × cover site, no one found cover for jar

📝 满 分 范 文

The article offers three potential explanations why there were so many jars in the Plain of Jars in Laos, all of which are challenged by the lecturer.

First, the lecturer rejects the fermentation hypothesis, because in ancient Laos pots used for fermentation were traditionally made of clay. While it is true that fermentation devices could be made of stone, the creation process would be much more time-consuming and more expensive. It's unlikely that people expended excessive effort making these stone jars when they could have gone for a much easier but equally effective alternative.

Second, the lecturer does not believe that the jars were used to store water for travelers either. Even though the Plain is located near ancient trade routes, but the routes were also quite close to rivers and streams, indicating that there was no need for ancient travelers to seek additional water sources. Therefore, the jars were probably not storage devices for water.

Finally, the lecturer considers unilluminating the theory that the jars were tombs used for burying human remains and burial artifacts. Tombs were usually covered in order to protect the human body and the artifacts from unfriendly weather and from thieves. However, no one found signs of covers for the jars. Therefore, it is quite unlikely that the Plain was an ancient burial site.

TPO 60

阅读解析与听力预测

> **总　论：**
> 提供了三个保护 rhino 的方案。问题解决型文章。

> **方案1：**
> dehorn rhino（去除角），rhino 没有角的话那些人自然就不盗猎了。[1]

> **方案2：**
> educate consumers，让他们觉得买犀牛角对他们没有医用价值。[2]

> **方案3：**
> 使贩卖犀牛官方合理化（禁不了就想办法程序化、正规化）。[3]

[1] 1) 不可行，角去不了；2) 无效，角去了那些人也会盗猎；3) 副作用，去除了角会伤害犀牛，或引起其他什么坏处，伤害犀牛是我最容易想到的。

[2] 1) 不可行，没有办法 educate consumers；2) 无效，educate consumers 了也保护不了犀牛；3) 副作用，教育消费者有坏处，这个听起来很不合理，直接从脑海中排除。

[3] 1) 不可行，政府没法管；2) 无效，政府管了也救不了犀牛；3) 政府管理会有副作用。

[4] ×practical, ×good for survival, have to find, prepare for surgery then remove horn, < time, money > likely reduce chance for survival, horn for good reason, dig water, break branches, guide protect young, protect territory, <unattractive to poacher> disadvantage to wild

听力解析

solutions... have significant weaknesses，无用信息。

First, ...neither practical nor good for rhino's survival，既不可行又有副作用。To dehorn rhinos, you have to find them in the wild, prepare them for surgery, and then remove their horns，这是不可行的部分。even if we have time and money，让步，就算可行，等会儿要吐槽副作用了。reducing... chances for survival，降低存活率，等会儿肯定会解释。dig for water, to break branches when looking for food, to guide and protect their young, and to protect territories，这是具体讲 rhino horns 的必要性，可以推断出 rhino 没有 horn 就很难活。disadvantaged in the wild，无用信息。[4]

◆ **本段逻辑梳理：** 去除角是不可行的，也对犀牛有危害。要去除角，得首先找到野生犀牛，还得做好术前准备，然后才能执行。就算有时间、有金钱完成这些麻烦操作，没有角的犀牛很难活。它们无论是找水、破坏树枝去找食物，照顾幼崽，还是保护领地，都需要角。

TPO 60

Second, educating consumers is unlikely to be effective, 无效。 Many people have strong cultural beliefs about the healing powers, health benefits of rhino horn, 人们对犀牛角的作用的认知根深蒂固。very ancient, go back thousands of years, 展开根深蒂固。Educating works best when... don't have strong ideas about something, 在人们还没有预设的想法时，教育是有用的，暗示现在想法已经根深蒂固了，很难通过教育去改变。when consumers have very old and very strong beliefs, new scientific evidence is unlikely to easily change mind, 无用信息，可以预期到的。[5]

◆ **本段逻辑梳理**：教育没用。人们对犀牛角的药用价值的想法可谓是根深蒂固、积习难改，这是几千年来老祖宗传下来的老方子了，怎么可能错呢？教育能有用，纯粹是因为人们还没有形成根深蒂固的陋习；像这种抱着老祖宗的旧观念不放的，再多科学发现都改不了他们的想法。

Third, the effect... actually be unpredictable, 有效性不确定。Currently, many people who want... may not buy it, because it's illegal, 人们现在之所以想买但不买，纯粹因为不合法，其实已经暗示了反驳策略，很有可能未来合法化之后，想买的人自然就会买，需求就多了。But if governments start selling rhino horn, buying... would become acceptable, more people might start buying, 顺理成章的因果链，没什么好解释的。demand... might grow, creating a much larger market, larger demand would increase prices, high prices... attract poachers, poaching might not stop, instead... continue killing rhinos and sell their horn, 还是顺理成章的因果链。政府许可了，人们就敢买，市场需求就大了，犀牛角就更贵了，盗猎就更猛了。[6]

◆ **本段逻辑梳理**：犀牛角合法化的操作效果未知。现在一些人想买不敢买的原因就是购买犀牛角不合法，而如果未来合法了，他们很可能就会买，就会增大市场需求，使得犀牛角更值钱，盗猎就更猖狂。

[5] ✎ ✗ effective, cultural belief, health benefit, ancient thousands of years, works best when don't already have strong idea, when have old strong belief, new science evidence ✗ change mind

[6] ✎ unpredictable effect, ✗ buy because illegal, if gov, become acceptable, start to buy, demand might grow dramatic, larger market, increased demand would increase price, attract poacher, might continue and sell, because govs sell would create large lucrative market

满分范文

The lecturer points out weaknesses with each of the methods proposed in the article about saving rhinos.

First, she considers dehorning rhinos neither practical nor good for rhinos' survival. The method requires finding rhinos in the wild first, preparing them for surgery, and then removing their horn. Even with sufficient time and money, rhinos' chance of survival would reduce, because they need horns to dig for water, break branches, guide and protect their young, and protect territories. Dehorned rhinos would thus be at a very disadvantaged position in the wild.

Second, the lecturer does not believe that educating consumers would be effective. The beliefs that rhino horn has practical health benefits is deeply rooted in many traditional cultures, lasting thousands of years. Education could be effective, if ideas weren't already established in people's minds, but when they have such strong and ancient belief, new scientific evidence is unlikely to change people's mind.

Finally, the lecture believes that legalizing horn business might lead to unpredictable effect. The reason why many people don't buy horn products now might just be that this trade is illegal. If it becomes legalized, they might consider purchasing horn products acceptable and start buying them. Consequently, demand for rhino horns might grow, and increased demand would increase prices, in turn attract more poachers to a large, lucrative, and legalized market.

TPO 61

阅读解析与听力预测

▶ **总 论：**
conservationists 为帮助 golden frogs 解决 fungus problem 提出了 3 种解决方案。典型的问题解决型题目。

▶ **方案 1：**
bacterial protection，引入抗真菌细菌。[1]

▶ **方案 2：**
圈养 golden frogs 然后再将它们放归大自然，等圈养的无真菌 frogs 形成自然规模。[2]

▶ **方案 3：**
等 golden frogs 自然形成防御机制，某些青蛙会发烧以抵抗真菌。[3]

[1] 👎 不可行；没用；有副作用。

[2] 👎 不可行；没用；有副作用。

[3] 👎 不可行；没用；有副作用。

听力解析

none... very effective，无用信息。

First, ...bacteria not work，无效。did have a positive effect, but it did not last very long，没有长期效果，反驳策略已经明了。protection against the fungus only temporary，重复上文。"... produces a chemical that attacks the fungus. Unfortunately, ... produces this chemical early in its colonization of frogs' skin，具体展开为什么只产生短期效果，因为细菌产生抗真菌物质的时间只在其渗透青蛙皮肤的初期阶段。After this brief period, ...stop producing chemical, and therefore stops protecting the golden frogs from the fungal infections，无用信息总结。[4]

[4] ✍ ✗ work, introduce, + effect, ✗ last long, temporary protection, chemical attacks, only produces early in colonization of skin; after, stop producing, stop protecting

◆ **本段逻辑梳理：** 靠引入抗真菌细菌的策略并不会长期有效，因为这种细菌的抗真菌模式是：在渗透青蛙皮肤后的初期产生一种抗真菌的化学物质，但这个时期结束之后，它就不产生该物质了，自然也就无法保护青蛙了。

TPO 61

Second, if we release... new frog population is not going to stay healthy, 将人工繁育的青蛙放归到野生环境，它们并不会保持健康，暗示第二个方案最后也是没有用的。other animals living in that environment carry the same disease, causing fungus, 听到这儿，反驳思路已经明了，别的物种也带真菌（会传染给这些青蛙的）。So if we release ... into that environment, ... soon get infected by the fungus, 可以预见到的无用信息。[5]

◆ **本段逻辑梳理**：把人工繁育的无真菌青蛙放归野外也没用，它们不会保持健康，因为野生环境下的其他物种也是带有这种真菌的，所以将青蛙放生之后，青蛙会很快接触其他野生动物，于是也会马上被真菌感染。

Third, ...heating up their bodies, big drawback, 靠青蛙自己发烧抗菌是有副作用的。use up lot of energy, weakens the frogs, easily get ill or die from other causes, 很自然的因果链，发烧要耗能，耗能就变虚弱，虚弱就容易病死。might be protected from the fungus, but they're not strong and healthy, unlikely... help... population to recover, 这种策略也许能不感染真菌，但会脆弱，无法让物种数量恢复。[6]

◆ **本段逻辑梳理**：靠青蛙自己发烧抵御真菌，这种策略也救不了青蛙。它们发烧就会大量耗能，这会让它们变虚弱，容易被其他疾病攻击而亡。所以就算它们免受真菌影响，它们还是很弱，所以种群数量还是无法恢复。

[5] if release to an area where wild frogs die out, × stay healthy, other animals carry same disease causing fungus, release captivity, soon infected, contact animals there

[6] defend by heating up bodies, drawback, use up lots of energy, expenditure weakens frog, easy ill, die from other causes, might be protected from fungus, × strong healthy, will not help recover

满分范文

The article offers three possible solutions to protect the golden frog population against fungal infection, all of which are questioned in the lecture.

The first possibility is to introduce anti-fungal bacteria to the frogs' skin. However, the lecturer does not believe that the effect can last, because the introduced bacteria produce anti-fungal chemicals only during the early stage of colonization of the frogs' skin. After that stage, they stop producing the chemical and the protection against fungus ceases.

Second, the lecture does not believe that breeding fungus-free frogs in captivity and sending them back to the wild can solve the problem. In places where golden frogs have died out from fungal problems, other wild animals also carry the same disease, causing fungus. Once the frogs in captivity were released to the wild, they will soon get into contact with other wild animals and become infected by the fungus.

Finally, the lecturer does not believe that we can count on frogs to develop a natural defense mechanism against the fungus. The frogs overcome the disease by heating up their body, but this process uses up a lot of energy. Such excessive energy expense weakens the frogs, so they easily succumb to other diseases and die. Therefore, while this defense mechanism might protect the frogs against fungus, they are not strong or healthy enough for their population to recover in the wild.

TPO 62

阅读解析与听力预测

▶ **总 论：**
人工 reefs 有三个好处。听力会否定这三个好处。

▶ **好处 1：**
人工 reefs 为鱼群提供了更多 gather 和 reproduce 的场所，从而使一些种群鱼的数量增加。[1]

▶ **好处 2：**
通过建造私有的、别人不知道的 reefs，提高小规模经营渔民的经济竞争力。[2]

▶ **好处 3：**
可以废物利用。[3]

[1] 鱼的数量并没有增加；或这不是什么好事。

[2] 并不能真的提高他们的竞争力；或这不是什么好事。

[3] 并不能废物利用；或这不是什么好事。

听力解析

create more problems than benefits，全文反驳策略是弊大于利。
First, ...more fish are reported... caught near... reefs doesn't... mean... populations... grown larger，反驳策略已出，阅读所说的捕获更多鱼并不能证明阅读的观点，即 reefs 帮助鱼群增长。reefs attract fish to them, fish that once lived in more distant... moved to and stay near，鱼其实是被吸引到 reefs 周围的。higher catch... mean... fish that once... lived somewhere else by attracting... fish。捕鱼数更多只能说明 reefs 把别处的鱼吸引过来了，基本上是完全可以预见到的反驳策略。may cause a decrease in fish populations, help fishers catch so many fish, cannot maintain populations，相反 reefs 反而使鱼数量减少，因为这种把鱼集中起来的过程会让渔民捕到更多的鱼。[4]

[4] more caught ≠ population larger, reefs attract fish, fish that once lived in distant locations move to stay near, higher catch No.s mean attracting else, cause a decrease in fish pop, help catch so many, cannot maintain

◆ **本段逻辑梳理：** 阅读所给的证据（即捕鱼量增大）并不能证明阅读的论点（即鱼数量增多）。因为 reefs 会吸引鱼，所以鱼的捕获量增多纯粹可能是别处的鱼被吸引过来的结果。且这种吸引使得渔民捕鱼更容易，所以恰恰可能带来的结果是鱼数量的下降而非增多。

TPO 62

bad idea to allow small-scale fishers to create... reefs in secret locations，就不应该让小渔民建造隐蔽的 reefs。Not knowing where... can cause... safety problems，下文肯定会展开有哪些危险。other fishers who use large nets to catch fish can get nets caught on reefs and destroyed as a result，渔民的网可能会缠上 reefs 而被毁掉。In shallow waters, boats might crash into secret reefs，船会触礁，这个很好理解。the only way... safe is to make... known，要是为了安全肯定会公开，那公开之后阅读所说的经济优势就不存在了，完全可以预见。But when ... public, small-scale fishers have no competitive advantage，这是无用信息。[5]

◆ **本段逻辑梳理**：让 small-scale fishers 自己偷偷建造 reefs 很危险。别的渔民捕鱼时，鱼网可能会缠到 reefs 上而被毁掉，船甚至都可能触礁。于是为了安全，reefs 就得公开，可是公开了以后，small-scale fishers 也别想有什么经济优势了。

environmental damage, even when harmful chemicals ... removed，就算回收利用时把有害物质去除了，还是会有环保问题。happened to the Osborne Reef，举例。made of used car tires, bound together，具体介绍 Osborne Reef 的情况，等待 environmental damage。when a storm came, parts ... came loose，风暴来了把 reefs 给刮散架了。started crashing into the... seafloor，散掉的部分就沉入海底。caused... environmental damage, harming ... plants and animals living on the seafloor，基本是无用信息。[6]

◆ **本段逻辑梳理**：废物重复利用建造 reefs 会有环保危害，就算回收利用时已经去除了有害化学物质。以 Osborne Reef 为例，它是由旧轮胎拼接制造而成，结果风暴来临，reefs 就散架了，散落的部件被风暴刮到了海底，造成了严重的环境灾难，威胁海底的动植物。

[5] ✏ a bad idea ... secret locations × tell, cause safety problems, other fishers' nets caught & destroyed, boats crash, only way ... safe, made known, when public, small scale no advantage

[6] ✏ serious environ damage, even when chemicals removed, Osborne Reef. car tires bound together, reef came loose when a storm came, crash onto seafloor, cause damage, harm plants and animals living on the seafloor

📝 满分范文

The article presents three possible benefits of artificial reefs, each of which the lecturer believes is outweighed by potential problems.

First, the article suggests that the reefs increase population of some fish species, but the lecturer believes that since reefs attract fish, the article's evidence that more fish have been caught do not prove increased fish population. Instead, it only indicates that fish living in distant areas have been attracted nearby. In fact, the reefs help fishers catch so many fish, leading to potential decrease in fish population.

Second, the article claims that by creating secret artificial reefs, small-scale fishers become more economically competitive. However, the lecturer argues that if the reefs are kept secret, they pose serious safety problems. Other fishers' nets can be caught onto the reefs and destroyed; boats might even be crashed by the reefs. Therefore, the only safe way is to make the reefs public, but in that case small-scale fishers wouldn't have any economic advantage.

Finally, the article presents the reefs as a good way to recycle unused materials, but the lecturer believes that it causes serious environmental damage, presenting the Osborne Reef as an example. The Osborne Reef used old car tires bound together, but it was torn apart by the storm. The loose pieces crashed onto the seafloor, harming the creatures living there.

TPO 63

📖 阅读解析与听力预测

○ 总 论：
生态学家给出了几种方案，以解决入侵北美的未来物种 cheatgrass 所造成的危害。典型的问题解决型文章。

▶ 方案 1：
鼓励 cattle 以 cheatgrass 为食。[1]

▶ 方案 2：
焚烧。[2]

▶ 方案 3：
引入寄生真菌专攻 cheatgrass。[3]

[1] 不可行，无法引入 cattle；无效，cattle 也搞不定 cheatgrass；cattle 会带来副作用。

[2] 不可行，没法焚烧（听起来不是什么难以做到的事情，估计不会这么反驳）；无效，焚烧搞不定 cheatgrass；焚烧有严重的副作用。

[3] 不可行，无法引入真菌；无效，真菌也搞不定 cheatgrass；真菌有副作用。

📝 听力解析

not likely to work well，无用信息。

First, not a plant that grazers prefer, 其实这一句一出现这一段基本都是无用信息了，grazers 不爱吃 cheatgrass 呀，那怎么消灭 cheatgrass 呢。if grazers are released in a field that has a lot of cheatgrass but that also has other kinds of plants, eat the other kinds of plants first, grazers 也会挑喜欢的先吃啊，那就把其他植物都先吃完了，反而剩下 cheatgrass 呗。might eat some of the cheatgrass, only after native grass and plants that were trying to protect ... destroyed, 就是无用信息。So releasing grazing animals ... will have the opposite effect, 无用信息总结，这个方法最后会和目标背道而驰。fewer native grasses, plenty of cheatgrass, 无用信息总结。[4]

◆ **本段逻辑梳理**：grazers 没用，甚至南辕北辙。grazers 并不爱吃 cheatgrass，所以把 grazers 丢到既有 cheatgrass 又有 native plants 的地里，grazers 一定会先吃 native plants，然后才吃 cheatgrass。所以

[4] not a plant grazers prefer, grazers release, also has other plants, eat other first, grazers may eat some cheat grass, only after native plants (protect) be destroyed, opposite effect of intended, fewer native, plenty cheat

TPO 63

grazers 反而会毁掉更多我们本想保护的 native plants，留下 cheatgrass。

Second, fire will destroy cheatgrass plants on the surface，已经暗示问题了，就是 surface 以下的 cheatgrass 火烧不到。but that doesn't mean cheatgrass won't quickly come back，cheatgrass 很快就会东山再起。Cheatgrass produces many seeds, can germinate a few years falling to the ground，草籽很多，几年内就能发芽。Many seeds get pushed down into the soil below the surface，前面暗示的东西出现了，草籽会存在于地表以下的土层中。fire cannot harm them，无用信息。after the fire has burned away… on the surface, seeds that are buried… below… sprout, give rise to new plants，土壤中的 seeds 就会发芽，完全可以预见到。soon again filled with cheatgrass，无用信息。[5]

◆ **本段逻辑梳理**：火只能烧表面，影响不到地下。cheatgrass 会产生很多草籽，一部分草籽会落到地表以下的土层中，不会被火影响到。在火将地表的植被烧光之后，地下的草籽很快就能发芽重生，很快地面上又都是 cheatgrass 了。

Third, cheatgrass and the fungal parasite have lived together in their native habitats for thousands of years，cheatgrass 和寄生真菌其实共生了很久。cheatgrass plants have… developed some resistance against the fungus，cheatgrass 已经形成了防御能力。while the fungus has the ability to harm cheatgrass，让步，承认 fungus 有一定能力伤害 fungus, in reality, only harms… already weak or sickly，但其实只能伤害老弱病残的 cheatgrass。The healthy and strong… can usually resist the fungal infection，健康强壮的 cheatgrass 是不太怕 fungus 的。will probably not be efficient，无用信息。[6]

◆ **本段逻辑梳理**：寄生真菌也没什么用，在 cheatgrass 的 native habitats，它与寄生真菌共生了几千年了，早已形成了抵御机制。所以虽然真菌能对一些 cheatgrass 起作用，但主要攻击的都是老弱病残，健康强壮的 cheatgrass 并不怎么会受 fungal parasite 的影响。

[5] fire will destroy cheat on the surface, will come back quickly, many seeds, germinate a few years, many get pushed down into the soil below the surface, fire cannot harm, after burn surface, buried seeds sprout give rise to new, soon filled with cheat

[6] lived together in native habitats 1000 years, cheat developed resistance to fungus, < ability to harm > only destroy sick, strong & healthy can resist, will not be efficient

满分范文

The lecturer does not believe that any of the methods proposed in the reading against cheatgrass will work very well.

TPO 63

First, he believes that the introduction of grazers to eliminate cheatgrass will backfire, eliminating more native plants that we intended to protect than cheatgrass, because cheatgrass is not a plant that grazers prefer. As a result, introduced grazers would more likely eat all other available plants before they start eating cheatgrass.

Second, he does not believe that fire will be able to eradicate cheatgrass either. Cheatgrass produces a lot of seeds, many of which are pushed down to the soil below ground surface. Since fire cannot harm these underground seeds, even if the ground-level cheatgrass has been cleared, the underground seeds will sprout and give rise to new cheatgrass within just a few years.

Finally, introducing the fungal parasite mentioned in the article is regarded as a futile effort as well. Cheatgrass has coexisted with the fungal parasite for thousands of years in their original environment, so they have developed resistance to the parasite. Therefore, while the fungus is able to hurt cheatgrass, it can only destroy the sick and weak ones, leaving the strong and healthy ones intact.

TPO 64

阅读解析与听力预测

- **总　论：**
  计划把西兰花种在美国炎热的东海岸，有三个好处。

- **好处1：**
  降低运输成本。[1]

- **好处2：**
  更加受消费者青睐。[2]

- **好处3：**
  更快被吃掉意味着人们更健康。[3]

[1] 运输成本不会降；或运输成本降了也不是什么好事。

[2] 不会被喜欢；或被喜欢也不是什么好事。

[3] 人们吃西兰花并不会更健康；或人们吃西兰花更健康也不见得是什么好事。

听力解析

not... successful or beneficial，无用信息。

First, it's true that growing and selling crops locally saves money on transportation，让步，承认节省了运费。not necessarily... cheaper for consumers，反驳策略明了，虽然运费便宜了，但是最后售价并不会低，等着听为什么售价不变。Yes, the new breed... survive the hot summers on the east coast，让步，承认新西兰花能长在东海岸。but unfortunately, lower yields，但产量会下降，这等会儿肯定会说售价没有下降。farmers... harvest less broccoli per hectare，继续展开减产。have to sell... at higher price，无用信息。cancel out the saving on transportation，无用信息。consumers... not save any money，无用信息。[4]

[4] <save transport cost >, × necessarily cheaper for consumers, < survive summer coast >, also lower yield than west, harvest less/hectare, higher price, cancel out saving on transport, east coast consumers ×save money

◆ **本段逻辑梳理：**虽然在东海岸种西兰花能减少运费，但消费者购买西兰花并不会便宜。因为在东海岸虽然西兰花能存活，但是其产量会下降，这就会导致农民必须抬价以维持收入，于是消费者并不会买到更便宜的西兰花。

TPO 64

Second, even though... using traditional breeding techniques, 承认用的是古法栽培。the public might still be suspicious, 大众还是不信, 反驳策略出现, 所以大众不会欢迎新西兰花, 等待大众为什么不信的展开。financial support for this research comes from the same companies that created genetically modified crops in the past, 关键展开, 解释了大众为什么不信, 因为这些研究是那些转基因公司赞助的, 那大众肯定不信啊。because... used... modification techniques with other crops, consumers distrust, 基本是无用信息了。might distrust any project... involved in, 还是无用信息, 消费者不会相信那些公司相关的任何产品。reject the new broccoli, 无用信息。5

◆ **本段逻辑梳理：** 就算新西兰花用的是古法栽培, 民众也不见得相信新西兰花。这项新研究的赞助公司之前正是做转基因农作物的, 民众本来就不相信他们, 很可能也就不信他们连带的任何产品, 包括现在的新西兰花。

Third, it's true... broccoli... greatest... nutrients, 确实西兰花营养价值很高。"But... good argument for creating a new breed of broccoli ... on the east coast?" 作者设问：这个论证足够证明要在东海岸种西兰花吗？我们知道答案肯定是否定, 等她继续说。Not necessarily, 无用信息。Other vegetables that are already grown on the east coast contain similar nutrients, 策略出现, 已经有替代物了。For example, kale... provides comparable health benefits, 列举了一个替代品的例子, kale。kale is in some respects better, kale 还有优势, 等待听优势。grown... not only during summer, but also during the fall and winter, 很多季节都可以种, 那西兰花肯定不行。Instead of wasting... resources on... new vegetables, we should educate people about eating fresh... vegetables that are already locally, 因此不应该关注什么新植物, 应该劝人们好好吃现有的这些健康蔬菜。6

◆ **本段逻辑梳理：** 西兰花是很健康, 但问题是东海岸已经有差不多的其他植物了, 比如 kale。kale 营养价值和西兰花差不多, 但是不仅可以在夏天种, 还可以在秋冬季种, 西兰花就只能在夏天种。所以, 我们不应该浪费一大堆钱研究什么新作物, 应该宣传教育并鼓励人们好好吃这些本来就有的健康蔬菜。

5 ✎ <traditional breeding technique> public still suspicious, financial support research comes from same company that... genetically modified crops, consumers distrust those companies, distrust any project, reject new broccoli as well

6 ✎ fresh nutrients, good argument for creating a new breed? Other grow on the east, contain similar nutrients, kale provides comparable health benefit, better, east × just summer, also fall and winter, × create new, educate peo about eating fresh vegetables already local

The article believes that growing broccoli on the east coast carries three potential benefits, all of which are questioned by the lecturer.

The first benefit cited in the article is a lower transportation cost, but the lecturer does not believe that this reduction entails lower prices for consumers. The growing technique that allows broccoli to survive the hot summer on the east coast also results in lower yield than the west coast counterpart. Reduced harvest would force farmers to increase prices, canceling out the saving from transportation.

Second, while the article claims that the new broccoli would be desirable to consumers, the lecturer is skeptical. Even though growing the new broccoli relies on traditional breeding techniques, the public might remain suspicious, because the research is funded by the same companies that used to grow genetically modified crops. Consumers' distrust toward those companies might extend to anything they are connected with, including the new broccoli.

Finally, while the lecturer concedes that the fresh broccoli contains valuable nutrients, she points to other vegetables with comparable health value that already grow there, like kale. In fact, kale is better in that it can grow in summer, fall, and winter, unlike broccoli, which grows only in summer. Therefore, the lecturer believes that we should educate people more on consuming healthy vegetables already available locally, instead of wasting resources creating a new crop.

TPO 65

📝 阅读解析与听力预测

总　论：
tuna farming 有几个主要问题。听力肯定会指出这些都不是问题。

问题 1：
被捕获的雌鱼是不产卵的，所以必须捕幼鱼，会导致野生 tuna 进一步减少。[1]

问题 2：
养殖的 tuna 贵，因为 tuna 吃的食物贵。[2]

问题 3：
tuna 被寄生生物感染。[3]

[1] 并不会产生这个结果，或这并不是什么坏事。

[2] 并不贵，或这不是什么坏事。

[3] 并不会被感染，或这不是什么坏事。

📝 听　力　解　析

researchers are finding promising solutions，反驳策略是：阅读提的问题都可以解决，所以不再会有那些问题。

it's true that tuna farms need to be stocked with wild young，让步，tuna farms 要囤野生幼鱼。but this may soon no longer be the case, thanks to a breakthrough，重点听以后怎么变。can get captive females to lay their eggs by injecting… hormones，解决了，注射激素。get the females to lay eggs without posing health risks to tuna or to consumers，安全的激素，不用担心。tuna farming can be done without… reducing wild populations，无用信息总结。

◆ **本段逻辑梳理：** 现在 tuna farms 需要囤幼鱼，因为成年雌鱼在捕获状态下是不产卵的，但之后就不会这样了。一个新的科技突破使得我们可以给 tuna 注射激素，这种激素可以让成年雌鱼稳定产卵，而且这种激素对 tuna 以及人类都无害。以后，tuna farming 就不会导致野生 tuna 减少了。[4]

[4] ✎ < stocked young > soon breakthrough, inject hormone, lay eggs reliable, no health risk to tuna and consumer, without further reduce wild pop

yes, must eat a high-protein diet, 让步，承认确实得吃高蛋白。usually from fish, 蛋白质也确实通常来自鱼。but the protein that tuna need doesn't have to come from fish, 但那种蛋白并不见得非得来自鱼。also… from plants, 其实也可以来自植物。Certain plants… high in protein can be processed to make an inexpensive food for tuna, 解决了，可以以低廉的工艺将某种植物处理成 tuna 的食物。could supply captive tuna with all the… nutrients they need, 营养充分。since… inexpensive, cost… low, 无用信息总结。[5]

◆ **本段逻辑梳理**：tuna 确实要吃高蛋白，通常得是鱼，但这种蛋白其实也可以来自植物。某种植物就可以以廉价的工艺处理成 tuna 的食物，提供其日常所需的营养。这样，tuna farming 的成本就降下来了。

parasites attack many ocean fish farms, 寄生虫是常见的 fish farms 存在的问题。but steps can be taken to treat infestations, 但可以解决。scientists… in southern Australia discovered how to greatly reduce… infestations there, 澳大利亚的科学家就发现了大幅度减少某种寄生虫的方案。when tuna cages were moved farther offshore into deeper waters, far fewer tuna had… in their bodies, 当把 tuna cages 挪到更远的深海里时，感染就少了。It turns out that… need to stay close to shore to do well, 这种寄生虫得离海岸近才能活得好。because certain resources… require… not available farther offshore, 在离海岸远的地方得不到某种关键营养。cages were moved into deeper waters, infestations… basically stopped, 无用信息总结，挪到深海了，感染基本就没了。[6]

◆ **本段逻辑梳理**：寄生虫问题很常见，但可以解决。澳大利亚的 tuna farming 的科学家做了个研究，显示当把 tuna cages 挪到离岸远的深海后，某种寄生虫感染大幅减少。他们发现这些寄生虫所需的某种关键养料在深海中是无法获得的，所以把 tuna cages 挪到深海后，感染基本就没了。

[5] < high protein > usually fish, doesn't have to fish, also from plants, certain can be processed to make not expensive, supply all nutrients × expensive, cost kept low

[6] attack many ocean farms, studying in Australia, removed further offshore in deep waters, fewer have in body, need to close to shore to do well, resources require for life × available far from shore, basically stopped moving far

满分范文

The article mentions three potential problems regarding tuna farming, all of which the lecturer believes can be addressed.

TPO 65

First, regarding the article's concern that captive tuna would not procreate, so tuna farming entails excessive catch of the young, leading to reduced wild tuna populations. While tuna does have to be stocked young, the lecturer believes that a scientific breakthrough could soon change the case. A certain hormone, which is safe to both tuna and consumers, can be injected into female tuna so they could lay eggs reliably, so wild tuna population wouldn't be affected.

As for the concern that feeding tuna with fish can be very expensive, the lecturer concedes that tuna requires a high protein diet, which in the natural environment usually consists of fish. However, captive tuna can rely on certain plants, which can be processed inexpensively and which supply all the nutrients tuna need. The cost therefore can be kept low.

Regarding the article's concern about parasites, the lecturer points to a study conducted in southern Australia, which suggests that after tuna cages were moved further offshore into deep waters, far fewer tuna had certain infestations. It turns out the parasites need to be close to shore to acquire the resources they need to survive, resources unavailable far from shore. Consequently, when the tuna cage was moved far, parasite infection almost stopped.

TPO 66

阅读解析与听力预测

总　论：
airships 会再次流行，因为其相较于飞机与直升机有三个好处。听力肯定会说这些不是好处，或这些好处不足以让 airships 流行。

好处 1：
用 balloon 而不是 engine 来升空，所以用 less fuel，所以更 economical。[1]

好处 2：
可以去更难去的地方，做一些困难的工作。[2]

好处 3：
可以用更廉价的 airships 替代 satellites。[3]

[1] 并不见得省油；省油也并不 economical；更 economical 也不代表就会流行。

[2] 并没有更容易去难去的地方或做困难的工作；这不足以使 airships 流行。

[3] 并不能替代 satellites；这不足以使 airships 流行。

听力解析

several reasons... not likely... widely used in the future，反驳重点已经说明，这些因素并不足以说明未来 airships 会广泛使用。

Yes, use less fuel，让步，承认用燃料少。but... require special lighter-than-air gases，已经敲定反驳策略了，那肯定是这些轻气体燃料有问题。hydrogen and helium, each has... problems，接下来要一个一个说氢和氦的问题。Hydrogen catches fire easily，氢气容易着火，这个我们应该本来都知道。led to many airship accidents in the past，很容易想象。Helium is safer, but it is difficult to obtain, expensive, and it doesn't provide as much lifting power，氦也有各种问题。So finding a truly economical solution... balances safety and cost is not an easy matter，无用信息总结。[4]

[4] <less fuel> require special lighter than air gases lift, H & HE, H: catch fire, tragic accidents past, HE: difficult to obtain, expensive, ×enough lifting power, truly economical solution, balance safe & cost, ×easy

◆ **本段逻辑梳理：** airships 使用燃料确实少，但它用的燃料很特别，必须比空气轻才能飘起来，所以只能是氢气或氦气，但两者真的是卧龙凤雏。氢气容易点燃，历史上发生过的坏事已经数不胜数了；

TPO 66

氢气安全，可稀有啊，贵啊，而且提供的动力不如氢气那么多。所以，要想使燃料平衡安全性与成本，实在是不容易。

using airships for picking up loads off the ground has its challenges, 用 airships 来抓取重物并不容易。an airship picking up tree logs in a forest, has to slowly come down, pick the logs up, and then safely rise again, throughout this process, has to be kept steady, 整个抓取过程都必须非常稳健。but airships are large and light, difficult to keep them steady, especially under windy conditions, a gust of wind can easily blow... against... trees, airships 又大又轻，一阵风就可以把它吹到树上而毁了。[5]

◆ **本段逻辑梳理**：用 airships 从地面抓取重物并不容易，比如从深林里抬起树干，得先缓慢下降，抓取树干，再稳健地提起。整个过程必须非常稳定，否则可能会撞树而被毁掉。但问题是 airships 又大又轻，一阵疾风就可能被吹到树上去而毁了。

not quite ready to replace satellites, 还不能替代卫星。the types of airships currently in use can only rise to... 14km above the surface, at that height, very strong winds, 现在的 airships 只能飘到 14 公里的高度，但这个高度风很大。have to spend a lot of fuel to resist those winds, 抵抗风力需要耗能。stay in one place, to carry on telecommunications or surveying functions, 它得稳定才能完成各种使命。quickly use up the fuel, have to descend and refuel, 可以预见了，耗能很快，得下来重新补充燃料。right now, cannot provide... uninterrupted service satellites can, 无法像卫星一样持续作战。[6]

◆ **本段逻辑梳理**：airships 暂时还无法替代卫星。现在流行的 airships 只能到达 14 公里的高度，这个位置风力很大。所以 airships 需要消耗额外的能量来对抗风力以稳住自己的位置，否则就无法完成各种通信或搜集数据的工作。过快的耗能就使得 airships 得频繁回到地面补给，于是就不能像卫星一样保持持续的工作。

[5] pick up loads off ground challenge, pick up tree log, slowly come down pick up, slowly up, must be kept steady × crash, large, light, difficult to keep steady, especially windy, easily blow against trees damage

[6] × ready to replace, the types in use rise only to 14 km up, very strong wind, spend lots of fuel to stay in place, in order to do telecommunication or surveying function, use up fuel cannot, have to descend to refuel, cannot perform function as satellites do uninterruptedly

满分范文

The article believes that airships would be widely used again because of three advantages over airplanes, all of which are challenged in the lecture.

For starters, the lecturer does not agree that airships are more economical. Although they use less fuel, the fuel has to be lighter than air, being either hydrogen or helium. Unfortunately, hydrogen is highly flammable, having caused many tragedies before. Helium is difficult to obtain, expensive, and does not provide as much lifting power. Thus, it's hard to balance safety and cost.

Second, regarding the purported advantage that airships can perform difficult jobs like carrying forest logs, the lecturer argues that it would be quite a challenge for airships. They would have to descend slowly, pick up the logs, and ascend slowly, and be steady the entire time. Unfortunately, this would be a difficult task, especially during windy time, when these large and light vehicles are easily blown away and damaged against trees.

Finally, the lecturer does not think that airships are ready to replace satellites. The airships currently in use only rise up to 14 kilometers above the ground, a height where wind is very strong. Consequently, airships would have to spend excessive fuel to stay in place, so that they could perform telecommunications or surveying functions. As a result, they easily use up the fuel and have to descend for refuel. Thus, they cannot perform functions uninterruptedly as do satellites.

TPO 67

阅读解析与听力预测

> **总　论：**
> Brendan the Navigator（之后简称 BN）是第一个航行到北美的欧洲人，将有三个论证。典型的观点理由型文章。

> **理由 1：**
> BN 的航行故事所提到的他去过的地方是合理的路线（岛屿到岛屿，避开长期在 open sea 航行）。[1]

> **理由 2：**
> 研究者重现当年的船，是可以航行到北美的。[2]

> **理由 3：**
> 有一些北美的石头上有 marking，接近古爱尔兰文字。[3]

[1] 这不是他的真实航行路线；就算是这种路线，也不代表他真第一个到了北美。

[2] 当年也造不出这种船；造出来也到不了北美。

[3] 根本就不是古爱尔兰文字；或者就算是，也不是 BN 他们留下来的痕迹。

听力解析

Did Brendan really get to North America, none of the evidence… particularly strong，全是无用信息。

First, can we be sure that the stories refer to the Faroe Islands or Iceland，反驳策略出现，那些故事并不与法罗群岛或冰岛有关。stories… Brendan visited…"an island of sheep", a reference to the Faroe Islands, because sheep were raised there，有人觉得故事提到了"an island of sheep"，就认为 Brendan 去了法罗群岛，因为法罗群岛有羊，but sheep were raised in other locations，但别的地方也有羊啊。"a burning hill" … refers to Iceland, active volcanoes，有人觉得"a burning hill" 就指代冰岛，因为冰岛有活火山，but a burning hill may not mean a volcano, could be a hill where people have set many fires，但 a burning hill 可能就是人们放了火的山。not… really refer to islands… along the way to America，故事里的地点并不见得就是去北美沿线的岛屿。[4]

[4] sure story refers to Faroe or Iceland? Story: island of sheep, Faroe, sheep were raised there, but other locations too, a burning hill -> Iceland, active volcano, could be a hill where peo set fire, × sure refer to these islands to America

TPO 67

◆ **本段逻辑梳理**：故事里提到的那些地点不见得真的就是法罗群岛或冰岛什么的。所谓的关于法罗群岛的片段是"an island of sheep"，但虽然法罗群岛有羊，别的地方也可以有羊啊。所谓的关于冰岛的片段是"a burning hill"，确实有可能指的是火山，而冰岛火山很多，可这也可能指的就是人们放火烧山啊。所以，这些故事不见得真的能指向去北美沿线的岛屿。

although the researchers... using old... building methods，确实用的是古法造船，not an exact copy of... Brendan's time，但和 BN 那会儿的船并不一模一样。researchers' ship is quite a bit longer, 12 meters long, more sails than... 6th century，比当年长，帆还多。this... powerful ship... make an 8,000 kilometers voyage, doesn't prove... could do the same，这艘新船可以航行那么远，不代表以前的船能。⁵

◆ **本段逻辑梳理**：研究者们用的确实是古法造船，但问题是造出来的船还是和古代的不一样。新船比古船长，还有更多风帆，所以新船可以航行 8000 千米的里程，不代表古船可以。

some of those markings may resemble an old Irish alphabet，确实有标志和古爱尔兰语文字相像，but many others do not，但还有很多不像的。some... look like pictures, images of a son, a hand, a tree, Irish script was an alphabet, not... pictures，古爱尔兰文字没有图片，但很多 markings 有图片。So... probably not made by the Irish, but by native Americans, who did carve pictures into stone，所以其实 markings 更有可能是印第安人留下的，印第安人会这么做。⁶

◆ **本段逻辑梳理**：确实一些标记和古爱尔兰文字相似，但还有很多标记并不像古爱尔兰文字。比如，有很多图像标记，类似孩子、手、树，但爱尔兰古文字并没有图像。所以这些东西并不像爱尔兰人留下的，而像土著印第安人留下的痕迹，因为他们真的会在石头上刻图案。

5 ✎ <old Irish method> × copy, researchers' ship longer 12 meters, more sails than 6th, <powerful make 8,000 voyage>, × do the same

6 ✎ markings may resemble Irish alphabet, some: picture, image, son, hand, tree, real Irish alphabet × pic only letter, probably × Irish but native America, did carve pic into stone

📝 满分范文

According to the lecturer, none of the arguments presented in the article really proves that Brendan the Navigator reached North America.

First, the lecturer does not believe that the written stories about Brendan's voyage necessarily link to places like the Faroe Islands and Iceland. For example, while the quote "an island of sheep" could refer to the Faroe Islands, where sheep were raised, sheep were raised elsewhere too. Likewise, while the quote like "a burning hill" might represent active volcanoes in Iceland, it could simply be a hill where people set fire. Therefore, the stories do not necessarily point to locations along the way to America.

Second, while the article is correct that researchers today did manage to sail to North America with a boat made with materials and techniques available in the past, the boat itself was different from Brendan's, being much longer and having many more sails. Therefore, while the researchers' boat is powerful enough to cover 8,000 kilometers, Brendan's boat might not be.

As for the markings that resemble old Irish letters, they were more likely left by native Americans. Besides the markings similar to Irish letters, there are other markings that showed pictures and images like a son, a hand, or a tree, symbols that don't belong to the ancient Irish alphabet, which contains only letters and no images. It's the native Americans that would carve pictures into the stone.

TPO 68

📝 阅读解析与听力预测

总 论：
negatives 是 Ansel Adams（AA）制作的，有三个论证可以支持。典型的观点理由型文章。

理由 1：
negatives 里面的 images 包含某些 AA 拍摄过的地点。[1]

理由 2：
negatives 的信封署名像 AA 老婆 VA 的笔记。[2]

理由 3：
negatives 有被火烧过的痕迹，而 AA 的 studio 被火烧过。[3]

[1] 并不是 AA 拍摄过的东西；就算拍过，也不代表是他的 negatives。

[2] 并不是 VA 的笔记；就算是，也不代表是 AA 的 negatives。

[3] 被烧过也不代表就是 AA 的 negatives。

📝 听力解析

arguments ... not convincing，无用信息。It's true ... some similarities to Adam's work, but there are explanations，全是无用信息。

First, the leaning pine tree, not just a random tree that Ansel Adam's took a liking to, a famous landmark in Yosemite National park，基本的反驳策略已经明了，这是棵有名的树，那不是谁都可以拍么，AA 拍过不代表这张图片就非得是 AA 拍出来的。hundreds of thousands of visitors in the 1920s, the pine tree ... most visited sites, a popular symbol of Yosemite, a lot of photographers, taken photograph of it，基本就是可以预见的无用信息。[4]

◆ **本段逻辑梳理**：底片上的椰子树可不是棵普通的树，这是约塞米蒂国家公园最著名的地标，数以百万计的游客去参观这棵树，在这棵树前拍照，很多摄影师都拍过，不非得是 AA 拍的。

[4] <lean pine tree> × a random tree, famous landmark in Yosemite, happened to be most visited site, many photographers take photo

TPO 68

as you read, some envelopes have a place name written on them, 有些信封上署了地点, names of famous Yosemite landmarks, 有一些著名的 Yosemite 的地标。did not spell some of them correctly, 但有些地点名有很多拼写错误。Virginia Adams grew up in Yosemite, 听到这里反驳策略就很明了, VA 生长在 Yosemite, 怎么会拼错。her father was an artist to have an art studio in the park, so she knew Yosemite very well, 更加强了她熟悉这些地点的判断。Does it really make sense that she would misspell...? 无用信息。[5]

◆ **本段逻辑梳理**：信封上签署的一些地名是 Yosemite 的著名地标，但问题是拼写错了。VA 生长在 Yosemite，父亲在这里还有工作室，她怎么可能把自己生长的地方的名字拼错呢？

process that photographers used... in the 1920s was dangerous, 当年摄影师用来冲洗胶片的过程是很危险的。using highly flammable chemicals, 很多化学物质是易燃的, could cause fire... easily, 无用信息。a fire in a photographer's studio was not an unusual occurence, 经常着火, 无用信息。a great number of ... photographers had work that was damaged by fire, 也都是可以预见的无用信息。[6]

◆ **本段逻辑梳理**：20 世纪 20 年代冲洗胶片的过程本来就很危险，摄影师们要用到一些易燃的化学物质，所以那会儿摄影工作室着火是很正常的事情，很多摄影师都有作品被火烧的经历。

[5] some place names, landmark, did not spell correctly, VA grew in Yosemite, dad has an art studio in park, misspell familiar names?

[6] process 20s, dangerous, highly flammable chemical, cause fire easily, fire usual, many had work damaged by fire

满分范文

The lecturer believes that the arguments presented in the article do not suffice to prove that the negatives were created by Ansel Adams.

First, it's true that the leaning pine tree in the image of the negatives is something Adams' have photographed, but the tree is a very famous landmark in Yosemite National Park. It is the most visited site, one that many photographers have filmed. Therefore, the negatives could have easily been created by someone else.

Second, regarding the handwriting similar to Virginia Adams', some place names of famous Yosemite landmarks written on the envelopes were spelled wrong. However, Virginia Adams grew up in Yosemite, where her dad even had an art studio. It is quite unlikely she would misspell a place with which she was so familiar.

Finally, the lecturer does not believe that the fire damage strongly links the negatives to Ansel Adams, because the process to develop negatives in the 1920s was quite precarious. Photographers usually used highly flammable chemicals, so fire damage was quite frequent. In fact, many photographers had work damaged by fire.

TPO 69

📝 阅读解析与听力预测

- **总　论：**
  Lascaux 的洞穴壁画目的是保证狩猎成功，有三个理由。典型的观点理由型文章。

- **理由 1：**
  壁画主题为动物（猎物）。[1]

- **理由 2：**
  人物形象有兽首，说明是猎人。[2]

- **理由 3：**
  很多文化认为画可以影响现实，所以画猎物可以使狩猎成功。[3]

[1] 主题不止这些；就算主题是这些，也不代表其目的是保证狩猎成功。

[2] 不代表一定是猎人；就算是猎人，也不代表壁画目的是保证狩猎成功。

[3] 该地并不见得有此种文化；有此种文化也不代表这个壁画的目的是保证狩猎成功。

🖊 听 力 解 析

while this view is popular, there is little actual support, 无用信息。

First, animals in the paintings, yes, some… hunted by the cave painters, 让步，承认壁画上的一些动物确实是被捕猎的, but many of … probably not hunted, 但也有很大一部分没有被捕猎, rhinos and cats, 列举没被捕猎的动物出现在了壁画上。reindeer were the most hunted animals, aren't painted at all, 而最常被捕猎的动物没出现在壁画上, only a small percent… shown wounded by spears or arrows, 壁画上也只有一小部分动物有被捕的伤痕。cannot support the view… associated with hunting, 无用信息总结。[4]

[4] <hunted by painters>
many painted × hunted, rhino & cats, reindeer most hunted × painted, only a small percent wound, × support hunting

◆ **本段逻辑梳理**：壁画上的一些动物是被捕猎的，但还有很多动物不是被捕猎的，比如犀牛和猫，以及最常见的猎物 reindeer，并没有出现在壁画上。而且，壁画上只有很小一部分动物呈现了被猎杀的伤痕。

落笔生花
新托福综合写作高分范文精讲

TPO 69

Second, the human figures, some ... may have used animal heads while hunting，确实有人会用兽首来捕猎，but the human figures... not shown hunting, they are not even standing up，但壁画上的那些有兽首的人根本不是在打猎，他们都不是站着的。Instead... shown in a horizontal position on their backs, like they were asleep，这些人是平躺着的，像睡着了似的。not presented with other images that may help us interpret them，并且周围也没有其他图片帮助我们解读这些图片的目的。just don't know what... about，我们没法知道这些图片的目的。[5]

◆ **本段逻辑梳理**：确实有些古人会用兽首来打猎，但图片里的这些人就不是在打猎，他们干脆就是躺着的，应该是在睡觉。而且，也没有其他图片能帮我们解读这些图片的目的。所以，没有办法知道这些图片的意义到底是什么。

Third，...doesn't... mean the purpose of the magic was to ensure ... hunting，图片有魔法意义，不代表这个意义就是捕猎。may have had a different type of magical use，这些壁画可能的魔法意义就不是捕猎。For example, ... believed ... spirits of their ancestors live on some animals around them，有些古人相信祖先的灵魂会在动物周围，believe they can communicate with ancestors' spirits through ceremonies，他们相信是可以通过仪式和祖先交流的，in which images of the animals play an important role，此时，动物的图片就很有价值。may have played a role in these... ceremonies，我们所谈的这些壁画上的图案可能就是类似的作用。

◆ **本段逻辑梳理**：古人确实觉得绘画可以有魔法意义，但意义不代表一定是狩猎。有些远古部落相信祖先的灵魂会游荡在动物周围，且他们可以通过仪式去和祖先的灵魂沟通。所以，L壁画的意义可能就是在这样的仪式上，帮助他们去和祖先的灵魂沟通。[6]

[5] <used animal heads while hunting> × standing up, horizontal position, like asleep, × other images, can't interpret, don't know

[6] doesn't mean the purpose of the magic hunting, different types of magical use, sprits of ancestors live around animals, communicate with ancestors through ceremonies, animal images play an important role, may play in these magical ceremonies

满分范文

The lecturer does not believe that the evidence cited in the article suffices to prove that the Lascaux cave paintings were intended to secure hunting success.

First, while some of the painted animals could have been hunted by the painters, the lecturer does not believe the painting was necessarily linked to hunting. Many of the animals painted were probably not hunted, including rhinos and cats; also, the most hunted animal, reindeer, did not appear on the painting. Also, only a small percent of painted animals were depicted with wounds.

Second, regarding the images of humans with animal heads, the lecturer concedes that people might use animal heads while hunting, but the figures in the paintings were not even standing up. They lied in horizontal positions like they were asleep, and there were not other accompanying images that could help support the hunting interpretation. Thus, he is not sure what these images were about.

Finally, while ancient cultures did believe that paintings could have magical purposes, the author argues that the magical purposes weren't necessarily about hunting. Ancient people believed that the spirits of their ancestors lived around animals, and they could communicate with these spirits through ceremonies. Therefore, the animal images might play an important role in these magical ceremonies.

TPO 70

📝 阅读解析与听力预测

▶ 总 论：
palm oil production 应该扩大，因为它有以下三个好处。观点理由型文章。

▶ 好处1：
palm tree farming 需要的土地少，所以毁林少，有助于森林保护。[1]

[1] 并不会占地少；就算占地少，也不见得保护森林。

▶ 好处2：
palm oil 可以作为生物燃料，减少化石燃料导致的碳排放。[2]

[2] palm oil 并不怎么会被当作生物燃料；就算作为生物燃料，也不能减少碳排放。

▶ 好处3：
帮 small-scale farmers 脱贫，因为种植 palm trees 比种田更赚钱。[3]

[3] 种 palm trees 并不赚钱；或者并不能帮 small-scale farmers 脱贫。

📝 听 力 解 析

negative effects, should not be expanded, 无用信息。

true, require... less land than some other crops, 让步，承认 palm trees 需要的土地较少。doesn't mean that palm oil farming is helping us preserve ... forest, 无用信息。palm oil ... extremely desirable for use in food and cosmetics, 太受欢迎, much more ... than other ... oils, 比其他植物油受欢迎多了。worldwide demand ... grown very fast in recent years, 因此需求量大, 这个时候反驳策略已经完全明了, 需求增长意味着要种更多树, 那肯定要毁更多森林。to keep up with ... demand, farmers have to clear more ... forested land, 无用信息。in just one country, 7,000 square meters cleared every minute to make room ... in short, 无用信息总结, growing demand ... led to an increased rate of deforestation。[4]

[4] <less land than other crops > × mean help preserve forest, extreme desirable for food and cosmetic, much desirable, demand worldwide, grow fast recent yrs, to keep up with demand, have to clear more land, in 1 country, = to 7thousand m² /m make room, led to an increased rate of deforest worldwide

◆ **本段逻辑梳理**：确实种植 palm trees 需要的土地较少，但不代表 palm oil production 会帮助保护森林。palm oil 作为食物和化妆品原

Part 2 237
综合写作高分范文精讲

TPO 70

材料实在是太受欢迎了，全世界范围内它的需求都在大幅增长，农民们因此毁掉更多森林以便能满足这种市场需求。在一个国家，每分钟就有超过 7000 平方米的森林被毁掉，以给 palm trees 种植腾地方。简而言之，palm oil production 带来了更严重的毁林。

  It's true that using biodiesel… produces fewer emissions than using other fuels, 确实用生物燃料会产生更少的碳排放。However, the process… in growing the palms generate… additional carbon emissions, 但种植 palm trees 的过程会产生额外的碳排放。To prepare land, farmers… clear the land first, means that they burn the vegetation that existed… before, 为了种 palm trees, 农民得先清理土地，意味着要把已有的植物先烧光。includes burning plant material called peat, 这个过程还会烧掉 peat。[5]

 ♦ **本段逻辑梳理**：用 palm oil 做燃料是比其他燃料要减排，但种植 palm trees 的过程中会产生额外的碳排放。农民们种 palm trees 之前要先把土地清理干净，意味着会烧掉之前生长的植物，这个过程中还会烧掉 peat 这种东西。

  true that small-scale… clear… land to start palm tree farms, but … don't control the farms for very long, small-scale farmers 确实会为了种 palm trees 清理掉土地，但他们通常不会长期持有这些农田。large… companies see a great commercial opportunity, obtain the land… for themselves, controlling profits, 大公司虎视眈眈，会趁机持有这些土地，之后就会控制利润空间。small-scale farmers …get little in return, 个体农民最后就得不到什么利益。[6]

 ♦ **本段逻辑梳理**：small-scale farmers 是会清理掉土地来种植 palm trees, 但他们通常不会长期持有这些农田，于是大公司觊觎很久，就会伺机进入，把持这些土地，然后控制利润空间，这些个体农民就不能从中明显获利。

[5] < fewer emissions than other fuels > grow … generate additional C emission, prepare, clear land first, burn vegetation existing before, burn plant material called peat

[6] < small-scale clear land > don't control farms for long, large companies see opportunity, obtain land themselves, control profit, small farmers lose control, get little in return

📝 满分范文

  The article presents three advantages supporting the expanded production of palm oil, but the lecturer presents the following arguments why the accompanying problems more than offset those advantages.

First, while it's true that growing palm trees require less land than growing other crops, expansion of palm oil production will only increase deforestation. Palm oil is so desirable for food and cosmetic products, making its demand worldwide grow very fast recently. To meet this demand, farmers would have to clear more land, speeding up global deforestation. In fact, just in one country, approximately 7,000 square meters of forest is destroyed every minute to make room for growing palm trees.

Second, although palm oil generates fewer emissions than other fuels in vehicle engines, using palm oil for fuel won't help reduce emissions. The process to grow palm trees results in additional carbon emissions, because to prepare for planting, farmers would have to clear the land first by burning down vegetations that existed on the land before. It includes burning a plant material called peat.

Finally, palm oil production won't solve small-scale farmers' financial problems as the article suggests. While small-scale farmers would clear land to grow palm trees, they don't often control the farms for very long. Large-scale farming companies see these opportunities and would obtain the land for themselves. Afterwards, they would control profits so small-scale farmers lost control of the market, gaining little in return.

TPO 71

📝 阅读解析与听力预测

> **总　论：**
> 科学家们提出了三种理论，解释为什么 L 龙有 bony crests。现象解释型文章。

> **解释 1：**
> 为了提升嗅觉，因为其 structure 像 modern nose。[1]

> **解释 2：**
> 为了 cool。[2]

> **解释 3：**
> 为了发声，间接证据是 L 龙听力很好。[3]

[1] 不是为了提升嗅觉。

[2] 不是为了降温。

[3] 不是为了发声。

📝 听力解析

not clear... real function，无用信息。

not supported by the structure of... brains，下文肯定要讲 L 的 brain structure 为什么不能支持 improve smell 这个理论。In animals with a strong sense of smell, the brain area next to the organ of smell tends to be well-developed，这个地方已经可以预期 L 的 brain area next to the crest 是 not well-developed 了。because the brain area contains a lot of nerves that process the information from the organ of smell，解释上一句，因为需要大脑神经元来处理这些 smell 信息。from fossils of lambeosaur skulls, brain cavity next to the crest was small, underdeveloped，已经预期到了。hardly... likely... improve the sense of smell，无用信息。

◆ **本段逻辑梳理：** crests 不太可能是用来提升嗅觉的，一般来说，嗅觉好的动物，嗅觉器官附近的大脑结构会比较发达，因为需要丰富的脑神经元来处理嗅觉信号。而 L 龙的 crest 附近大脑结构并不发达，说明其 crest 不太可能有用来提升嗅觉的作用。[4]

[4] ✗ support structure of brain, strong smell, brain next to organ of smell tends to be well-developed, brain contains nerves process information from that organ, from fossil of skull, brain cavity next to the crest underdeveloped, unlikely used to improve smell sense

TPO 71

difference between lambeosaurs and stegosaurs，要讲 L 龙和 S 龙的区别，肯定是说 S 龙可以 cool，但 L 龙不可以。Stegosaurs had many bony plates along their back, added together, large amount of body surface area，S 龙的 plates 那么多，加在一起就是很大的表面积，可以降温，而 L 龙肯定不会增加那么多表面积，就不会降温，完全可以预见到的方向。Lambeosaur had just one crest, additional surface area... small, not... cooling，无用信息。[5]

◆ **本段逻辑梳理**：L 龙的 crest 可不是用来降温的，别拿它和 S 龙比，人家 S 龙有一堆 plates，加在一起表面积很大，所以可以降温，L 龙就一个 crest，能增加多少表面积，根本无法辅助降温。

All lambeosaur species had crests, if this theory is true, all the lambeosaur species should have a good sense of hearing，如果真是用来交流声音的，那按照这个理论，既然所有 L 龙亚种都有 crests，那么它们都应该有 good hearing，听到这里就可以预见到下文肯定要说并不是所有 L 龙亚种都有 crests。So far... discovered just the one fossil, suggesting one lambeosaur species had a good sense of hearing，目前只有一副 L 龙的化石，只能知道一种 L 龙亚种听力好。not... evidence... other... species，无用信息。unless evidence from other... found, should remain skeptical，无用信息。[6]

◆ **本段逻辑梳理**：crest 不一定是用来传递声音的，按照阅读的说法，其依据是 L 龙听力很强，那按照其逻辑，鉴于所有 L 龙亚种都有 crests，那应该所有 L 龙亚种的听力都很好。但问题是，现在只找到一副 L 龙化石，只能说明有一种 L 龙亚种听力好。其他亚种呢，没证据，所以我们没法判断。

[5] difference between L and S, S had many bony plates, added all together, add large surface area, L just one crest, additional area, so small, no advantage in cool

[6] All L had crests, then all should had a good sense of hearing, just 1 fossil discovered, suggest 1 species had a good sense of hearing, no evidence from other L species, unless found other, skeptical

满分范文

The lecturer does not believe that evidence is strong enough to support any of the interpretations offered in the article of the function of lambeosaur crests. The following is his argument.

First, the function of the crest is unlikely to improve smell. Normally, for a species with a strong sense of smell, its brain structure next to the organ of the smell would be highly developed, because

brain contains the nerves necessary for information processing. However, lambeosaur had a quite small, underdeveloped brain cavity next to the crest, suggesting that the crest's purpose is unlikely to improve smell.

Second, the cooling hypothesis is unfounded either. The reading draws a comparison between lambeosaurs and stegosaurs. However, while stegosaurs had many bony plates, which when added together, provide large surface area to serve the cooling function, lambeosaurs had only one crest, adding little additional area to provide extra cooling function.

As for the speculation that the crests were used to make sounds, the article relies on the finding that lambeosaurs had good hearing. However, under the same rationale, since all lambeosaur species had crests, they all should have a good sense of hearing. Unfortunately, so far just one fossil was found, suggesting that one lambeosaur species had good hearing. Until more evidence is found regarding other lambeosaur species' hearing ability, this speculation remains questionable.

TPO 72

📝 阅读解析与听力预测

▶ 总 论：
三个理论解释 TLP。现象解释型文章。

▶ 解释 1：
观测意外，由望远镜缺陷造成。[1]

▶ 解释 2：
陨石。[2]

▶ 解释 3：
月球岩石产生的光，thermoluminescence。[3]

[1] TLP 不可能是由观测错误造成的。

[2] TLP 不可能是由陨石效果造成的。

[3] TLP 不可能是由月球岩石产生的光造成的。

📝 听 力 解 析

none… explained TLP，无用信息。

if… caused by random flaws, reports of TLP would be pretty random as well，假如 TLP 真是由于随机观察错误发生的结果，那 TLP 的报告也应该是随机的。这个地方已经可以预期等会儿肯定会讲 TLP 报告不是随机的，是有规律的。observers … report TLP at many random places on the moon surface，继续讲完刚才的理论预期，应该如何随机。but… not what observers reported，完全预期到的无用信息，等进一步展开。Most … reported TLP from two very specific locations，直接和 random places 的预期对立，完美。Since TLP are closely associated with specific places, they probably reflect real events happening, not flaws of telescopes，无用信息总结。[4]

◆ **本段逻辑梳理**：TLP 并不是由观察者的偶然错误造成的，因为如果是偶然错误，TLP 的观察报告也应该是随机的，可能出现在月球任何一个地方。但实际上人们报告的 TLP 都发生在月球的两个具体地点，这种和具体地点的关联说明 TLP 不太可能是由随机的观察错误造成的，而是真实的月球事件的表现。

[4] if caused by flaws of tele, then reports would be random, observes would report many places on moon, not what observers reported, most from 2 specific locations, specific association, probably reflect real events, not clawed tele

TPO 72

flashes of light meteor impact produces usually last just one second, 陨石撞击产生的炫光只会持续一秒，已经可以预期 TLP 肯定更久。average... TLP is 20 minutes, 符合期望。It's true that meteor showers... can occur, could cause... longer duration, 让步，承认流星雨有可能带来更长时间的炫光。But most TLP are not reported during meteor showers, 把流星雨这条解释也封死了。So while... possible a few TLP are caused by meteor impact, great majority... certainly have other causes, 无用信息总结。[5]

◆ **本段逻辑梳理**：陨石撞击产生的炫光也不太可能解释 TLP，因为陨石的炫光只会持续一秒，而 TLP 一般会持续 20 分钟之久。流星雨确实是有可能带来更长时间的炫光，但大部分 TLP 都没有发生在流星雨期间。因此，陨石撞击产生的炫光确实能解释一小部分 TLP，但绝大部分 TLP 不会是陨石撞击的产物。

certain rocks... do emit... light, 确实有石头可以发光，but... weaker than the glare of the moon..., 但这种光比月光弱多了。the moon... reflects light from the sun, 无用信息。brighter than thermoluminescence, 无用信息。So we would not be able to see... against this bright background, 无用信息。like... trying to see the light from the candle in front of powerful spotlight, 做了个类比而已。[6]

◆ **本段逻辑梳理**：月球上确实有岩石可以发光，但我们看不到啊。月球反射的太阳光是我们平时看到的月亮的光，这光线那么强，月岩的光那么弱，我们不可能看到，这简直就像在探照灯前想要看到烛光一样。

[5] *meteor impact produces last 1 second, avg TLP 20 minutes, <meteor showers can occur> can cause longer, most TLP not reported during shower, <some cause>, majority other causes*

[6] *certain rocks do emit light, weaker than moon glare, surface reflects sun, fairly bright, much brighter than thermos, wouldn't be able to see, try to see the light of candle in front of powerful spotlight*

📝 满分范文

The lecturer believes that none of the theories presented in the article can explain TLP. The following is a recapitulation of his argument.

First, TLP cannot be explained by random errors from telescopes, because otherwise the reports of TLP should be random as well, for example, occurring at many places on the moon. However, the actual TLP reports mostly come from two specific lunar locations, and such a specific geographic association suggests that TLP reflects real events, not random flaws from observers.

Second, meteor impact is an unlikely explanation, because the light produced by such impact normally lasts just one second, but the average TLP lasts twenty minutes. Sure, meteor showers last longer and may explain this duration, but most TLP reported did not occur during a meteor shower. Therefore, most TLP instances should not be attributed to meteor impact.

Finally, thermoluminescence cannot be the cause of TLP. It's true that some moon rocks emit light, but the light is much weaker than moon glare. The light we normally observe from the moon is reflected sunlight, which is significantly brighter than thermoluminescence. We wouldn't possibly observe the latter, because it would be like trying to see candle light in front of a powerful spotlight.

TPO 73

📝 阅读解析与听力预测

总 论：
三种方式阻止 yellow crazy ants 肆虐 Seychelles 的 palm forest。问题解决型文章。

方案 1：
用涂上灭蚁化学物质的 ant traps。[1]

方案 2：
砍掉阔叶树，让 ants 没有好的栖息环境。[2]

方案 3：
减少人类活动。[3]

[1] 不可行；无效；有副作用。

[2] 不可行；无效；有副作用。

[3] 不可行；无效；有副作用。

📝 听力解析

suggestions… unlikely to work，无用信息。

cause… unintended harm，副作用要出现了。traps do not differentiate between the yellow crazy ants and other native… ants，反驳策略已经明了，traps 会灭掉当地蚂蚁，这肯定是人们不想要的结果。native ants can be harmed，无用信息。The island near Australia does not have any native ants，阅读所提的澳大利亚的例子当中，是没有 native ants 的，所以才能用 traps，而 Seychelles 有当地 ants，所以不能用 traps，这个逻辑可以轻松在大脑中完成。no unintended harm was done there，无用信息。But… on Seychelles, there are native ant species present that we want to protect，无用信息。these ants would… be killed by the… traps，无用信息。[4]

◆ **本段逻辑梳理**：traps 会有副作用，它们无法区分不同的蚂蚁物种，所以一方面它们会灭掉 crazy yellow ants，但也会灭掉当地蚂蚁。在阅读所提到的澳大利亚案例当中，之所以可以用 traps，是因为没有

[4] ✍ cause unintended harm, × differ yellow crazy & native ants, native can be harmed, AU island no native, palm Sey native present, want to protect, will be killed

落笔生花
新托福综合写作高分范文精讲

native ants，所以不会有不良后果，但在 Seychelles 是有当地 ants 的，所以不能这么用 traps。

Second, cutting... might not solve..., 无效。can thrive in several different... habitats，策略已经出现，砍了阔叶林还有别的地儿可以生存。Yes, they thrive in... broad leaved trees，承认阔叶林适合 ants 生存，让步。However, they also do well in... open areas with increased sunlight，但也适合阳光充足的开阔地。If we cut down broadleaved trees, we would create areas with increased sunlight，砍了一个栖息地，就会创造出新的栖息地，讽刺。destroy one, creating a new habitat，无用信息。[5]

◆ **本段逻辑梳理**：砍掉阔叶林没用，crazy yellow ants 又不是只能在这种栖息地生存，它们还喜欢阳光充足的开阔地。恰好砍了阔叶林之后，就会在 palm forests 当中开辟出一块阳光充裕的开阔地，ants 岂不是美滋滋。

limiting human... slow... spread a little，让步，承认限制人类活动可以减少一点蚂蚁的传播。but... serious economic problem，副作用。palm forest... main tourist attraction，这是旅游胜地。unique trees and animals... attract not just tourists but also scientists，具体解释吸引力。tourism and visits from scientists are the most important sources of income，主要的收入来源。trying to limit human presence ... negatively affect the economy，无用信息总结。[6]

◆ **本段逻辑梳理**：减少人类活动当然可以一定程度上减少蚂蚁的传播，但这会造成严重的经济困难。palm forest 是当地的重要旅游胜地，其独特的动植物吸引着大量的游客和科研人员。而这就是当地最重要的收入来源。因此，限制人类活动势必会造成当地巨大的经济困难。

[5] ✗ solve, thrive different habitats, <broad thrive> also well in an open area with increased sunlight, cut down broad → create sunlight in palm forests, destroy 1, create a new habitat, ✗ rid ants

[6] <slow down ants spread a little> lead to serious economic problem, main tourist attraction, unique trees and animals attract tourists and studies rare species, tou + sci important source income, limiting human negatively affect eco of whole region

满分范文

The lecturer believes that none of the proposals presented in the article offers satisfactory solution to the problem of the yellow crazy ants. Here is a recapitulation of her argument.

TPO 73

First, ant trap with toxic chemicals is not a good solution, because it causes collateral damage to the local ants that we want to protect. The chemicals do not distinguish between different ant species. In the case mentioned in the article, the Australians adopted the chemicals, because there was no native ant species on that island, but the situation does not pertain to the Seychelles.

Second, cutting down broad-leaved trees will not solve the ant problem, because these trees are not the only preferred habitat for the ants. If these trees are cut, open areas with increased access to sunlight will be created in the palm forests, and these areas happen to be another favorable habitat for the ants.

Finally, reduced human activity might slow down the spread of the yellow crazy ants a little, but it will lead to serious economic problems for the entire region. The palm forest, with its unique trees and animals, attracts both the tourists and scientists studying rare species and thereby offers the most important source of income. Limiting human activity will thus negatively affect the regional economy.

TPO 74

📝 阅读解析与听力预测

▶ 总　论：
Mystery Hill 的 stone structures 是一千多年前欧洲人建造的，三个论据支持。观点理由型文章。

▶ 理由1：
与欧洲知名的石质结构相似。[1]

▶ 理由2：
有一块石头上似乎雕刻有早期的欧洲文字。[2]

▶ 理由3：
石头的切割改造技术与欧洲过去流行的模式形似。[3]

[1] 并不相似；相似也不代表是欧洲人造的。

[2] 并不是欧洲文字；就算是也不代表是欧洲人造的。

[3] 并不相似；相似也不代表是欧洲人造的。

📝 听力解析

Most... don't think... built by ancient Europeans，无用信息。

true... arranged in the same way... European，承认确实和欧洲的石质结构模式相似。upright standing stones ... no longer in their original positions，但这是被挪位置了。belonged to a private owner in the 1930s，以前私有。owner moved... stones around, make... more like... stonehenge，所有者可能故意将许多石头挪位模仿巨石阵。hoped to attract more tourists, make a financial profit，为了吸引游客赚钱。[4]

[4] ✏️ <similar arrange EU>, upright MH not in original position, 1930s belonged to a private owner, owner move stones around, make site more like England's Stonehenge, attract more tourists make a financial profit

◆ **本段逻辑梳理**：确实 Mystery Hill 的石质结构和欧洲的石质结构形式相似，但这很可能是20世纪30年代 Mystery Hill 的主人挪动石头的结果。他当年很可能是想模仿英国的巨石阵，让这里能吸引游客赚钱。

a few straight lines might look like a simple writing system，石头上刻的线看起来像文字。Most... don't believe that those... ancient

TPO 74

European writing, 但大部分人并不信那些标记是古代欧洲文字。probably... accidental scratches made by farming equipment, 可能只是农具留下来的痕迹。area was used for farming for a long time, 这个地方农耕历史悠久。a meadow plow rode over the stones several times and left some scratches behind, 假想了一种农具可能留下痕迹的场景。[5]

◆ **本段逻辑梳理**：石头上刻的线乍一看可能像欧洲文字，但没几个人真的这么想。这些痕迹很可能只是农具偶然擦出来的效果，因为这个区域很久以前就是农业区域了。meadow plow 随便划拉几下，就可能产生这样的痕迹。

though... quarrying... suggests European work to some people, 也许有人觉得那些石头的切割技术反映了欧洲起源。found other... objects... clearly made by native Americans, 但找到了其他一些物体，很明显是北美土著制造的。Specifically, they found smaller stone objects such as jewelry that native Americans wore as decorations, 找到了小的珠宝物件，这是土著人的装饰。had the same type of toolmarks as the largest ones, 和大石头上的痕迹一样。same kind of ... tool was used to work both the large stone structures and the jewelry, 说明这些小石头和大石头都是一样的工具制造出来的。strong evidence that native Americans created the smaller objects as well as largest, 说明大小石头都是土著人打造的。[6]

◆ **本段逻辑梳理**：石头的切割技术也许看起来像起源于欧洲的，但是在当地找到了一些其他物品，明确指向这些石头是北美土著人造的。具体来说，当地发现了一些小的石质器物，比如土著人穿戴的珠宝。这些珠宝上的工具痕迹和大石头上的痕迹是一样的，这说明是同样的工具打造了这大小石器，也说明很有可能北美土著人既造了这些小珠宝，也造了那些大石头。

[5] not an expert, a few straight might look like writing system, not conclusive evidence, × believe ancient EU, accidental scratch farming equip, area used for farming, meadow plow rode over left scratch

[6] other ancient objects, clearly made by native Americans, small stone jewelry native wear as decoration, jewry has same toolmark as large stones, same tool used to work large stone and jewelry, native create small as well as large

📝 满分范文

The lecturer believes that none of the evidence presented in the article suffices to show that the stone structures at Mystery Hill were created by the ancient Europeans. Here is her argument.

First, even though the arrangement of tones at Mystery Hill resembles European structures, the upright standing stones today might have been the result of rearrangement. Mystery Hill used to belong to a private owner in the 1930s, who might have moved the stones around to replicate England's Stonehenge in order to attract tourists and make a financial profit.

Second, while a few straight lines in the stone carvings might appear similar to European writings, few experts believe that they are really created by the ancient Europeans. They might more likely be accidental scratches from farming equipment. This area has been long used for farming, and a meadow plowing riding over could have easily left such scratches.

Finally, the quarry technique doesn't decisively prove the European origin either. There are other ancient objects clearly indicating a native American origin. Specifically, small stone objects were found including the jewelry native Americans wore for decorations. The jewelry has the exact same toolmarks as the large stones, suggesting that the creators, more likely the native Americans, used the same tools for both the large and the small objects.

TPO 75

📝 阅读解析与听力预测

> **总　论：**
> 三种防止 Northern Pacific sea star 入侵的方案。问题解决型文章。

> **方案 1：**
> 引入有毒的 quicklime。[1]

> **方案 2：**
> 引入寄生生物。[2]

> **方案 3：**
> 处理 ballast water（船倾倒这些水之前把里面的 sea stars 处理掉）。[3]

[1] 🐾 不可行；无效；有副作用。

[2] 🐾 不可行；无效；有副作用。

[3] 🐾 不可行；无效；有副作用。

📝 听 力 解 析

none will stop… from spreading，无用信息。

quicklime doesn't hurt… mollusks, doesn't mean it's safe for the entire marine ecosystem，反驳策略是有副作用，quicklime 会伤害整个生态系统，虽然它不会伤害 mollusks。destroys not only… Northern Pacific sea stars, but also native ones，不仅伤害入侵物种，还会伤害当地海星。critical to maintaining their local ecosystems，当地海星很重要。Once quicklime is spread over the sea floor, it remains active for a long time，这种毒素是长效的。after… kills the invasive sea stars, native… will move into…, they will die too，杀死入侵物种之后，当地海星就会过来，它们就也会被杀死。[4]

♦ **本段逻辑梳理：** quicklime 虽然不会伤害 mollusks，但它仍然有害于当地生态系统，因为它不仅仅攻击入侵海星，还会杀死当地海星，而后者是当地生态系统中关键的一环。quicklime 的主要问题是它太长效了，它杀死一片地方的入侵物种之后，当地海星就会过来，然后当地海星就会死掉。

[4] ✏ < doesn't hurt mollusk > × mean safe ecosystem, not only sea stars, also destroy native sea stars, maintain system, active for a long time, problem for native, kill invasive, then native move in, they will die too

natural enemies... unlikely to work, 无效。parasites ... do not completely destroy male... reproductive system,并不会真的彻底毁掉雄性的生殖系统。male ... infected ... will still be able to fertilize ... female,还是能够让雌性受孕。given that a single female can produce up to 20 million eggs, unlikely... impact on the population,鉴于雌性繁殖能力这么强, parasites 的效果不会很好。⁵

◆ **本段逻辑梳理:** 引入寄生生物没用,因为它并不能真的彻底毁掉雄性海星的生殖系统,这意味着雄性海星还是能够让雌性受孕,而雌性海星一只就能产两千万颗卵,那寄生生物并不会真的对减少海星数量产生什么影响。

sterilizing... unlikely to prevent... from spreading, 无效。ballast water is not the only way... transported, 因为 ballast water 可不是海星移动所利用的唯一工具。while floating, stick to objects around, 它们会附着在周围的物体上。bottom of small boats or to equipment used for fishing, 列举了几个物体的例子。will likely continue to spread, regardless of whether ships sterilize ballast water or not, 所以无论如何, 海星还是能传播开来。⁶

◆ **本段逻辑梳理:** 处理 ballast water 也没什么用,因为海星不非得靠 ballast water 传播,它们漂浮在海中,会黏附在周围的物体上,比如渔具、船底,然后就会跟着到处走,所以无论 ballast water 是否被处理掉,海星还是能传播开来。

5 ✎ ✗ work, not completely destroy male reproductive system, male infected will still fertilize female, female can produce 20 million eggs, ✗ much impact on population

6 ✎ sterilize ✗ prevent, B water ✗ only way to transport from place to place, floating, stick to objects around, bottom boats, fishing equipment, continue to spread to new areas regardless of sterilizing

满分范文

The lecturer does not believe that any of the measures proposed in the reading will signiflcantly help prevent the spread of the Northern Pacific sea star. The following recapitulates his main arguments.

First, even though the poison quicklime doesn't hurt mollusks, it does not mean that it is safe for the marine ecosystem. It destroys not only the invading sea stars, but also the native ones, which are critical to maintaining the local ecosystem. The problem with quicklime is that it is active for a long time, so after it kills the invasive species, the native ones will move in place and be seriously affected by the poison.

Second, introducing parasites won't work well against the invading sea stars, because it does not completely destroy the male sea stars' reproductive system. The males infected with the parasites will still be able to fertilize the females. Since each female can produce up to 20 million eggs, the measure won't significantly affect the sea star population.

Finally, sterilizing ballast water is not going to stop the spread of the sea star, because ballast water is not the only method sea stars rely on to travel around. As sea stars float in the ocean, they stick to objects to move around, like the bottom of boats or fishing equipment. Consequently, they will be able to spread whether or not ballast water is treated.